sweets and desserts
from the middle east
arto der haroutunian

Grub Street • London

acknowledgements

Many thanks are due to all the authors, translators and publishers from whose works
I have quoted, and apologies to those who unintentionally may
have been overlooked.

Published in 2013 by
Grub Street
4 Rainham Close
London
SW11 1HT
Email: food@grubstreet.co.uk
Twitter: @grub_street
Web: www.grubstreet.co.uk

Text copyright © Arto der Haroutunian 1984, 2013
Copyright this edition © Grub Street 2013

Photography: Michelle Garrett
Food Styling: Jayne Cross
Design and Jacket Design: Sarah Driver

First published in Great Britain in 1984 by Century Publishing
A CIP record for this title is available from the British Library
ISBN 978-1-909166-07-3

Printed and bound by Berforts Group, UK

contents

introduction

*'If Choregs (dry breads) were good enough for our ancestor
Noah, they are good enough for us mere mortals on the barren hills
of ours, waiting for night to become day, snow to melt, howling winds
to disperse, the return of the holy sun and the resurrection of our Lord;
so we can celebrate with the honey of wild roses, the fruit of the trees,
milk of our sheep, the fragrance of spring air and huge, huge
mouthwatering trays of Bahki-halva (Baklawa). Praised be the Lord.
Praised be the dry bread of our ancestors.'*
Armenian Wisdom

There is a charming Armenian legend about how old Mrs Noah, when informed by her husband of their impending cruise to the unknown, rushed home, gathered her daughters and daughters-in-law around and hurriedly prepared vast quantities of choregs (small dry breads that keep for months); for who could tell how long the journey would take? I have always found this brief glimpse into our ancestral past utterly delightful in its cosy domesticity; with women of all ages pouring large jugs of water on to coarse flour in earthenware containers, kneading, rolling the dough, some shaping with their delicate fingers the patterned bread, others baking the bread in a small oven in one corner of an old house with old Mrs Noah supervising the proceedings. I can smell the sweet aroma of bread mingled with perspiration, the fresh desert air with the odour of sheep and mules. I can sense the fear and excitement of the forthcoming journey, while Noah and his sons busied themselves in the courtyard putting the finishing touches to their boat.

All this from a legend passed down through the ages from mother to daughter, from my grandmother to my mother. It will also have passed to the mothers of many other Middle Eastern people mostly unknown to me, some related, many friends or friends of friends, without whose tenacious conservatism, deep-rooted traditionalism and undoubted love of food these recipes could not have survived. For one of the most interesting points to be discerned from the legend of Noah's wife and her choregs is the strength of traditionalism in the Middle East where the cuisine (to date) is basically unchanged from time immemorial. The next point is that the source whence most Middle Eastern food is derived is in the shared ancestry of the people whatever their nationality, tongue or habitat today.

In this book I have gathered a selection of Middle Eastern desserts and sweets (by no means a comprehensive collection since the actual list would run into thousands). I have reluctantly omitted certain recipes which would not only be time-consuming, but also impracticable to create due mainly to the lack of necessary ingredients in the West. I have also tried to keep true to the spirit of the dishes and have not attempted to 'improve' or 'improvise' for the sake of convenience – one should only adapt out of sheer necessity and not for its own sake.

The little that is known in Europe and America of Middle Eastern sweets is dismally lacking in finesse and abominably false in representation. This is due in part to the commercialism of most Middle Eastern restaurants and delicatessens. Only a handful of famed specialities such as baklava, kunafeh (kadayifi), galatabourego and rahat lokum (Turkish delight) are known. I hope this book will help to lift the silky veil of ignorance through which the Middle East is often viewed by westerners. Gone are the days of camel caravans carrying spices and exotic carpets from one end of the desert to the other. Gone are the days when the langorous nymphs of the harems joined days into nights by munching Turkish delight, splitting *passotame* (toasted pumpkin seeds) and drinking ice cool sweet sherbets. Today the entire Middle East has woken to the realities of our age and the people of the deserts, with those of the hills, are striving to catch up with the industrialised West not only materially, but also (each in his own way) socially by updating his moral and political concepts in tune to this technological age of ours.

Very little is known of the food of our ancestors. A few hieroglyphic recipes from Egypt, Sumer and Urartu, where beer, wine, many types of bread and honey-based sweets were known, have come down to us. When Rome conquered and subjugated vast areas of the known world of her day she also created the first 'international cuisine' where 'Pumpkin Alexandrine-style' (*Aliter cucurbitas more Alexandrino*) was often served with 'Parthian chicken' (*Pullum Parthicum*) and 'Cilician bread'. The Roman cuisine was in turn equally influenced by her conquered territories. Apicius, in his *de re coquinaria* (a compendium of dishes from all over the then known world) notes several dishes of his day which are still (almost intact) prepared in the Middle East. One such recipe is *Dulcia domestica et melcae*, a confection of dates which, after the stones have been removed, are filled with nuts, sprinkled with salt and candied in honey – similar to the stuffed date recipes of Iraq and the Gulf States.

The second and most influential style of cooking was that of the Arabs who spread via Arabia in the 7th century and in a short time dominated the entire Middle East barring Byzantium and certain mountain regions of the Caucasus. The Arab cuisine at this early stage in history was limited and poor, for the desert could not offer much. The social structure of the 'Tent people' was equally primitive, while in Byzantium and to a lesser extent in Persia there had been large cities with a sophisticated urban population. The desert only had nomads without roots or a sense of belonging. However, it did not take long for these Arabs to settle down in the green valleys and pastures of the Mediterranean coastline. They absorbed all the social infrastrucrure of the natives, who were Christian Syrians and Assyrians as well as Copts, Persians and Greeks. Thus in the matter of a few centuries not only was Arabic the dominant language in the East, but also the religion and social make-up was that of the Muslims. All food acquired an 'Arabised' name and what was once perhaps an Assyrian speciality from northern Iraq soon spread to all corners of the Muslim Arab empire. Thus the popular sweet named *ghorayebah* (lover's pastry) so called because of its traditional heart shape, which was most probably of north Syrian origin, appears in name and basic content today as far away as Morocco, Tunisia and southern Iran. Another example is baklava[1] which is mentioned in Armenian folklore of the 10th-12th centuries, spread throughout the Arab world and later on further still to the Balkans during the Ottoman rule.

The Arab world was gradually subjugated by the Mongolian-Turks. They first appeared on the scene in the 9th and 10th centuries as mercenaries fighting for the Caliphs of Baghdad, but in time emerged as conquerors in their own right. Over the next few centuries most of the Turkish tribes (they were not formed into a nation until the 20th century) gave up their nomadic way of life and settled primarily in Asia Minor (modern Turkey). Here, by the end of the 18th century, the dominant language was Turkish and the majority of the populace were Muslims. Yet when the first Turkish-speaking tribes arrived in the Middle East they too were as primitive socially, and more so culturally, than the first 'Arab' conquerors. Turks took from the Arabs the Muslim religion and the Arabic alphabet; from the Persians and Armenians the food and folklore; from Byzantium administrative and naval skills and from Greeks and Armenians their arts and basic architectural skills. As the Ottoman empire expanded she also took with her the 'Ottomanised culture' of the subject races[2] and once again we can see how, for example, a dish of aubergines cooked with minced meat and pistachio nuts, *moussaah* of the Abbasid Arabs[3], appears in Romania, Greece,

Turkey and other adjacent lands as *mussaka*; or how the 'wine' of the desert Bedouins as 'Turkish coffee' throughout the Balkans up to Vienna and beyond[4].

Today these empires of the Arabs and Turks have disappeared. The map of the region is divided into many independent countries, most of them Arabic speaking and Muslim in religion. Although most sweets, as well as the cuisine in general, have one main source there are regional and local specialities which more or less reflect the climatic and religious as well as the ethnic origins of the food. Thus in general the north is the mountainous region while the south contains almost all the desert, the west has the Mediterranean sub-tropical coastline and the east has the Indian subcontinent as a neighbour.

The mountainous region is rich in honey-based sweets, as well as fruits – dried and fresh. Much use is made of almonds and walnuts and many dry cakes, biscuits and fruit pastes are made. The south has dates and is where most milk-based puddings, *muhallabieh* or *malabi*, originate. The west is rich in pastries, indeed almost all of the finest pastries originate in this region which stretches from southern Turkey to northern Egypt. It is here that pistachios, pine kernels, sesame seeds and fruits are made best use of. In the east rice and unusual combinations such as saffron, cardamom and dried fruit appear. But there are few pastries, for if the Syrian and Lebanese love sweet pastries the Iranians prefer fresh fruit; if a Turk or an Armenian loves nuts, dried fruits and sugared biscuits, a Saudi Arabian is happy with a few fresh dates. Most Middle Eastern desserts are very sweet – literally soaked in honey or syrup or a combination of the two – this is at its extreme in Morocco where almost everything is covered in honey. Great use is made of nuts especially walnuts, almonds, pistachios, hazelnuts, pine kernels and coconuts, the latter appearing prominently in Iranian and Gulf States recipes.

Middle Eastern desserts and sweets are exciting and different from those of the West. They are also, by and large, simple to prepare, being mostly of peasant origin. In days past perhaps only the caliphs and sultans could indulge (or afford) luxurious dishes prepared with almonds, sugar, rosewater and expensive spices. One such dish would be *faludhaj* – originally a Persian sweet that spread throughout Abbasid lands and about which a humorist once remarked 'had Moses come to Pharoah with *faludhaj* he would have accepted Moses' mission, but, alas he came to Pharoah with a stick.'[5] However, Moses' pharoah certainly knew how to tantalise his palate for as far back as 2600 BC King Unas' bill of fare mentions (amongst other goodies) 'milk, three kinds of beer, five kinds of wine, ten kinds of loaves, four of bread, ten of cakes, fruit cakes . . . figs, ten other fruit, three kinds of corn (wheat), barley, spelt, five kinds of oil and fresh plants.'[6]

No synthetic additives are used and maximum use is made of every ingredient. Nothing is added merely for the sake of appearance – a disease from which so many European desserts unfortunately suffer.

With the establishment of the State of Israel in 1948, 'new' European-inspired desserts have been added to the rich repertoire of the region and though as yet they are only found in Israel the best of these will, in time, spread throughout the adjacent lands. The Turks on the other hand have, for generations, tried to imitate the Europeans, particularly the French. Consequently a large section of their cuisine has been Europeanised[7]. Turkish cuisine is rich, but unfortunately little of it is local. I have completely discarded several popular recipes for the simple fact that they are not Middle Eastern in origin and giving a recipe a Turkish or an Arab name does not make it authentic. The Lebanese too have tried (unsuccessfully) to imitate the French, producing only a few 'interesting' dishes in the process.

Western influence is unavoidable, but blatant imitation – a nasty habit of middle class Lebanese and Iranians – is wrong and usually unsuccessful. The only way is to use western cooking techniques, ingredients and equipment while retaining the true spirit or essence of the East; for after all most of Europe's food came from the Middle East and its environs in the first place. The popular dumplings, the use of fruit in pastry, use of spices and ices were all of Middle Eastern origin, penetrating Europe via Spain, Greece or the Balkans.

I do hope you will make good use of these recipes. They will open a new world filled with delicate wafer-thin pastries, crunchy honey and nut balls, sesame-coated triangles, syrupy shredded pastries and rice puddings that taste out of this world, worthy only of Paradise where

'Are two fountains flowing,
therein are pairs of every fruit
Reclining on beds, whose inner coverings are of silk brocade.
And the fruits of the two gardens are within reach . . .
therein are fruits, palms and pomegranates,
therein are goodly beautiful ones,
Pure ones confined to pavillions.
Before them man has not touched them, nor jinni,
Reclining on green cushions and beautiful carpets.'
***Koran* – Ar-Rahman**

NOTES

1   Also known as 'baklavah' or 'bahlawah', It is made from two words – 'Bahk' and 'Halva', The first is Armenian for Lent and the second is from the Akkadian 'helou', Arabic 'halweh', meaning sweet. Traditionally baklava consists of 40 layers of pastry – one for each day of fasting – filled with nuts and soaked in honey or syrup; it is eaten on Easter Sunday,

2   Till the formation of the Turkish Republic (1923), the Turkish speaking element was a minority in the Ottoman empire.

3   Abbasid rule based in Baghdad lasted from 786-902 AD though the Caliphate (under Turkish rule) survived up to the time of the Mongolian invasions (12th-13th centuries).

4   Turks being of Mongolian extraction were, in essence, tea drinkers, coffee originated in Arabia and is the drink of the nomadic Arab. It acquired its Turkish name because it was introduced to Europe in the 16th century by subjects (Jews and Armenians) of the Ottoman empire – hence 'Cafe Turque'.

5   Quoted from Abu'l-Faraj ibn al-Jawzi *Akhbar al-Ziraf wa-l-mutamajinin* Damascus 1928.

6   *The Pyramid Texts in translation and Commentary* Mercer SAB 1952·

7   This trend is apparent in Istanbul, Ismir and Ankara more than the rest of the country where traditionalism still dominates.

baklavas and kunafehs

baklava

flaky pastry with nuts or fruits

Baklava (Paklava) or in its original form *Bahki-halva* is the most famous of all Middle Eastern sweets. This is not surprising since it is one of the great desserts of the world.

Traditionally there should be 40 layers of pastry, 20 below and 20 above the filling – symbolising gastronomically the 40 days of Lent. *Bahk* means Lent in Armenian. There are numerous variations of this sweet, several of which I have included. The recipe below is a classic one from my family, prepared and served on Easter Sunday when Lent was broken.

The pastry (phyllo or filo or strudel pastry) can be purchased from most Indian and continental shops. It normally comes in 450g (1 lb) packets. However, if you wish to be more authentic use the recipe Home-made Baklava filo on page 235.

450g (1 lb) packet filo pastry
225g (½ lb) unsalted butter, melted and with froth removed
225g (½ lb) walnuts, chopped or coarsely ground

Syrup
350g (12 oz) sugar
1 tablespoon lemon juice
2 tablespoons rosewater

First prepare the syrup. Place the sugar, lemon juice and 350ml (12 fl oz) water in a saucepan and bring to the boil. Lower the heat and simmer for about 10 minutes or until the syrup leaves a slightly sticky film on a spoon. Add the rosewater and set aside to cool.

Most packets of filo pastry have sheets 53 X 28cm (21 X 11in), but it is not easy to find a tin with these dimensions. I use one 30 X 20cm (12 X 8in) and trim the sheets to make them fit. As I am loathe to waste good food I slip the trimmings between the sheets, maintaining an even thickness. The one important point is that the tin should be at least 2.5cm (1in) deep. Grease the baking tin with a little melted butter.

Open out the sheets of pastry and cover with a tea towel. Lay 2 sheets of the pastry on top of each other in the tin, keeping those not in use covered so that they do not dry out. Dribble a tablespoon of the melted butter over the second sheet. Repeat in this way until you have 6-8 sheets in the tin. While layering the sheets try to press on them as little as possible. This ensures that air is trapped between the layers and so enables the sweet to rise.

Spread half of the chopped nuts over the top sheet of pastry. Continue with layers of pastry and spoonfuls of butter until you have laid down a further 6-8 sheets. Spread the remaining nuts over the last sheet.

Continue layering the pastry with spoonfuls of the melted butter dribbled over alternate sheets until you have used up all the pastry. Spoon any remaining butter over the last sheet, discarding the milky residue at the bottom of the pan. Lightly brush the butter all over the last sheet so that every bit of pastry is covered.

Cut the baklava into lozenge shapes, using a sharp knife and taking care to press as little as possible on the pastry. Place in an oven preheated to 180C (350F) gas 4 and cook for 30 minutes. Lower the temperature to 150C (300F) gas 2 and cook for a further hour or until the pastry is golden.

Set aside until the baklava is warm and then pour the cold syrup all along the gaps. Set aside until completely cold. To serve first run a sharp knife along the gaps to make sure that all the layers have been completely separated.

Makes 24-30 pieces

ALTERNATIVE FILLINGS

Here on the following pages are eight different baklava fillings. Follow the method in the recipe above and substitute the filling of your choice. The proportions below are all for 450g (1 lb) packet of filo. Mix the fillings well before using.

baklava-bil-fistuk halabi

pistachio filling

225g (½ lb) pistachio nuts, coarsely chopped
3-4 tablespoons caster sugar

noushi-baklava

almond filling

225g (½ lb) almonds, chopped or coarsely ground
3-4 tablespoons caster sugar
1 teaspoon ground cinnamon

bahlawa-bil-joz el hind

coconut filling

225g (½ lb) desiccated coconut
6-7 tablespoons caster sugar
2 teaspoons vanilla essence
2-3 tablespoons water

There is no reason why other nuts, eg. hazelnuts, brazil nuts or a mixture of nuts, should not be used, so long as you avoid peanuts! The use of this latter nut is recent, popularised by the lower grade Cypriot restaurateurs and delicatessens – I assume to keep prices down. The taste is almost revolting. I exaggerate? Try one – they are sold in many Greek and Indian stores. Better still, don't waste your money!

portakali baklava
baklava with oranges

Fruits are often used as fillings in baklavas although they are not as popular as their nutty counterparts. Some of these recipes are highly prized, for example this recipe for baklava with oranges which is a speciality from Istanbul, Turkey. This is an absolutely marvellous sweet with the addition of orange blossom water giving it a wonderful refreshing aroma.

450g (1 lb) oranges

When preparing the syrup flavour with 2 tablespoons orange blossom water instead of rosewater.

To make the filling place the oranges in a saucepan half filled with water, bring to the boil, cover, lower the heat and simmer for 30 minutes. Drain, return the oranges to the pan with fresh water and cook for a further 30 minutes. Drain and leave until cool enough to handle.

Quarter the oranges and remove and discard the pips. Using a blender, liquidise the quartered oranges, including the peel. Add a tablespoon or two of water if this will make it easier. Place the pulp in a muslin bag and squeeze out as much liquid as possible. Set the pulp aside to cool.

Prepare the baklava according to the usual method, but when you have laid down 8 sheets of filo spread all the orange pulp evenly and gently over them and then layer all the remaining sheets and butter.

elmali paklava
apple filling

Apple strudel *à la turque*! The Austro-Hungarian Empire was greatly influenced by the Ottoman cuisine and it is quite possible this recipe for apple baklava was the progenitor of the famed Viennese apple strudel.

350g (¾ lb) apples, peeled and grated
225g (½ lb) caster sugar
1 teaspoon ground cinnamon

Mix the grated apples and sugar together, put into a muslin bag and squeeze out as much juice as possible. Empty the mixture into a bowl, stir in the cinnamon and make the paklava using all the apple to make 1 layer of filling rather than 2.

gerasov baklava

cherry filling

450g (1 lb) fresh cherries, stones removed
110g (¼ lb) caster sugar
1 teaspoon vanilla essence

Liquidise the cherries, place in a muslin bag and squeeze out as much juice as possible. Mix in the sugar and vanilla essence and make the baklava, making 1 layer with the filling instead of 2.

bahlawah-bil-annanas

pineapple filling

Particularly popular in Lebanon and the Gulf States.

450g (1 lb) pineapple flesh

Liquidise the pineapple, place in a muslin bag and squeeze out as much juice as possible. Make the baklava as usual, making 1 layer with the filling instead of 2.

tutumi baklava

pumpkin and walnut filling

A regional speciality from Southern Turkey which is unusual and devastatingly tasty.

225g (½ lb) pumpkin, peeled and grated
225g (½ lb) caster sugar
110g (¼ lb) walnuts, chopped or coarsely ground
1 tablespoon rosewater

Mix together and make the baklava as usual, making 1 layer with the filling rather than 2.

baklawah min semsem

sesame baklava

A Lebanese recipe in which sesame seeds are fried and then mixed with chopped almonds and spices to form a filling for the baklava. It has an earthy and wholesome flavour about it.

450g (1 lb) packet filo pastry
350g (¾ lb) unsalted butter, melted and with froth removed

Filling
50g (2 oz) sesame seeds
225g (½ lb) almonds, coarsely chopped
75g (3 oz) sugar
½ teaspoon ground cinnamon
¼ teaspoon ground nutmeg

Syrup
350g (12 oz) sugar
1 tablespoon lemon juice
½ teaspoon ground allspice
1 tablespoon rosewater
1 tablespoon orange blossom water

First prepare the syrup. Place the sugar, lemon juice, allspice and 350ml (12 fl oz) water in a saucepan and bring to the boil. Lower the heat and simmer for about 10 minutes or until the syrup leaves a slightly sticky film on a spoon. Add the rosewater and orange blossom water and cool.

Place 3 tablespoons of the butter in a small saucepan, add the sesame seeds and fry, stirring frequently until the sesame seeds are golden brown. Remove from the heat and stir in the remaining filling ingredients.

Brush a baking tin about 30 X 20cm (12 X 8in) and at least 2.5cm (1in) deep with a little of the melted butter. Open out the sheets of filo and cover with a tea towel to prevent them drying. Lay 2 sheets of pastry on top of each other in the tray. Trim the sheets to the correct size and slip the trimmings between the layers, maintaining an even thickness. Dribble a tablespoon of the melted butter over the second sheet. Now lay down a further 4-6 sheets, dribbling a tablespoon of butter over each one.

Sprinkle half the nut mixture over the buttered filo. Cover with 6-8 more filo sheets, dribbling a little butter over each one. Sprinkle with the remaining nut mixture. Continue layering and buttering the pastry. Pour any remaining butter over the last sheet and brush all over the surface.

With a sharp knife cut the baklava into lozenge shapes, taking care to press as little as possible on the actual baklava. Place in an oven preheated to 180C (350F) gas 4 and cook for 30 minutes. Lower the heat to 150C (300F) gas 2 and cook for a further hour or until the pastry is golden.

Remove from the oven and leave to cool for 10-15 minutes. Then slowly pour the syrup along all the gaps in the baklava. Set aside until completely cold and then serve.

Makes 24-30 pieces

galatabourego

cypriot baklava

450g (1 lb) filo pastry
2-3 tablespoons unsalted butter, melted

Syrup
175g (6 oz) sugar
1 tablespoon lemon juice
2 tablespoons orange blossom water

Filling
900ml (1½ pints) milk
250g (9 oz) sugar
110g (4 oz) fine semolina or rice flour
225g (½ lb) unsalted butter, cut into small pieces
1 tablespoon grated orange rind
6 eggs, separated
pinch of salt

First prepare the filling. Pour the milk into a saucepan and stir in 175g (6 oz) of the sugar and the semolina or rice flour. Add the pieces of butter and cook over a moderate heat, stirring constantly, until the mixture thickens like a custard. Stir in the grated orange rind, pour into a large bowl and leave to cool. When the custard is cool place the egg whites in a bowl with the salt and whisk until stiff. Place the egg yolks in another bowl with the remaining 75g (3 oz) sugar and whisk until pale and creamy. Fold the egg whites and egg yolks gently but quickly into the custard.

Open out the filo pastry, take out 7-8 sheets of filo and cover with a tea towel to prevent drying. Wrap well and refrigerate or freeze the remaining pastry for future use. The sheets of pastry are usually about 53 X 28cm (21 X 11in); cut them in half to give sheets about 26 X 28cm (10½ X 11in). Stack the sheets on top of each other and cover again with the tea towel.

Lay one sheet of the pastry out flat on a work top and place 2 tablespoons of the filling in a ridge about 12.5cm (5in) long, 6cm (2½ in) in from the edge nearest you. Fold the edge of the pastry over the filling, fold the 2 sides in over the ends of the filling and carefully roll the pastry up. Roll it loosely as the filling will expand as it cooks. Repeat with the remaining pastry and filling.

Grease 2 large baking trays and arrange the pastries, openings underneath, on them at least 2.5cm (1in) apart. Brush the surface of the pastries with the melted butter and place in an oven preheated to 180C (350F) gas 4. Cook for 30-40 minutes, until the custard filling puffs up and the pastry is a light golden. Remove from the oven and leave to cool.

Prepare the syrup. Place the sugar, lemon juice and 450ml (¾ pint) water in a saucepan and bring to the boil. Simmer for 10 minutes, remove from the heat and stir in the orange blossom water. Pour the syrup over the galatabourego and leave to cool. These are delicious on their own or with cream.

Makes 14-16

saray baklavasi

palace baklava

A Turkish speciality from the days of the Ottoman sultans who could afford to indulge themselves with luxurious titbits in their over-ornate, dark, hermit-like palaces. This is not a true baklava. It is really a crescent-shaped pastry filled with nuts or semolina custard or fruits. I have given the recipe for the traditional Saray Baklavasi dough with a nut filling, and for Kaymakli Saray Baklavasi – palace baklava with cream. However, there is no reason why other fillings cannot be used.

Basic dough
350g (12 oz) plain flour, sifted
½ tablespoon icing sugar
½ tablespoon salt
30ml (1 fl oz) melted butter, with froth removed
1 egg
½ egg yolk
50g (2 oz) margarine, softened

Filling
225g (½ lb) chopped walnuts or shredded coconut or chopped, blanched almonds or chopped pistachio nuts or chopped hazelnuts
225g (½ lb) icing sugar
1-2 tablespoons orange blossom water

Syrup
450g (1 lb) sugar
1 tablespoon lemon juice

Glaze
1 egg, beaten

Place the flour in a large bowl and make a well in the centre. Add the icing sugar, salt and butter and knead. Add the egg and egg yolk and mix well. Gradually add 120ml (4 fl oz) water and knead for about 10 minutes or until you have a smooth dough.

Lightly flour a work top and divide the dough into 2 equal portions. Roll each ball into a 30cm (12in) long stick. Cover with a damp cloth and leave to rest for 20 minutes.

Now cut the rolls of dough into 2.5cm (1in) pieces. Roll the pieces into walnut-sized balls, arrange on a greased baking tray, cover with the damp cloth and leave to rest for a further 20 minutes. Flour the work top again and, taking 1 ball at a time, roll it into a disc 3mm (⅛in) thick. Spread a little of the softened margarine over each disc and fold in half.

One at a time take the folded discs, open and gently pull and stretch with your hands to make them as thin as possible. Finally loosely and lightly roll each circle of dough up like a cigarette and place on the baking tray. Refrigerate for at least 30 minutes before using.

Lightly flour a work top and remove the prepared dough from the refrigerator.

Mix the filling ingredients together in a bowl. Unroll one roll of dough and flatten it, with a floured rolling pin. Place 1 tablespoon of the nut mixture in one half of the round of dough.

Fold the dough over to form a semi-circle and press the edges together with your fingertips. Continue with the remaining dough and filling.

Arrange the baklava on greased baking trays and brush the surface of each one with the beaten egg. Place in an oven preheated to 200C (400F) gas 6 and bake for 30-35 minutes or until golden.

Meanwhile place the sugar, lemon juice and 300ml (½ pint) water in a saucepan, bring to the boil and simmer for about 10 minutes or until the syrup forms a sticky film on a spoon.

Remove the trays from the oven and pour the hot syrup over the baklava immediately.

Leave to cool on the trays and serve cold, ideally sprinkled with a little ground pistachio nuts mixed with cinnamon.

Makes 24

kaymakli saray baklavasi

palace baklava with cream

Similar in principle to the Greek galatabourego.

Dough
Prepare as for Saray Baklavasi

Filling
600ml (1 pint) milk
40g (1½ oz) fine semolina

Prepare the filling first. Bring the milk to the boil in a saucepan, add the semolina and cook over a low heat, stirring constantly, until the mixture thickens. Remove from the heat and set aside to cool. It will continue to thicken.

Prepare this sweet as described in the method for Saray Baklavasi.

Makes 24

antep suarzesi

'bird's nest' pastries

Antep (Gaziantep) is a medium-sized town in Southern Turkey famed for her rich culinary traditions – derived from centuries of intermingling of Arab, Armenian and Turkish cultures. The recipe below is of Arab origin. *Suarzes* means bird's nest in the Syrian dialect.

10 sheets filo pastry
225g (½ lb) unsalted butter, melted and with froth removed

Syrup
450g (1 lb) sugar
1 tablespoon lemon juice

Garnish
6-7 tablespoons very finely chopped pistachio nuts

Lay the sheets of pastry out flat, on top of each other, on a work top.

Each sheet is approximately 53 X 28cm (21 X 11in). Mark the top one into 6 portions each about 18 X 13cm (7 X 5½in) and then cut down through all 10 sheets. Stack the 60 pieces of pastry on top of each other and cover with a cloth to prevent them drying out.

Remove 1 piece of pastry and brush all over with a little melted butter. Roll the pastry up as you would a cigarette so that you have a roll 13cm (5½in) long.

Carefully bend the roll into a circle and squeeze the 2 ends of the pastry together. They will stick easily if you dampen your fingers first. Repeat with all the remaining pieces of pastry.

Arrange on lightly greased baking trays about 1cm (½in) apart and brush the outer surfaces of the circles with any remaining butter. Place in an oven preheated to 170C (325F) gas 3 and bake for 20-25 minutes or until they are just turning a light golden colour.

While they are cooking prepare the syrup. Place the sugar, lemon juice and 450ml (¾ pint) water in a saucepan and bring to the boil. Boil quite vigorously for about 5 minutes and then remove from the heat. When the suarzesi are cooked place them in a shallow dish, pour the boiling syrup over them and leave for 2 hours to cool.

Lift from the syrup and arrange the pastries on a large serving plate.

Dust with the finely chopped pistachio nuts.

Makes 60

istanbul bulbulu

istanbul nightingale pastries

This is the Turkish version of Suarzesi – bird's nest pastries. Here the pastries are filled, as well as topped, with nuts. If possible use pistachio nuts, otherwise almonds or walnuts will do. Make a point of packing the filling as tightly as possible.

6 sheets filo pastry
110g (4 oz) unsalted butter, melted and with froth removed

Filling
175g (6 oz) chopped pistachio nuts
50g (2 oz) caster sugar

Syrup
350g (¾ lb) sugar
1 tablespoon lemon juice
1 tablespoon orange blossom water or rosewater

Garnish
a little thick honey
2-3 tablespoons finely chopped pistachio nuts

First prepare the filling by mixing the nuts and sugar together with 2 tablespoons water. Set aside.

Lay the sheets of filo out flat, one on top of the other. Cut down through the sheets lengthways. Place the lengths on top of each other and cut crossways to divide into 3 equal parts. Stack all the pieces on top of each other and cover with a cloth to prevent the pastry from drying out.

Remove one piece of pastry and brush with melted butter. Take a long, thin rolling pin (even a very thick knitting needle will do) and place it across the pastry about 2.5cm (1in) in from the edge nearest you. Spread ½-1 tablespoon of the filling along the inside edge of the pin, finishing 1cm (½in) in from either side. Fold the edge of the pastry over the rolling pin and roll the pin over the filling, pressing lightly. Roll once more over the filling and then carefully pull out the rolling pin.

Press the nut filling tightly and, like rolling a cigarette, roll up in the remaining pastry. Now, very carefully, bend the roll into a circle and stick the 2 ends together, slightly overlapping, with a touch of honey. Continue in this way until you have used up all the pastry and filling.

Arrange the pastries close together on a greased baking tray and brush the tops with any remaining butter. Place in an oven preheated to 170C (325F) gas 3 and cook for 20-30 minutes or until the pastries are a light golden brown.

Meanwhile prepare the syrup. Place the sugar, lemon juice and 450ml (¾ pint) water in a saucepan and bring to the boil. Simmer for 10 minutes or until the syrup forms a slightly sticky film on a spoon.

Remove from the heat and stir in the orange blossom water or rosewater.

When the pastries are cooked, remove from the oven and immediately pour the hot syrup over them. Leave to cool for ½ hour. Arrange the pastries on a large serving dish and sprinkle with the finely chopped pistachio nuts.

Makes 3

asabeti-el-arous

almond fingers

This pastry appears throughout the region. It is called Vezir's Fingers in Turkish, Zainab's Fingers and simply Fingers in Armenian. This recipe is from Syria and makes use of almonds, although walnuts are often mixed in. In Iraq hazelnuts are usually used. Simple to make, these fingers make an excellent after-dinner dessert.

450g (1 lb) packet filo pastry
225g (½ lb) unsalted butter, melted and with froth removed

Filling
225g (½ lb) coarsely ground almonds
2 teaspoons ground cinnamon
2 teaspoons sugar

Syrup
450g (1 lb) sugar
juice of 1 lemon
2 tablespoons rosewater

First prepare the syrup. Place the sugar, lemon juice and 450ml (¾ pint) water in a saucepan and bring to the boil. Lower the heat and simmer for 10 minutes or until the syrup forms a slightly sticky film on a spoon. Add the rosewater and set aside to cool.

Mix the filling ingredients together in a bowl. Brush 2 baking trays with a little of the melted butter. Open out the filo pastry and cut along the fold so that each sheet is divided into 2 rectangles. Stack on top of each other and cover with a tea towel to prevent them drying out.

Lay a rectangle of pastry on the work top, a short side nearest you, and brush the 2 long edges with butter.

Arrange a teaspoon of the almond mixture in a ridge across the short side nearest you. Fold the 2 long edges inwards over the ends of the almond mixture and then roll up to form a cigar shape. Continue until the pastry and filling are all used up.

Place the rolls on the baking trays, openings underneath. Brush all over with any remaining butter. Cook in an oven preheated to 190C (375F) gas 5 for 20-30 minutes or until golden. Dip the hot rolls in the cold syrup and then arrange on a serving plate. Serve when cold.

Makes 40-50

saray burma

palace twist pastry

These are rolled pastries filled with nuts and sugar. They are usually prepared with a special dough which, though similar to baklava dough, is slightly thicker. However, I suggest that you make these sweets using a double thickness of filo pastry.

225g (½ lb) filo pastry
225g (½ lb) unsalted butter, melted and with froth removed

Filling
225g (½ lb) chopped pistachio nuts or chopped walnuts,
almonds or hazelnuts or shredded coconut
3 tablespoons icing sugar
2 tablespoons orange blossom water

Syrup
450g (1 lb) sugar
juice of 1 lemon

First prepare the syrup. Place the sugar, and 600ml (1 pint) water in a saucepan and bring to the boil. Lower the heat and simmer for about 10 minutes or until the syrup forms a slightly sticky film on a spoon. Set aside to cool.

Place the nuts, icing sugar and orange blossom water in a bowl and mix well.

Brush a large baking tray with a little of the melted butter. Lay the filo out flat on a work top and cover with a tea towel to prevent it drying out.

Take one sheet of the filo, lay it out flat and brush the surface all over with melted butter. Lay another sheet of filo over the buttered one. Using a long, thin rolling pin about 1cm (½in) in diameter (or a long, round stick) position it 2.5cm (1in) in from one of the shorter ends. Sprinkle a little of the filling all along the inner edge of the stick, as evenly as possible. Carefully fold the pastry over the stick and then roll the stick over the filling.

Fold over once more and then brush the edge with butter. Fold over once more and then cut along the edge with a knife. Do not fold more than 4 times. You should get 3 rolls from each 2 sheets of filo.

Carefully push the rolled pastry from both sides in towards the centre to make the roll smaller and to create wrinkles and folds. Take care or the filling will burst through the pastry. Carefully pull out the stick. Transfer this pastry to the baking tray and place with the edge downwards.

Continue in this way until you have finished the filling and filo. Arrange all the pastries on the baking tray quite close together and brush the tops with any remaining melted butter. Bake in an oven preheated to 180C (350F) gas 4 for about 30 minutes or until the pastries are lightly golden.

Remove the pastries from the oven and leave to rest for 10 minutes.

Cut each pastry in half and then pour the syrup over them.

Set aside to cool and then serve.

Makes 30-36

Below I have suggested 2 alternative fillings, but you can experiment with any of the fillings suggested on pages 10-12, halving the quantities.

bademli samsa tatlisi

almond-filled samsa sweets

Filling
225g (½ lb) blanched almonds, chopped
3 tablespoons icing sugar
½ teaspoon ground cinnamon
2 tablespoons almond essence

Mix the filling ingredients together in a bowl and prepare the sweets as described in the recipe above.

elmali samsa tatlisi

palace apple twists

Filling
225g (½ lb) apples, peeled and grated
110g (4 oz) caster sugar
½ teaspoon ground cinnamon

Put the grated apple in a muslin bag and squeeze to remove as much juice as possible. Put the apple pulp into a bowl, mix in the sugar and cinnamon and then prepare the sweets as described in the recipe above.

m'hencha

serpent rolls

M'hencha means 'like a serpent' and this pastry is arranged in the pan in such a way that it looks like a coiled snake. It is one of the classics of North African cuisine and its appearance is most attractive. The paper-thin pastry used in North Africa is called *ouarka*, but baklava filo is ideal.

12 sheets filo pastry trimmed to about 30 X 20cm (12 X 8in)
1 egg yolk

Filling
225g (½ lb) ground almonds
175g (6 oz) icing sugar
2 tablespoons orange blossom water
50g (2 oz) unsalted butter, melted
1 egg yolk
2 teaspoons ground cinnamon

Garnish
2-3 tablespoons icing sugar
1 teaspoon ground cinnamon

Place the almonds, sugar, orange blossom water and butter in a saucepan and mix to a paste. Cook over a low heat for 10-15 minutes or until the sugar dissolves.

Remove from the heat, add the egg yolk and cinnamon and mix thoroughly.

Stack the filo sheets on top of each other on the work top and cover with a cloth.

Remove 1 sheet and place on the work top with one of the longer sides nearest you. Brush all over with egg yolk and lay another filo sheet on top of it.

Take one sixth of the almond mixture and arrange it in a ridge 3.5cm (1½in) in from the edge nearest you and reaching right to the 2 shorter ends.

Fold the 3.5cm (1½in) of pastry over the filling and then roll up in the rest of the pastry. Brush the top edge with egg to stick it down. Repeat with remaining filo and filling.

Brush a round baking tray about 22.5-25cm (9-10in) in diameter with a little melted butter. Take one roll and very carefully curl it around itself to form a coil. Do this gently or the filling will burst out. Place this coil in the middle of the tray. Take another roll, place one end of it next to the outside end of the coil on the tray and coil this roll around the first one.

Continue using the rolls to extend the coil, sticking the ends of each roll together with a little of the egg yolk.

When all the rolls are on the tray brush all over with the remaining egg yolk.

Place in an oven preheated to 190C (375F) gas 5 and bake for about 30 minutes or until golden brown in colour. Remove from the oven and leave to cool. Place on a serving plate, sift the icing sugar over the top and decorate with the cinnamon.

Serves about 8

kunafeh

shredded pastry with nuts

Poets have sung the praises of this sweet. In the courts of the caliphs of Baghdad trays of kunafeh were served amongst rapture as the ivory-skinned maidens moved their bellies to the rhythms of tambours and flutes, while the poet whispered 'God has not given my belly half of the words it would utter of kunafeh's sweetness'.

Kunafeh pastry looks like shredded wheat or fine vermicelli and it is sold in 450g (1 lb) packets under the name of kadayifi fila. Kadayifi is the Greek name of this sweet – in Turkish it is known as Tel-kadayif, but both are misnomers derived from the Arab word for pancake *ataif*. In most Middle Eastern households even today kunafeh pastry is still made at home by the time-honoured process of passing a batter of flour and water through a brass-plated sieve on

to a hot metal sheet. The dough sets in seconds and the shredded pastry is swept to one side.

The recipe below – a family one – is also known as Zadgi kunafeh since it is traditionally prepared around Christmas and the New Year.

450g (1 lb) kadayifi pastry
350g (¾ lb) unsalted butter, melted and with the froth removed

Filling
175g (6 oz) chopped or coarsely ground walnuts
2 tablespoons sugar
2 teaspoons ground cinnamon

Syrup
350g (¾ lb) sugar
juice of 1 lemon
2 tablespoons rosewater

First prepare the syrup. Place the sugar, lemon juice and 350ml (12 fl oz) water in a saucepan and bring to the boil. Lower the heat and simmer for about 10 minutes or until the syrup forms a slightly sticky film on a spoon. Remove from the heat, stir in the rosewater and set aside to cool.

Lightly brush a baking tin about 30 X 23cm (12 X 9in) or about 25cm (10in) in diameter and at least 2.5cm (1in) deep, with a little of the melted butter. Put the pastry into a large bowl and gently ease apart the strands without breaking them. Remove any hard nodules of pastry which you may find in some brands.

Pour three-quarters of the melted butter into the bowl and gently rub all the strands between your fingers until they are well coated with the butter.

Divide the pastry into 2 equal parts and spread 1 part evenly over the base of the tin. Mix the filling ingredients together and spread evenly over the pastry.

Press the filling down firmly. Arrange the remaining pastry evenly over the top, tuck in any strands hanging over the sides and press the pastry down firmly.

Spoon the remaining melted butter evenly over the top, discarding the white residue in the bottom of the pan.

Place in an oven preheated to 180C (350F) gas 4 and cook for ½ hour.

Lower the heat to 150C (300F) gas 2 and cook for a further 1½ hours or until golden. Remove from the oven and pour the syrup slowly over the kunafeh, covering as much of the surface as possible. Cover with silver foil, place a heavy board over the top and add a heavy weight in order to flatten the kunafeh. Leave to cool and then cut into squares or lozenges 3.5-5cm (1½-2in) in size.

Makes 24-30 pieces

kunafeh mabrouma

rolled kunafeh with whole pistachio nuts

A Syrian speciality, these kunafehs are shaped into rolls, baked and then cut into smaller pieces. This dry, very rich sweet is best eaten with coffee or, as is the custom in the Orient, with orange or mulberry sherbet. In Turkey it is known as Burma Tel-kadayif from the Arab word to 'whirl' or 'twist'.

450g (1 lb) kadayifi pastry
350g (¾ lb) unsalted butter, melted and with froth removed

Filling
350g (¾ lb) whole, shelled pistachio nuts
75g (3 oz) finely chopped almonds
3 tablespoons sugar

Syrup
350g (¾ lb) sugar
juice of 1 lemon
1 tablespoon orange blossom water

First prepare the syrup. Place the sugar, lemon juice and 350ml (12 fl oz) water in a saucepan and bring to the boil. Lower the heat and simmer until the syrup begins to leave a sticky film on a spoon.

Remove from the heat, stir in the orange blossom water and cool.

Put the pastry into a large bowl and gently ease apart the strands without breaking them. Divide the pastry into 3 portions. Take 1 of the portions and lay it out on a clean work top. Flatten it as much as possible with your hands until it is about ½-1cm (¼-½in) thick and then shape it into an oblong approximately 30 X 15cm (12 X 6in).

With a pastry brush, brush the surface with some of the melted butter.

Take a flat stick about 45cm (18in) long and approximately 2.5cm (1in) wide and lay it diagonally across the flattened pastry. Mix the filling ingredients together and then lay one-third of the mixture evenly along the stick. Roll the strands of dough around the stick as tightly as possible. Carefully slide the stick out leaving the filling inside. Brush some melted butter all over the roll of pastry. Prepare the other portions of pastry in the same way.

Lightly butter a baking tray about 30 X 20cm (12 X 8in).

Arrange the 3 pastry rolls on the tray and pour any remaining butter over the rolls, taking care to discard the milky residue. Cook in an oven preheated to 180C (350F) gas 4 for 30 minutes.

Lower the temperature to 150C (300F) gas 2 and cook for a further 1½ hours or until the kunafeh is golden. Remove from the oven and pour the cold syrup evenly over the rolls, turning each one so that it is covered all over with the syrup.

Leave to cool and then cut each roll, at a slant, into 5-7.5cm (2-3in) long pieces.

Makes 15-18 pieces

kunafeh mafrouke

rubbed kunafeh

In this sweet the pastry is shredded as small as possible, rubbed in butter, flavoured with rosewater and orange blossom water and topped with nuts and icing sugar. A traditional Lebanese sweet, it is light and quick to make. Serve as it is or with cream.

110g (4 oz) unsalted butter
25g (1 oz) pistachio nuts
25g (1 oz) blanched almonds
25g (1 oz) pine kernels
225g (½ lb) kadayifi pastry
2 teaspoons rosewater
2 teaspoons orange blossom water
110g (4 oz) icing sugar
1 teaspoon ground cinnamon

Melt half the butter in a small saucepan and remove any froth. Add the pistachio nuts and fry for a few minutes, stirring frequently, until golden. Remove with a slotted spoon, drain and reserve. Fry first the almonds and then the pine kernels in the same way.

Place the shredded pastry in a large bowl and use your hands to keep tearing the pastry until it forms small strands about the size of rice grains. Alternatively pass the pastry through a mincer. Melt the remaining butter in a large saucepan and spoon off any froth. Add the pastry and, over a low to moderate heat, rub the butter into the pastry until all the shreds are as fine as possible and covered with butter. Remove from the heat and leave to cool.

Add the rosewater and orange blossom water and mix thoroughly.

Stir in three-quarters of the icing sugar and the cinnamon and transfer the sweet to a serving bowl. Sprinkle the nuts over the top and dust with the remaining icing sugar.

Serve cold with or without cream. Eat on the day it is prepared.

Serves 8

'When he had opened his shop in the cobblers' market, he lifted his hands on high, praying: "O lord, grant that I earn enough to buy an ounce of kunafeh, and save myself from the hands of that vile woman!" But, in spite of this, no man brought him any work that day and he did not earn even enough to buy a crust of bread for supper. It was with trembling fingers that he locked his shop, and upon trembling feet that he set out towards his home.

'But his way lay past the shop of a pastrycook whose shoes he had often mended, and the man, seeing him walk by in evident despair with his back bent under some heavy weight of grief, called to him, saying: "Master Maaruf, why do you weep? What is your trouble? Come in here and rest while you tell me all about it." Maaruf approached the delightful counter, and exclaimed after greeting: "There is no power or might save in Allah, the Merciful, the Compassionate! Destiny pursues me and will not even allow me supper." Then, as the pastrycook insisted all further details, he told him of his wife's demand and how impossible it was of obedience.

'When the man had heard all, he answered with a good-natured laugh: "At least you might tell me how many ounces of kunafeh your good lady requires." "Perhaps five would be enough," answered Maaruf. "Then let it not trouble you," cried the benevolent cook. "I will let you have the five ounces and you can give me the price when Allah returns to you with His favour." He cut off a large slab of kunafeh and set it in a dish, where it swam among butter and honey. As he set the dish in Maaruf's hand, he said: "This is worthy of a king's table. I have not made it with bee honey but with sugarcane honey, a change from the usual which improves it greatly."

'But the calamitous woman had no sooner set eyes on the dish than she uttered a cry of strident indignation and, beating her cheeks, exclaimed: "Allah curse the Stoned One! Did I not tell you it must be made with bee honey? You have brought me golden syrup to spite me! Did you imagine that I could not tell the difference. Do you wish to thwart me into my grave, you dog?" Poor Maaruf said: "O daughter of excellent parents, I did not buy this kunafeh; one of Allah's compassionate pastrycooks had pity on me and gave it to me with indefinite credit." But, even so, the terrifying shrew thus broke in upon him: "These are but words and help you not at all! Take your dirty treacle kunafeh!" With that she threw the confection at her husband's head, dish and all, and bade him rise up for a pimp and bring her another made with honey. At the same time she buffeted him so heartily all the jaw that she broke one of his front teeth and caused the blood to spurt over his beard and breast.'

1001 Nights. J. C. Mardins

kunafeh min jibn
shredded pastry with cheese

An Arabic speciality which is also popular with Turks. This is a Syrian recipe. To make it you need a soft, unsalted cheese – akkawi, ricotta or any other sweet cheese will do. You can also use feta cheese but, if you do, first soak it in water for several hours, changing the water several times. The syrup can either be poured over the kunafeh when it is removed from the oven or you can serve the syrup separately.

450g (1 lb) kadayifi pastry
150g (5 oz) unsalted butter, melted and with froth removed

Filling
350g (¾ lb) sweetened cheese, eg. ricotta, akkawe or feta
(soak the latter in water for several hours)
1 tablespoon rosewater

Syrup
450g (1 lb) sugar
1 tablespoon lemon juice
1 tablespoon rosewater
1 tablespoon orange blossom water

First prepare the syrup. Place the sugar, lemon juice and 450 ml ($^3/_4$ pint) water in a saucepan and bring to the boil. Lower the heat and simmer for about 10 minutes or until the syrup forms a slightly sticky film on a spoon. Set aside to cool after stirring in the rosewater and orange blossom water.

Grate the cheese into a bowl and mix in the rosewater.

Place the pastry in a large bowl and pull apart the strands, loosening them and breaking them into smaller pieces. Brush a baking tin about 30 X 20cm (12 X 8in) and at least 2.5 cm (1in) deep with a little of the melted butter. Pour the remaining butter over the pastry, discarding any white residue in the bottom of the pan. Rub the butter into the pastry until all the strands are well coated.

Spread half the pastry evenly over the bottom of the tin. Spread the cheese filling evenly over the pastry. Spread the remaining pastry evenly over the top and press it down lightly, tucking in any loose strands hanging over the edge of the tin.

Place in an oven preheated to 160C (325F) gas 3 and bake for 45 minutes or until the kunafeh is a light golden colour. Remove the tray from the oven, place a larger tin over the top and invert, thus turning the sweet over into the larger tin. Return to the oven and cook for a further 30-45 minutes or until the top of the kunafeh is dark golden. Remove from the oven and either pour the syrup over it immediately or allow the sweet to cool and serve separately with the syrup. Cut into 5cm (2in) squares when cold.

Makes about 24

sarma tel-kadayif
nuts wrapped in shredded pastry

Middle Easterners have a mania for wrapping things inside other things. This recipe does exactly that – the shredded pastry is wrapped around a nut and cinnamon filling. Delicious with fresh cream poured over the top.

450g (1 lb) kadayifi pastry
225g (½ lb) unsalted butter, melted and with froth removed

Filling
175g (6 oz) walnuts, coarsely ground or almonds or a mixture of the two
3 tablespoons sugar
2 teaspoons ground cinnamon
1 egg, lightly beaten

Syrup
450g (1 lb) sugar
juice of 1 lemon
1 tablespoon rosewater
1 tablespoon orange blossom water

Prepare the syrup. Place the sugar, lemon juice and 450ml ($^3/_4$ pint) water in a saucepan and bring to the boil. Lower the heat and simmer for about 10 minutes or until the syrup forms a slightly sticky film on a spoon. Stir in the rosewater and orange blossom water and set aside to cool. Place the filling ingredients in a bowl and mix until the nuts are well moistened.

Place the kadayifi pastry on the work top and gently loosen the strands without pulling them completely apart. Discard any coarse bits. Divide the dough into 4 equal portions and lay 1 portion out in front of you.

Gently ease into an oblong shape about 10cm (4in) wide.

Place about $^3/_4$ tablespoon of the filling in a ridge about 3.5cm (1$^1/_2$in) in from one of the short sides and 1cm ($^1/_2$in) in from the long ends. Wrap the 2 sides over the filling and then fold over the 3.5cm (1$^1/_2$in) pastry, thus covering the filling from 3 sides. Roll the pastry over twice and then cut off the remaining oblong of pastry with a sharp knife. The result should be a sausage-shaped sweet about 6-7.5cm (2$^1/_2$-3in) long.

Lightly grease a large baking tray with a little of the melted butter. Place the rolled sweet on the baking tray. Repeat three times with the remaining pastry in that portion. Each portion should produce 4 rolled sweets.

When you have used up all the pastry and filling arrange the sweets on the baking tray. Pour the melted butter evenly over the rolls, discarding any white residue in the bottom of the pan. Place in an oven preheated to 160C (325F) gas 3 and bake for 30-40 minutes or until lightly golden. Remove from the oven and pour the cool syrup evenly over the rolls.

Allow to cool and then serve with cream.

Makes about 16

ballorieh

white kunafeh

'She has a ballorieh skin' – a compliment implying the lady in question is light-skinned – in contrast to the swarthy or dark-skinned majority. A Syrian speciality, ballorieh is the 'Queen of all kunafehs' – milk white in appearance and tightly packed with pistachio nuts this is the sweet that is always reserved for the most honoured guests.

150g (5 oz) unsalted butter, melted and with froth removed
1 tablespoon clear honey
450g (1 lb) kadayifi pastry

Filling
175g (6 oz) coarsely chopped pistachio nuts
40g (1½ oz) sugar
½ tablespoon ground cinnamon

Syrup
450g (1 lb) sugar
1 tablespoon lemon juice

Garnish
2 tablespoons very finely chopped pistachio nuts

Pour the melted butter into a bowl, discarding the milky substance in the bottom of the pan, and place the bowl in the refrigerator until the butter is semi-solid. Remove from the fridge, add the honey and whisk until the mixture begins to foam. Pour the mixture into a baking tin about 30 X 20cm (12 X 8in) and at least 2.5cm (1in) deep.

Open up the packet of pastry and lay it out on a clean work top. In order to loosen the strands I suggest that you divide the pastry into 4 portions and squeeze each portion between the palms of your hands – as though making a snowball – for about 2 minutes. Take 2 sections of the pastry and, without breaking the strands, gently ease the pastry out spreading it over the bottom of the tray.

Mix the filling ingredients together in a bowl. Spread this filling evenly over the pastry in the tray. Gently ease apart the 2 remaining portions of pastry and arrange them evenly over the filling. Press the pastry down firmly and tuck in any strands of pastry hanging over the edge of the tin. Place in an oven preheated to 150C (300F) gas 2 and bake for 20 minutes. Keep the door ajar – this will prevent the balourieh from changing colour.

Meanwhile prepare the syrup. Place the sugar, lemon juice and 450ml (³/₄ pint) water in a saucepan and bring to the boil. Boil vigorously for 5 minutes and then remove from the heat.

After the balourieh has been cooking for 20 minutes take it from the oven.

Very carefully lift the tin to an angle and pour the butter and honey mixture into a bowl. Now completely cover the sweet with another flat surface, e.g. a chopping board or the back of another tin, and turn the balourieh over on to this surface. Very gently and carefully slide the sweet – now bottom side up – back into the tin.

Return to the oven and, still keeping the door open, cook for a further 20 minutes.

Remove from the oven.

Pour the boiling syrup evenly over the surface of the sweet. In order to get the tight and compact appearance of the sweet, put an empty tray over it and hold it down with a heavy weight while the sweet cools. When cold cut into 3.5-5cm (1½-2in) squares. Sprinkle some of the very finely chopped pistachio nuts over each square and serve.

Makes 24-30

kaymakli tel-kadayif

kunafeh with cream

Although this recipe is called kunafeh with cream the filling is in fact made with milk and semolina. A light and delicious sweet, it is popular throughout the Middle East but especially so in Turkey. It should be eaten within 48 hours or the cream will harden.

450g (1 lb) kadayifi pastry
175g (6 oz) unsalted butter, melted and with froth removed

Filling
600ml (1 pint) milk
40g (1½ oz) fine semolina
1 tablespoon rosewater

Syrup
450g (1 lb) sugar
1 tablespoon lemon juice

First prepare the syrup. Place the sugar, lemon juice and 450ml (¾ pint) water in a saucepan and bring to the boil. Lower the heat and simmer for about 10 minutes or until the syrup forms a slightly sticky film on a spoon. Set aside to cool.

To prepare the filling bring the milk to the boil in a small saucepan.

Place the semolina in a small bowl, add a little of the milk to make a smooth paste and then stir into the rest of the milk. Cook over a low heat, stirring constantly, until the mixture thickens. Stir in the rosewater and set aside to cool.

Brush a baking tin about 30 X 20cm (12 X 8in) and at least 2.5cm (1in) deep with a little of the melted butter. Place the kadayifi pastry in a large bowl and pull the strands apart to loosen them. Remove any coarse bits of pastry found in some brands. Pour the butter over the pastry, discarding any white residue in the bottom of the pan. Rub the butter into the pastry until all strands are well coated.

Spread half the pastry evenly over the bottom of the tin. Pour the cool filling over the pastry and spread it out evenly with the back of a spoon. Spread the remaining pastry evenly over the filling. Press down lightly and tuck in any strands hanging over the edge of the tin.

Place in an oven preheated to 180C (350F) gas 4 and cook for 1 hour or until the kunafeh is a dark golden colour. Remove from the oven and pour the cold syrup evenly over the sweet. Allow to cool and then cut into 5cm (2in) squares and serve.

Makes 20-24

kiz memesi tel kadayif

'young girls' breasts'

The Turks lovingly call these pastries young girls' breasts. They are small, firm, rounded pastries each topped with half a walnut – it has to be a Turk to think of such imagery! The filling suggested below is chopped almonds, but you can substitute hazelnuts, pistachio nuts or a mixture of coconut and chopped walnuts. Pour the syrup hot over the pastries – it will then trickle down through the pastry and, when cold, will help the sweets to maintain their shape.

450g (1 lb) kadayifi pastry
225g (½ lb) unsalted butter, melted and with froth removed
about 12 walnut halves
50-75g (2-3 oz) almonds, finely chopped

Syrup
675g (1½ lb)
1 tablespoon lemon juice

Open out the shredded pastry on a work top and discard any coarse bits.

Now shred the pastry very finely with your hands, or pass it through a mincer. The aim is to get very small, fine pastry shreds. Drop the pastry into a large bowl and then pour most of the melted butter over the top. Mix and rub with your hands until all the pastry shreds are coated with the butter.

Lightly brush 2 baking trays with a little of the remaining butter.

To make these sweets in the correct shape you need a soup ladle about 6cm (2½in) in diameter or a container of a similar size and shape. Lightly brush the inside of the ladle with a little melted butter. Put one of the walnut halves in the bottom of the ladle. Fill the ladle with shredded and buttered pastry and press down. Make a hole with your index finger in the centre of the pastry, large enough to take 2 teaspoons of the chopped nuts. Push the nuts in.

Add a little more pastry to cover the nuts and press down as hard as possible to make a firm mould. Place your fingers over the mouth of the ladle, turn it over and then lift the ladle off. Transfer the pastry to the greased baking tray.

Continue making pastries until you have used up all the ingredients. Place in an oven preheated to 180C (350F) gas 4 and bake for about 40 minutes.

While they are cooking prepare the syrup. Place the sugar, lemon juice and 450ml (¾ pint) water in a saucepan and bring to the boil. Simmer for about 10 minutes.

When the pastries are cooked, remove from the oven. Bring the syrup back to the boil and then ladle the syrup over the pastries.

Set aside to cool and then serve by themselves or with cream.

Makes about 12

halvas

In the Aleppo of my childhood one of the most important men was a thickset, middle-aged Turk with a long moustache and an even longer red fez tilted to one side. He was called Osman, but better known as 'Halvaji Osman'. Osman the halva-maker was undoubtedly one of the greatest unsung chefs of the East. In his dark, gas-lit shop (under the large 'bar dawah' hanging from the ceiling which a youngster of my own age manoeuvred by pushing and pulling his foot forward, backward and forward again thus ventilating the dry air of the desert and frightening the famed 'Aleppo flies' away to some other Godforsaken abode) were gathered, in tray after tray, some of the most delicious culinary masterpieces of the Middle East. When a mere stripling I gorged, in utter delight, halva with pistachio nuts, or walnuts, or almonds, plain sesame halva, vanilla or chocolate halva, halva with raisins, fruits or honey, or my childhood favourite – the unsurpassable, unbeatable 'Ruz-el-Bint' (young girl's hair) – a delicacy of pistachio nuts covered in layers of spun sugar.

Halva – from the ancient Akkadian word 'Helou' – means sweet and is usually today applied to sweetmeats and sweet dishes in general. The name appears throughout the region including Greece and as far away as India. Yet in the Middle Ages halva as a dessert was the prerogative of the rich and was unknown to the poor, who had to make do with dates and oil-cakes. One day Caliph Muqtadir was journeying by boat. At lunchtime he was invited by the crew to share their food. The Caliph thanked and joined them. Having finished the meal he asked for his customary halva. The sailors apologised saying that they were not accustomed to sweet dishes and could only offer dates and dry cakes. (Told in *Nishwar al-Muhadara of Al-Tanukhi* ed D. S. Margoliouth, Cairo 1921.)

Today halvas are the fare of the poor for they are simple and cheap to prepare. They are made with semolina or plain flour although the latter is usually substituted with couscous in North Africa or riceflour or chickpea flour in Iran. They are wholesome, delicious sweets that can be eaten warm or cold. The first recipe is a family one from Armenia. It is one that I often prepare as a great treat for my friends.

imrig khavitz

semolina halva

Syrup
t75g (6 oz) sugar
1 tablespoon rosewater
75g (3 oz) butter
175g (6 oz) fine semolina
2 tablespoons raisins
2 tablespoons blanched almonds
2 tablespoons pine kernels
2 tablespoons ground cinnamon

First prepare the syrup. Place the sugar and 300ml (½ pint) water in a small saucepan and bring to the boil. Lower the heat and simmer for about 10 minutes or until the syrup forms a slightly sticky film on the back of a spoon. Remove from the heat, stir in the rosewater and set aside to cool.

Melt the butter in a saucepan, add the semolina and stir well. Cook over a medium heat for several minutes, stirring constantly, until the semolina has slightly browned. Add the raisins and almonds and half the pine kernels and cinnamon and stir well.

Gradually pour in the syrup, stirring constantly. Cook for about 5 more minutes until the syrup is absorbed and the mixture has thickened. Remove from the heat and allow to cool for about 5 minutes.

Now scoop a tablespoon of the mixture into the palm of your hand, close your fingers around it, press tightly and then place on a serving plate. Repeat until all the halva is thus arranged. Sprinkle the remaining cinnamon over the halva and stick 1 pine kernel into each piece. Serve warm with tea or coffee.

Serves 4-6

mamouniah

aleppan halva

This recipe from Syria is another personal favourite and is named after the famed Caliph Al-Mamoun. Mamouniah is eaten daily for breakfast as well as being given to the sick, the weak and to pregnant women. Some people like to serve it with kaymak or double cream.

110g (¼ lb) unsalted butter
110g (¼ lb) fine semolina
1 teaspoon ground cinnamon

Syrup
175g (6 oz) sugar
1 tablespoon lemon juice

First prepare the syrup. Place the sugar, lemon juice and 600ml (1 pint) water in a saucepan and bring to the boil. Lower the heat and simmer for 15 minutes or until the syrup forms a slightly sticky film on a spoon and then set aside.

Melt the butter in a large saucepan. Add the semolina and fry, stirring constantly, for about 5 minutes or until the mixture has become crumbly in appearance. Pour in the syrup and mix thoroughly with a wooden spoon. Cook for a further 2-3 minutes. Remove from the heat and set aside for 12-15 minutes.

Spoon into a serving bowl, sprinkle with the cinnamon and serve warm.

Serves 4-6

mal beyrouth
lebanese halva

Also known, amongst Turks and Armenians, as Şam Tatlisi – Damascus sweet, yet in Damascus they call it Mal Beyrouth – Beirut sweet! It is a heavily saturated halva which is sold by sweet vendors in large, round trays. I recall as a child that most vendors used to scatter small change under the halva thus tempting us children to spend more of our pocket money. If we had luck we could win an extra portion of the sweet. My *kismet* hardly ever came! Serve cold.

50g (2 oz) unsalted butter
200ml (6 fl oz) milk
1 egg, beaten
25g (1 oz) crushed walnuts
25g (1 oz) crushed hazelnuts
225g (½ lb) fine semolina or plain flour
25g (1 oz) caster sugar
½ teaspoon salt

Syrup
350g (¾ lb) sugar
juice of ½ lemon

Garnish
toasted almonds

Melt the butter in a large saucepan. Add the milk, egg and crushed nuts and stir thoroughly with a wooden spoon.

Gradually stir in the semolina and then the sugar and salt.

Lightly grease a round baking tin about 20-22.5cm (8-9in) in diameter. Turn the semolina mixture into the tin and smooth the surface over with the back of a spoon. Place in an oven preheated to 160C (325F) gas 3 and bake for 1 hour. Halfway through baking remove the tin from the oven and cut into lozenge shapes about 5cm (2in) square. Press a toasted almond into the centre of each lozenge. Return to the oven for the remainder of the cooking time.

Meanwhile prepare the syrup. Place the sugar, lemon juice and 200ml ($\frac{1}{3}$ pint) water in a saucepan. Bring to the boil and simmer for 5 minutes. Remove from the heat and leave to cool.

When the halva is golden, remove from the oven and immediately pour the cold syrup over the cake. Leave to cool and serve with cream.

Makes 12-14 pieces

In Egypt these kinds of halva are better known as Basbousa – the best known of which are the recipes below, one with yoghurt and the other, similar in principle to Mal Beyrouth, with almonds. They are very rich halvas drenched in butter and syrup.

basbousa-bil-laban
halva with yoghurt

75g (3 oz) blanched almonds
225g (½ lb) unsalted butter
150ml (¼ pint) yoghurt
110g (¼ lb) sugar
175g (6 oz) fine semolina
1 teaspoon baking powder
1 teaspoon vanilla essence

Syrup
225g (½ lb) sugar
2 tablespoons lemon juice

First prepare the syrup. Place the sugar, lemon juice and 150ml (¼ pint) water in a saucepan and bring to the boil. Lower the heat and simmer for about 10 minutes or until the syrup forms a slightly sticky film on a spoon. Set aside to cool.

Toast the almonds under the grill until golden, turning once. Chop the almonds finely. Melt the butter in a saucepan. Pour the yoghurt into a large mixing bowl; add half the melted butter, the sugar, semolina, baking powder, vanilla essence and almonds. Mix thoroughly until well blended.

Grease a round baking tin about 20cm (8in) in diameter. Pour the mixture into the tin and smooth over with the back of a spoon.

Bake in an oven preheated to 200C (400F) gas 6 for 30-35 minutes or until the surface is golden brown. Remove the basbousa from the oven and pour the cold syrup over the sweet.

Cut into squares and lozenges. Return the tin to the oven for a further 3-4 minutes.

Warm the remaining butter, remove the basbousa from the oven and pour the butter evenly over its surface. Leave to cool and serve with or without cream.

Makes 12-14 pieces

halawah-bil-loz

halva with almonds

110g (4 oz) blanched almonds
110g (4 oz) unsalted butter
175g (6 oz) fine semolina
2 tablespoons raisins

Syrup
350g (12 oz) sugar
1 tablespoon lemon juice
1 tablespoon rosewater

Garnish
whole almonds
cream (optional)

Place the sugar, lemon juice and 600ml (1 pint) water in a saucepan and bring to the boil.
Simmer for about 5 minutes then remove from the heat, stir in the rosewater and set aside.
Chop the almonds finely. Melt the butter in a large saucepan, add the almonds, semolina and raisins and fry, stirring constantly until golden in colour. Now add the hot syrup to the semolina mixture slowly, stirring constantly, until the mixture thickens – about 3-5 minutes. Remove from the heat, cover and leave for about 10 minutes. Pour into small dessert dishes and smooth over the tops. Decorate each with a few whole almonds and serve as it is or with cream.

Serves 4-6

halawah-bil-gibna

cheese halva

A deliciously flavoured and coarsely textured halva.

110g (4 oz) unsalted butter
175g (6 oz) fine semolina
3 tablespoons pine kernels or blanched almonds
75g (3 oz) feta cheese or any other mild white cheese, grated

Garnish
1 teaspoon ground cinnamon

175g (6 oz) sugar
250ml (8 fl oz) milk

First prepare the syrup. Place the sugar, milk and 250ml (8 fl oz) water in a saucepan and bring to the boil. Lower the heat, simmer for 10 minutes and then set aside.

Melt the butter in a large saucepan. Add the semolina, pine kernels or almonds and mix well. Fry for about 10 minutes, stirring constantly, until the mixture is golden.

Slowly stir in the milk syrup. Cover the pan and simmer over a low heat, stirring occasionally, until the syrup is absorbed and the mixture has thickened. Add the grated cheese and cook for a further 2-3 minutes, stirring frequently until the cheese has melted. Transfer to a serving dish, sprinkle with the cinnamon and serve warm.

Serves 4-6

revani

semolina cake

Revani is a popular semolina cake throughout Turkey, Greece and Armenia. It was first popularised during the time of Byzantium and her fratricidal emperors.

6 large eggs, separated
225g (8 oz) sugar
225g (8 oz) fine semolina
1 teaspoon baking powder
2 tablespoons blanched almonds, chopped finely
2 tablespoons brandy
pinch salt

Syrup
350g (12 oz) sugar
1 stick cinnamon 7.5-10cm (3-4in) long

Place the egg yolks in a large bowl, add the sugar and beat until smooth and light in colour. Add the semolina, baking powder and almonds and stir thoroughly. Stir in the brandy.

In another bowl whisk the egg whites until stiff. Add the salt and whisk until the egg whites stand up in peaks. Fold the egg whites gently into the semolina mixture. Grease a cake tin about 25cm (10in) square and 5cm (2in) deep, pour in the cake mixture and smooth over. Bake in an oven preheated to 180C (350F) gas 4 for 30-40 minutes or until golden.

Meanwhile prepare the syrup. Place the sugar, cinnamon stick and 600ml (1 pint) water in a saucepan and bring to the boil. Reduce the heat and simmer for 15 minutes. Set aside to cool. When the cake is cooked remove it from the oven and spoon the syrup over it. Use as much syrup as will be easily absorbed, but do not make the cake too soggy. Leave to cool and then refrigerate. Before serving cut into 5cm (2in) diamond shapes. Eat with or without cream.

Makes 25

limonlu revani

lemon semolina cake

This variation is flavoured with lemon. Follow the recipe above but omit the blanched almonds and brandy. Instead beat the grated rind of 3 lemons and 1 tablespoon of lemon juice into the mixture after stirring in the semolina, and then continue with the recipe.

un helvasi

flour-based halva

Halvas are also prepared with plain flour or rice flour. These are equally popular and there are many versions; most are lighter in colour and finer in texture. The simplest and most typical one is this recipe from Turkey.

110g (4 oz) unsalted butter
275g (10 oz) plain flour, sifted
blanched almonds

Syrup
175g (6 oz) sugar
1½ tablespoons honey
1 tablespoon lemon juice
1 tablespoon rosewater

First prepare the syrup. Place the sugar, honey, lemon juice and 250ml (8 fl oz) water in a saucepan and bring to the boil. Simmer for 5 minutes, remove from the heat, and set aside to cool.

Melt the butter in a large saucepan. Add the flour, stir well and cook over a low heat, stirring constantly, for about 20 minutes or until the flour is a light golden colour. Remove from the heat and slowly stir in the syrup. Mix until well blended.

Spoon the mixture on to a large serving plate and smooth the surface over with the back of a spoon. Mark into 5cm (2in) squares. Toast some blanched almonds until golden and press one into the centre of each square. When cold cut with a sharp knife and serve with tea or coffee.

Serves 4-6

halwa ajami

iranian halva

This recipe is traditionally served during the month of Ramadan when all good Muslims fast from dawn till dusk. 'Eat and drink until so much of the dawn appears that a white thread may be distinguished from a black; then keep the fast completely until night.' (*Koran 2:183*) The fast is broken with a cup of warm water, some dates, an egg, tea, bread, honey and cheese and this particular halva which can be eaten plain or spread on bread.

225g (8 oz) unsalted butter
225g (8 oz) plain flour, sifted

Syrup
175g (6 oz) sugar
1 tablespoon rosewater
1 teaspoon ground saffron dissolved in 1 tablespoon hot water

Melt the butter in a large saucepan. Lower the heat and gradually stir in the flour. Cook for about 15-20 minutes, stirring constantly, until the flour is golden, and then remove from the heat.

Place the sugar and 250ml (8 fl oz) water in a small saucepan, bring to the boil and simmer for 5 minutes. Remove from the heat and stir in the rosewater and dissolved saffron. Slowly pour the syrup into the flour mixture, stirring constantly until the mixture thickens – it should look like peanut butter. Transfer the halva to a large serving plate and smooth over the surface with the back of a spoon. Using the back of a soup spoon, imprint half circles on the halva at regular intervals in straight lines horizontally and vertically.

Allow to cool for 30 minutes before serving.

Serves 4-6

kachi

honeymoon halva

This golden coloured sweet is traditionally served at weddings –first to the bride and groom and then to the children and finally to the guests.

Prepare as for Halwa Ajami, but stir into the mixture.

25g (1 oz) seedless raisins
50g (2 oz) finely chopped dates

Garnish the halva with 2 tablespoons finely chopped pistachio nuts.

While on the subject of weddings and marriage celebrations I would like to quote some lines from *A Time in Arabia* by Doreen Ingrams about her experiences at an Arab wedding feast.

'"We are going to veil you and henna you, for you are to be the bride of Mashur." Sa'ud promptly burst into tears, which was expected of her, and was half carried to another room where she was dressed in red, the first time she had worn a coloured dress since going into purdah as a child of ten – The celebrations went on for almost a week. Every day hundreds of men and women were fed on the traditional rice and boiled mutton, while relatives and close friends had more elaborate meals in the family dining room. Teas were served all day long – cooking was done on the ground floor or in the back courtyard and I caught one nightmarish glimpse of four women sitting inches deep in onion skins, peeling for all they were worth.

'The morning after the wedding night the bridegroom is woken early and sent out of the room by the women servants who then wash the bride and allow her to sleep.

'Sa'ud, dressed in green and gold, sat on a mattress leaning against the two bridal pillows embroidered with gold tinsel and with propitious texts written on calico pinned to them.

'A servant passed around an incense bowl for us all to waft the smoke over our faces and another servant came in with freshly roasted coffee beans on a plaited straw tray over which we bent our heads to sniff the bouquet. Then came cups of coffee. Nothing at all was said and presently the men got up, placed money in the bride's lap and went out.'

sellou

festive halva

In North Africa large trays of Sellou are prepared on festive occasions such as the 40 days of Ramadan, a child's birth, a wedding. The halva is piled high like a cone and served generously to all relations, friends and passers-by. This sweet has a distinctive, earthy flavour with its combination of sesame seeds, honey and mastic (gum arabic).

225g (8 oz) plain flour, sifted
110g (4 oz) sesame seeds
75ml (2½ fl oz) vegetable oil
50g (2 oz) blanched almonds
2 teaspoons ground cinnamon
½ teaspoon aniseed
1 grain mastic, crushed with a little sugar
25g (1 oz) butter
60g (2½ oz) honey

Garnish
50g (2 oz) caster sugar
whole almonds and hazelnuts

Place the flour in a large saucepan and cook over a low heat for 15-20 minutes or until the flour is lightly browned, stirring constantly. Remove from the heat and pour into a large mixing bowl. Place the sesame seeds in a small saucepan and cook over a low heat, stirring constantly, until they are golden. Remove from the heat. Heat the oil in a small saucepan and fry the almonds until golden. Remove the almonds with a slotted spoon and place in a blender. Retain the oil. Add the sesame seeds to the blender and blend to a powder. Transfer this mixture to the mixing bowl. Add the cinnamon, aniseed and powdered mastic and mix well.

Melt the butter and honey in a small saucepan. Make a well in the centre of the flour mixture and add the butter-honey mixture and the remaining oil. Mix well with a wooden spoon until all the liquid has been absorbed. Transfer the halva to a serving plate and pile it up like a cone. Sprinkle generously with the sugar and decorate with the nuts. Serve with tea or coffee.

Serves 4-6

halawah bil-fawakeh

fruit halva

This recipe from Libya combines couscous and such fruits as melon, peaches, pears and grapes – delicious!

10-12 grapes, peeled, halved and seeded
1 pear, peeled, quartered, core removed, flesh cut into small pieces
1 peach, peeled, halved, stone removed, flesh cut into small pieces
5cm (2in) slice honeydew melon, flesh cut into small pieces
juice of 1 lemon
1 teaspoon ground cinnamon
2 tablespoons honey or carob syrup
75g (3 oz) raisins
50g (2 oz) unsalted butter
175g (6 oz) couscous

Garnish
2 tablespoons chopped walnuts

Place the prepared fruit in a large saucepan and stir in the lemon juice, cinnamon, honey or carob syrup and raisins. Cook over a low heat for about 5 minutes or until the fruit begins to give up its juices. Stir occasionally. Add the butter and allow to melt. Stir in the couscous, cover the pan and cook over a very low heat until the couscous is tender. Stir frequently, but gently. Spoon into a serving dish and leave to cool for about 15 minutes.

Sprinkle with the chopped walnuts and serve cool but not cold.

Serves 6

halawath-el-jazar

carrot halva

There are several such dishes in Iran and the Indian subcontinent where sweets made by reducing vegetables or fruits with sugar are called halva. An important ingredient in the preparation of these sweets is the addition of ghee (clarified butter). The Halvai of Northern India are the caste and profession of confectioners. Bananas, carrots, potatoes, marrows, oranges and many other fruits and vegetables are used in the making of these sweets. They are not, of course, true halvas in the Middle Eastern sense of the word, but the Akkadian-Arab name of the sweets show clearly the original source. The recipe below is from Iraq, but is also popular in Iran and the Gulf regions.

450g (1 lb) carrots, peeled and grated
3 tablespoons oil
110g (4 oz) fine semolina or sifted plain flour
3 tablespoons walnuts, coarsely chopped
1 teaspoon ground cardamom

Syrup
225g (8 oz) sugar
1 tablespoon lemon juice

Garnish
1 tablespoon finely chopped pistachio nuts

First prepare the syrup. Place the sugar, lemon juice and 350ml (12 fl oz) water together in a saucepan and bring to the boil. Lower the heat and simmer for 10 minutes and then remove and set aside.

Place the grated carrot in a large saucepan with 150ml (¼ pint) water and cook over a moderate heat, stirring occasionally, until the carrots are soft.

Drain the carrots. Heat the oil in the saucepan, add the carrots and fry for about 5 minutes, stirring frequently. Little by little add the flour, stirring constantly, and cook over a low heat, still stirring very frequently, until the flour is golden. Slowly stir in the syrup and continue cooking over a low heat until the syrup has been absorbed and the halva has thickened. Stir in the walnuts and cardamom.

Pour into a serving bowl or into individual glasses. Sprinkle with the chopped pistachio nuts and serve warm.

Serves 4-6

lar khavitz

string halva

Like the wine of Cana I have left the best halva to the last.

A classic of the Armenian cuisine Lar khavitz resembles a many threaded string. Preparing this sweet is a challenge as it is rather difficult, but well worth the effort and as it is fun to eat it will be very popular with the children.

'A sweet tongue will even bring the snake out of its hole.'
Proverb

50g (2 oz) unsalted butter
225g (8 oz) plain flour, sifted

Syrup
225g (8 oz) sugar
1 teaspoon lemon juice

To prepare
25g (1 oz) unsalted butter

Melt the 50g (2 oz) butter in a large saucepan over a low heat. Stir in the flour and fry for about 15 minutes, stirring constantly and breaking up any lumps. Spread the flour out over a baking tray and place in an oven preheated to 180C (350F) gas 4 for about 30 minutes, turning occasionally, until pale golden.

Sift the flour on to a large table top, pressing any lumps through the sieve with the back of a spoon.

Meanwhile prepare the syrup. Place the sugar, lemon juice and 150ml (¼ pint) water in a saucepan. Fasten a sugar thermometer to the saucepan. Bring to the boil, lower the heat and simmer until the temperature on the thermometer reaches 130C (260F). Remove immediately from the heat and pour into a ready-buttered cake tin about 20cm (8in) in diameter. Leave until cool enough to handle. Do not let it become too cool or it will be difficult to 'string'.

Butter your hands and lift the syrup from the tin. Pull the syrup into a strip about 25cm (10in) long. Fold in half and pull again. Repeat pulling and folding in this way until the toffee is lighter in colour and shiny. Butter your hands occasionally to make it easier to handle. Pull into a 25cm (10in) strip again, bring the 2 ends together to form a circle and press the 2 ends together to seal.

Place this circle on the toasted flour. Very carefully pull the circle out until it is about 50cm (20in) in diameter. Push flour over the top. Form the circle into a figure 8 and place one circle on top of the other. Continue pulling, folding and pushing flour over the top in this way until much of the flour has been absorbed and the halva is string-thin and made up of many threads.

Now pull the halva into a circle about 50-75cm (20-30in) in diameter.

With a sharp knife cut it into 5-7.5cm (2-3in) pieces. Squeeze each piece gently in the palm of your hand to stick the threads together.

Store in an airtight container.

Makes 24-30 pieces

fritters and pancakes

zalabieh
iranian fritters

At street corners in Tehran and most other Iranian towns, vendors using primitive utensils make a smooth, running batter of flour, yeast and yoghurt and then squeeze this mixture through a piping bag into a large cauldron of sizzling oil. Zalabieh are patterned doughnuts. The shapes vary. Usually it is the standard figure eight, but sometimes very elaborate ones symbolising religious and artistic concepts.

The Indian Jalebi is similar to this sweet except that the Iranians rarely add artificial colouring. In Lebanon a similar sweet, Mushabbak, is sold throughout the bazaars, patterned in never-ending circles. These fritters are thicker and come in red, golden or pink colours.

Fritters and doughnuts, as well as pancakes – ataif or kaygana – are very old fare in the Middle East, where they first appeared in the days of the Pharoahs and Babylonians. It is written that the prophet Nehemiah first introduced the Babylonian-Persian custom of 'something sweet' for the month of Tishri – the Jewish New Year when all kinds of fritters, doughnuts and other desserts were prepared. Zalabieh can be eaten warm, but I prefer them cold.

Batter
350g (12 oz) plain flour
15g (½ oz) dried yeast
150ml (¼ pint) yoghurt
oil for frying

Syrup
450g (1 lb) sugar
1 tablespoon lemon juice
pinch of ground saffron
4 cloves
1 tablespoon rosewater

Garnish
icing sugar

Sift the flour into a large bowl, add the yeast, yoghurt and sufficient warm water to form a batter about the consistency of double cream. Beat until really smooth. Cover and leave to stand in a warm place for 3-4 hours.

Meanwhile prepare the syrup. Place the sugar, lemon juice and 450ml (³/₄ pint) water in a saucepan and bring to the boil. Stir in the saffron and cloves, lower the heat and simmer for about 10 minutes or until the syrup forms a sticky film on a spoon.

Remove from the heat, stir in the rosewater and set aside to cool.

When the batter has risen and is spongy to the touch, pour about 5cm (2in) of oil into a large frying pan or saucepan and heat. Using a piping bag or narrow funnel with about a ½cm (¼in) nozzle, allow the batter to run into the hot oil to form either the traditional figure of eight or double circle whirls. Fry, turning constantly, for about 1 minute until crisp and golden on both sides.

Lift out with a slotted spoon and drop into the syrup. Leave to soak for 1-2 minutes, but no longer or the fritter will go soft and lift on to a plate.

When all the zalabieh are cooked and ready arrange on a large serving plate, dust with icing sugar and serve.

luqaimat-el-quadi

epiphany doughnut balls

These doughnut balls are known everywhere. They are called Lokma in Turkey, Zalabia in Egypt, Loukoumades in Greece and Awamat in Syria. All are based on the fact that the Quadi (Judge) liked them so much. I have included several recipes with variations and they are all delicious. The first is from Syria and Lebanon, where Christian minorities prepare it on the morning of Epiphany.

Syrup
350g (¾ lb) sugar
1 tablespoon lemon juice
1 tablespoon rosewater
1 tablespoon orange blossom water

Dough
½ teaspoon fresh yeast or 1 teaspoon dried yeast
1 teaspoon sugar
225g (½ lb) plain flour
½ teaspoon salt
150ml (¼ pint) milk
oil for frying

Garnish
½ tablespoon ground cinnamon

First make the syrup. Place the sugar, lemon juice and 300ml (½ pint) water in a saucepan and bring to the boil. Lower the heat and simmer for about 10 minutes or until it is slightly sticky and just coats a spoon. Remove from the heat, stir in the rosewater and orange blossom water and set aside.

Meanwhile place the yeast and sugar in a small bowl and dissolve in a little water, warmed, taken from 150ml (¼ pint). Set aside for about 10 minutes or until the mixture begins to froth.

Sift the flour and salt into a large bowl and make a well in the centre.

Pour the rest of the water and the milk into the yeast mixture and beat thoroughly.

Gradually add this liquid mixture to the flour and gradually beat the flour in until the dough is soft and smooth, but not quite a liquid.

Cover and leave to rise in a warm place for an hour. Beat the dough at least once more and leave to rest again. The final dough should be a well fermented, sponge-like mixture.

Pour about 5cm (2in) oil into a large saucepan and heat.

When the dough is ready, wet a teaspoon, take a teaspoonful of the mixture and drop it into the hot oil. Another method is to take up some of the dough in one hand and gently squeeze it up between thumb and forefinger to form small walnut-sized balls. Fry a few at a time. Turn them occasionally and remove when crisp, golden and cooked through.

Drain on kitchen paper.

Dip immediately into the cold syrup and lift out with a slotted spoon.

When they are all ready arrange them in a pyramid on a large plate.

Sprinkle with the cinnamon and serve while still warm.

Serves 4-6

lokma

turkish fritters

This is a standard from Anatolia which makes use of milk, egg and cinnamon.

Syrup
175g (6 oz) sugar
2 tablespoons honey
1 teaspoon lemon juice
5cm (2in) stick cinnamon

Dough
15g (½ oz) dried yeast or 8g (¼ oz) fresh yeast
½ teaspoon sugar
1 egg
120ml (4 fl oz) warm milk
400g (14 oz) plain flour, sifted
½ teaspoon salt
oil for frying

Garnish
1 teaspoon ground cinnamon
2 tablespoons finely chopped pistachio nuts

First prepare the syrup. Place all the ingredients in a small saucepan with 150ml (¼ pint) water and bring to the boil. Simmer for 5 minutes then remove from the heat and set aside to cool.

Dissolve the yeast and sugar in a few tablespoons of warm water and set aside in a warm place until the mixture begins to froth. Pour the yeast mixture into a large bowl and beat in the egg, 250ml (8 fl oz) warm water and milk. Gradually add the flour and continue beating until the batter is smooth. Cover the bowl with a cloth and leave to rest in a warm place until the mixture has doubled in size.

Pour about 5cm (2in) of oil into a large saucepan and heat.

Take a teaspoonful of the batter and drop it into the hot fat. Cook a few at a time.

Fry for 3-5 minutes, turning once, until golden and cooked through. Remove with a slotted spoon and drop into the cold syrup. Leave to soak for about 5 minutes, turning once. Remove with a slotted spoon and arrange on a serving dish.

Continue in this way until all the batter is used. Sprinkle with the cinnamon and chopped pistachios.

Serve with any remaining syrup and, if you like, with yoghurt or cream.

Serves 6-8

hanim gobegi

'lady's navel' fritters

These delicious fritters are seeped in syrup and filled with whipped cream. The depression in the centre which is filled with cream is meant to represent a lady's navel!

Syrup
450g (1 lb) sugar
1 teaspoon lemon juice

Dough
50g (2 oz) butter
½ teaspoon salt
225g (8 oz) plain flour, sifted
3 eggs
oil for frying
1 teaspoon almond essence

Garnish
150ml (¼ pint) double cream, whipped

First prepare the syrup. Place the sugar, lemon juice and 450ml (³/₄ pint) water in a saucepan and bring to the boil. Simmer for 10 minutes and then set aside to cool.

Place the butter and 300ml (½ pint) water in a large saucepan and bring to the boil, stirring all the time until the butter melts. Remove from the heat, add the flour and salt and, using a wooden spoon, stir vigorously until the mixture is well blended. Make a well in the centre of the dough and add the eggs, one at a time, and continue to beat until the mixture is smooth, shiny and comes away from the sides of the pan.

In another large saucepan pour enough oil to cover the bottom by about 5cm (2in).

Lightly oil your hands and then break off a lump of dough about the size of a walnut and roll between your palms to form a ball. Place the ball on an oiled baking sheet. Continue until you have used up all the dough. Heat the oil in the saucepan.

Flatten a few of the balls a little and then, dipping your forefinger in the almond essence, press it about 1cm (½in) into the centre of each one to make a depression. Place a few into the gently sizzling oil and leave to fry for about 8 minutes.

Turn once and fry for a further 8 minutes or until the fritters are golden. Do not fry too quickly or the insides will not be cooked. Remove with a slotted spoon and place on kitchen paper to drain, then drop into the syrup, turn once and leave to steep for 5 minutes before transferring with a slotted spoon to a serving plate.

Allow the oil to cool a little while you prepare a few more balls and then fry as described above. Continue in this way until all the fritters are fried and steeped in syrup.

Before serving drop a teaspoon of the whipped cream into the centre of each fritter.

Makes 12-16

dilber dudaği

'sweet lips' fritters

Once again from Turkey, the recipe below is for deep-fried semi-circles of dough which are either dipped in syrup or dusted with icing sugar. While cooking, the pastry puffs up to a shape resembling lips – hence the name Dilber Dudaği – meaning 'sweet lips'. Simple and cheap to prepare.

Syrup
225g (8 oz) sugar
1 tablespoon lemon juice

Dough
110g (4 oz) plain flour
pinch of salt
50g (2 oz) butter
2 large eggs, beaten
25g (1 oz) ground almonds
25g (1 oz) ground pistachio nuts and oil for frying

Garnish
if not using syrup mix 50g (2 oz) sifted icing sugar with 1 teaspoon cinnamon

If using syrup put the sugar, lemon juice and 350ml (12 fl oz) water in a saucepan and bring to the boil. Simmer for 10 minutes and set aside to cool.

Sift the flour and salt into a bowl. Put the butter and 250ml (8 fl oz) water in a saucepan, heat slowly until the butter melts and then bring to the boil. Pour all the flour in at once and, stirring constantly with a balloon whisk or wooden spoon, beat until the mixture comes away from the sides of the saucepan.

Cook over a low heat, stirring occasionally, for 5 minutes. Turn the mixture into a mixing bowl and leave to cool for 2-3 minutes.

Gradually beat in the eggs. It is easiest if you use a balloon whisk to break up the lumps and then use a wooden spoon to beat until the mixture is smooth and shiny.

Fold in the ground nuts.

Oil your hands, break off walnut-sized lumps of dough and roll into balls.

Take one ball and flatten it in one palm to a round about 6cm (2½ in) in diameter.

Fold in half and place on an oiled tray. Repeat with the remaining balls of dough. Pour enough oil into a large saucepan to cover the base by about 5cm (2in) and heat.

Add the dilber dudagi, a few at a time, and fry gently for about 15 minutes, turning occasionally so that they brown evenly. Do not cook too quickly or they will not cook through. Remove with a slotted spoon, drain on kitchen paper and then, if you wish, place in the cold syrup and leave for 2-3 minutes, turning once.

Then, with or without the syrup, arrange on a serving dish.

If serving without the syrup sprinkle the dilber dudagi generously with the icing sugar and cinnamon. Serve cold.

Makes 18-20

A variation called Tulumba Tatlisi has the dough put in a pastry bag with a 1cm (½in) nozzle. The dough is then cut off, with an oiled knife, into 7.5cm (3in) strips and fried according to the recipe above. When cooked they are steeped in cold syrup. In yet another version called Baghdad Hurma Tatlisi the dough is shaped like dates before cooking.

sufganiyot
fruit doughnuts

A doughnut filled with dates or prunes or jam.

450g (1 lb) plain flour
½ teaspoon baking powder
½ teaspoon salt
¼ teaspoon ground nutmeg
¼ teaspoon ground cinnamon
110g (4 oz) sugar
1 egg, beaten
2-3 tablespoons oil
150ml (¼ pint) milk
15-20 stoned dates or soaked and stoned prunes or jam of your choice
oil for frying

Garnish
caster sugar

Sift the flour twice with the baking powder, salt, nutmeg and cinnamon into a large bowl. Stir in the sugar, beaten egg and oil. Begin to knead and add sufficient of the milk to form a soft dough. Form into walnut-sized balls. With your forefinger form a depression in each ball and tuck in a date or prune or a teaspoon of jam and then close the opening and reform the ball.

Heat enough oil in a saucepan to deep fry the doughnuts. When hot drop 2 or 3 doughnuts into the oil and cook over a moderate heat until cooked through and well browned all over. Remove with a slotted spoon and drain on kitchen paper while the remaining doughnuts are being cooked. Sprinkle generously with caster sugar and serve.

Makes 15-20

gioush

sesame-honey fritters

These plaited Moroccan sweets are very rich. Dark brown when cooked, they are soaked in honey and generously scattered with sesame seeds. In Libya and Egypt they are known as Asslah. An ideal teatime treat.

225g (8 oz) plain flour
pinch of salt
¼ teaspoon fresh yeast or ½ teaspoon dried yeast
1 teaspoon sugar
1 egg yolk
110g (4 oz) sesame seeds
50g (2 oz) butter, melted
120ml (4 fl oz) vegetable oil
60ml (2 fl oz) wine vinegar
½ teaspoon saffron
1 tablespoon orange blossom water
oil for frying

Syrup
450g (1 lb) honey

Garnish
25g (1 oz) sesame seeds

The night before sift 110g (4 oz) of the flour and the salt into a bowl.

Place the yeast, 3 tablespoons warm water and the sugar into a small bowl, stir and leave in a warm place for about 10 minutes or until the mixture begins to froth.

Pour into the sifted flour and gradually add about 120ml (4 fl oz) tepid water to form a soft dough.

Knead vigorously for 10-15 minutes. Shape into a ball, place in a clean bowl, cover with a damp cloth and leave in a warm place overnight.

The next day spread the sesame seeds over a large baking tray and cook in the oven or under a grill turning several times, until browned all over. When the sesame seeds have cooled a little, place in a blender and grind until fine.

Sift the remaining flour into a large bowl, add the ground sesame seeds, the melted butter and the oil. Heat the wine vinegar in a small saucepan, remove and stir in the saffron and orange blossom water.

Place the yeast dough on a lightly floured work top and punch down. Make a well in the centre, add the vinegar and saffron mixture and knead well.

Add the egg yolk and knead for a further 2 minutes. Now add the sesame dough and knead one into the other for about 10 minutes.

Sprinkle the work top and a large baking tray with flour.

Break off a walnut-sized lump of dough and roll between your hands to form a ball.

Now roll it into a pencil-thin strip about 25cm (10in) long. Break off one-third of the strip and press one end of it into the centre of the remaining length. Now plait the 3 lengths together, press the ends together and place on the baking tray. Repeat until you have used up all the dough. Cover the gioush with a cloth and leave to rest for 20 minutes.

Heat enough oil in a large saucepan to deep fry and add 2-3 gioush. Fry gently for 10-15 minutes until brown and crisp. Turn gently half way through the cooking time. Meanwhile heat the honey in a saucepan wide enough to take the gioush. When cooked lift the gioush out with a slotted spoon, drain and place in the honey.

Leave to steep for 2-3 minutes, turning once. Keep the honey over a very low flame while there are gioush in it, but remove from the heat at other times or else it will become too thick and toffee-like. Remove from the syrup, place on a tray and sprinkle generously with sesame seeds.

Cook and prepare the remaining gioush in the same way. Serve cold.

Makes 16-20

ataif

pancakes

'When my friends are full of hunger
I have Ataif like soft sheets;
As flow of Lanbent honey brimming white
So amidst other delicacies it is bright,
And having drunk of almond-essence deep,
With oil it glitters, wherein it doth seep.
With rose-water floating as up a sea,
Bubble on bubble swimming fragrantly;
A foliated book laid fold on fold
Afficted hearts rejoice when they behold.'
Meadows of Gold

Pancake recipes turn up all over the world. In Russia they are called *blinis*, in Israel *blintzes* while in France they are known as *crêpes*. Turks call theirs *kaygana* while they are better known as *ataif* amongst the Arabs. One of my childhood favourites, they make an ideal after dinner dessert. You can either serve them with syrup poured over the top or you can fill them with:

a)   unsalted cheese, e.g. ricotta, akkawi or feta – the latter if it is first soaked in water overnight to remove most of the salt

b) nuts

c) a tablespoon of kaymak (see recipe) or clotted cream. Double or whipped cream will not do for this recipe.

Batter
8g (¼ oz) fresh yeast or 1 teaspoon dried yeast
½ teaspoon sugar
110g (4 oz) plain flour
oil for frying

Syrup
225g (8 oz) sugar
1 tablespoon lemon juice
1 tablespoon rosewater

First make the syrup. Place the sugar, 150ml (¼ pint) water and the lemon juice in a saucepan and bring to the boil. Lower the heat and simmer for about 10 minutes or until the syrup forms a slightly sticky film on a spoon. Remove from the heat and stir in the rosewater.

Place the yeast and sugar in a small bowl, add 3 tablespoons tepid water, mix to dissolve and then leave to rest in a warm place for about 10 minutes or until the mixture begins to froth. Sift the flour into a large bowl, add the yeast mixture and work it in with your hand. Little by little add another 250ml (8 fl oz) tepid water and continue kneading. When the mixture begins to become liquid, beat until you have a smooth batter.

Cover with a tea towel and leave in a warm place for 1 hour.

Lightly brush the insides of a large frying pan with oil and heat the pan for a few minutes until it is really hot. Reduce the heat to medium. Pour 1 tablespoon of the batter into the pan and tilt the pan around to allow the batter to spread. After a minute or two the batter will begin to bubble and become pale golden.

With a palette knife lift the pancake and turn it over to cook the other side.

Remove the pancake to a large plate and continue to make pancakes, piling them on top of each other when cooked.

The traditional method of eating ataif is to pour some syrup over each one and then to spread with a little kaymak or clotted cream and perhaps sprinkle with a few chopped nuts. Alternatively you can spread with honey (instead of syrup) and then sprinkle with chopped nuts or you can spread with a little melted butter, sprinkle with cinnamon and then add a tablespoon of mulberry syrup or *bekmez* (grape syrup). Finally you can stuff the ataif with one of the fillings suggested below. Note that if you are going to stuff the ataif then you only fry one side of each.

Makes 14-16 pancakes

ataif-bil-jibn
cheese-filled pancakes

Batter and Syrup
see Ataif

Filling
225g (8 oz) unsalted cheese, e.g. akkawi, ricotta or feta – the latter must be soaked overnight in water to remove saltiness

Grate the cheese and place in a bowl. Prepare the pancakes as described above, but only cook one side of each.

Take one ataif and place it on a work top, uncooked side upwards.

Place 1 tablespoon of the cheese in one half of the pancake.

Fold the other half over to make a half-moon shape and pinch the edges together very firmly. Heat some oil in a large pan until hot and then deep fry the ataif for 2-3 minutes or until golden. Remove with a slotted spoon and drain on kitchen paper. Dip into the cold syrup and then serve either warm or cold.

ataif-bil-joze
nut-filled pancakes

Batter and Syrup
see Ataif

Filling
**225g (8 oz) walnuts, coarsely chopped, or chopped
pistachios, almonds or a mixture
4 tablespoons sugar
2 teaspoons ground cinnamon
1 teaspoon orange blossom water
1 teaspoon rosewater**

Mix all the filling ingredients together in a bowl. Prepare the pancakes as described above, but only cook one side of each.

Fill and cook the ataif as described in Ataif-bil-jibn using the nut filling instead of the cheese. Dip in the cold syrup and serve warm or cold.

ataif-bil-eishta

cream-filled pancakes

Batter and Syrup
see Ataif

Filling
225g (½ lb) eishta – also known as kaymak – or clotted cream

First prepare the eishta or kaymak following directions on page 236 or use clotted cream. Prepare the pancakes as described above, but only cook one side of each. Place 1 tablespoon cream in one half of an ataif and proceed to fill and cook as described in Ataif-bil-jibn (page 58). Either dip the hot pancakes in the cold syrup or serve the syrup separately.

kaygana

anatolian sweet pancakes

Kaygana are thin pancakes made of a batter of eggs, milk and flour, fried on both sides and served hot. They are then Anatolian-style crêpes, for they have been made by the peasants for centuries; and although crepes can be savoury as well as sweet the latter seem to have been the most popular – so much so that there are scores of fruit, nut and cream-based kaygana recipes. Below I have given the basic dough recipe, as well as that for apricot kaygana, but I have also noted the basic ingredients for several other Anatolian fillings for these crêpes. In the villages the crepes are made much thicker than their wafer-thin cousins in Europe. I suggest you try and make them as thin as possible as you will then be better able to appreciate the flavour of the various fillings.

Dough
225g (½ lb) plain flour, sifted
½ teaspoon salt
4 eggs
4 tablespoons melted butter
475ml (16 fl oz) tepid milk
a little vegetable oil

Place the flour and salt in a large bowl. Make a well in the centre and add the eggs, one at a time, stirring them in with a wooden spoon. Add the melted butter and stir in thoroughly. Now gradually add the milk, stirring constantly, until you have a smooth batter with no lumps. Cover the bowl with a cloth and leave in a cool place for 1 hour.

With a pastry brush lightly grease a 15-17.5cm (6-7in) heavy-based frying pan with a little of the oil. Place the pan over a moderate heat and warm the oil until it is very hot.

Remove the pan from the heat and pour 4 tablespoons of the batter into it.

Tilt the pan in all directions to help the batter spread. Return the pan to the heat and cook for 30-40 seconds. Shake the pan gently to loosen the crêpe. With a palette knife gently lift the crêpe and turn it over. Brown the reverse side for 20-30 seconds and then slide the kaygana on to an ovenproof plate and keep warm. Continue making the kaygana, greasing the pan each time, until you have used up all the batter.

Serves 4-6

kayisili kaygana
crêpes with an apricot filling

Dough
see Kaygana

Filling
450g (1 lb) fresh apricots
350g (¾ lb) caster sugar
juice 1 lemon

Garnish
110g (4 oz) icing sugar, sifted

Prepare the kaygana following the recipe opposite and keep warm. Drop the apricots into a bowl of boiling water for 1 minute then remove and peel.

Cut the apricots in half, remove the stones and then halve the halves. Place the apricots in a saucepan, add the sugar, lemon juice and 120ml (4 fl oz) water, bring to the boil and then simmer gently for 15 minutes, stirring regularly.

Remove from the heat and leave to cool. Strain off the juice and reserve.

Take one kaygana, spread it out on a worktop and place 2 tablespoons of the apricots on to one half of the crêpe. Fold the crêpe in half and then over again into quarters. Continue until you have filled and folded the remaining kaygana. Arrange them in a shallow, ovenproof dish and reheat for 5 minutes in the oven preheated to 200C (400F) gas 6.

Remove from the oven, sprinkle generously with icing sugar and serve warm.

In a small pan reheat the apricot juice and pour a little over each kaygana as it is served.

Serves 4-6

elmali kaygana

apple-filled crepes

Dough
see Kaygana

Filling
450g (1 lb) apples, peeled, cored and sliced
350g (¾ lb) caster sugar
1 tablespoon lemon juice

Garnish
110g (4 oz) sifted icing sugar mixed with 1 teaspoon
ground cinnamon

Prepare the kaygana as described on page 60 and keep warm. Place the apples in a pan with the sugar, lemon juice and 60ml (2 fl oz) water and cook over a low heat until the apple slices are just soft, but still retain their shape.

Continue as with the recipe for apricot kaygana (page 61).

Serves 4-6

çilekli kaygana

strawberry-filled crepes

Dough
See Kaygana

Filling
450g (1 lb) strawberries, hulled and washed
225g (½ lb) caster sugar
110g (4 oz) cream crackers or sweet biscuits, crushed

Garnish
110g (4 oz) icing sugar, sifted

Prepare the kaygana following the recipe on page 60 and keep warm. Place the strawberries in a bowl with the sugar and mash. Stir in the crushed biscuits and fill the crêpes as described in the recipe for apricot kaygana (page 61).

Serves 4-6

limonlu kaygana

lemon crêpes

Dough
see Kaygana

Filling
110g (4 oz) unsalted butter
110g (4 oz) caster sugar
grated rind of 1 lemon
juice of 2 lemons
120ml (4 fl oz) milk

Prepare the kaygana as described on page 60 and keep warm. Put the butter, sugar and lemon rind into a saucepan and cook over a moderate heat for 5 minutes. Gradually pour in the lemon juice and the milk and simmer for a further 10-12 minutes. Pour the syrup into a large, shallow dish. Taking one crêpe at a time, dip into the lemon syrup and then arrange on a serving plate. Pour the remaining syrup over the kaygana and warm in a hot oven for a few minutes before serving.

Serves 4-6

fistikli kaygana

pistachio-filled crêpes

Dough
see Kaygana

Filling
60g (2½ oz) caster sugar
1 tablespoon baking powder
½ teaspoon salt
½ teaspoon vanilla essence
450ml (¾ pint) milk
3 egg yolks, beaten
50g (2 oz) ground pistachio nuts

Prepare the kaygana as described on page 60 and keep warm. Put the sugar, baking powder, salt and vanilla essence in a saucepan and slowly stir in the milk. Cook over a low heat for about 3 minutes, stirring constantly. Remove from the heat and stir in the beaten egg yolks. Return to a very low heat and cook, stirring constantly, for about 5 minutes.

Stir in the ground pistachio nuts, bring to the boil and simmer for 2-3 minutes, stirring constantly.

Arrange the warm crêpes over a large serving plate and pour most of the mixture over them. Serve the crêpes immediately with the rest of the syrup served separately in a small bowl.

Serves 4-6

There are several other such recipes using all kinds of fresh fruits, nuts, preserves and mixtures of different fruits and nuts.

banrov sankatah

cheese pancakes

This is an Armenian recipe. Traditionally goat or sheep's cheese is used, but standard cottage cheese is a good substitute. Some people like to pour a little *bekmez* (grape syrup) or carob syrup over them.

2 eggs
225g (½ lb) cottage or curd cheese; feta will also do if you soak it
overnight first to remove the salt and then grate
50g (2 oz) plain flour, sifted
½ teaspoon baking powder
1 teaspoon sugar
½ teaspoon salt (omit if using feta cheese)
½ teaspoon vanilla essence
about 50g (2 oz) butter

Garnish
2 teaspoons ground cinnamon mixed with 4 teaspoons sugar, or more
according to taste
2 tablespoons ground almonds

Place the eggs and 3 tablespoons cold water in a large bowl and whisk until frothy. Add the cheese, flour, baking powder, sugar, salt and vanilla. Mix thoroughly until a thickish batter is formed.

Melt a little of the butter in a 15-17.5cm (6-7in) frying pan. When the butter is hot add 2-3 tablespoons of the batter and spread it out with the back of a spoon. Fry gently until the bottom of the pancake is golden and then turn over and cook the other side. Remove to a plate, sprinkle with a little of the cinnamon-sugar mixture and then with some of the nuts. Serve hot.

Makes 6 pancakes

pastries

'Let us pamper our souls and taste of all that is good.'
Koran

In this chapter I have included pastries prepared with flour, semolina, nuts and fruits. They are usually cooked in the oven and will keep well when stored in airtight tins. Perhaps the most famous of these pastries is Ghorayebah (lover's pastries) – a name which appears, in one version or another, from North Africa and Greece through to the borders of Pakistan. The classic version is the one below from Syria-Lebanon. They are charming pastries which melt in the mouth. Ideal with tea or coffee.

ghoriba louze
almond pastries

Ghoriba Louze is a variation on Ghorayebah. It is made entirely of ground almonds and has a marvellous aroma and beautiful texture. This recipe is from Algeria, but there are similar ones from all parts of North Africa and they are the originals from which our own macaroons have developed. These are ideal with tea or coffee and will keep for a long time.

1 small egg
150g (5 oz) icing sugar, sifted
finely grated rind 1 lemon
1 teaspoon vanilla essence
¼ teaspoon ground cinnamon
225g (½ lb) ground almonds
plain flour (optional)

Garnish
icing sugar

Place the egg and icing sugar in a large bowl and whisk until the mixture is white. Add the lemon rind, vanilla essence and cinnamon and mix well. Now stir in the ground almonds. Gather the mixture up into a ball and knead for a few minutes until soft and workable. If you find it a little sticky add just enough plain flour to bind.

Lightly oil your palms and shape the mixture into balls slightly larger than a walnut. Pass each ball from one palm to the other gently flattening it into a round 6-7.5cm (2½-3in) in diameter. Put on a greased baking tray and continue until you have used up all the mixture. Sprinkle each round generously with icing sugar and place in an oven preheated to 180C (350F) gas 4. Bake for 15-20 minutes or until golden. Remove and set aside to cool. Store in an airtight tin when cold.

Makes 12-14

ghorayebah

lover's pastries

225g (½ lb) unsalted butter
110g (¼ lb) icing sugar, sifted
225g (½ lb) plain flour, sifted
blanched, halved almonds

Melt the butter in a small saucepan over a low heat. Spoon off any froth and pour the yellow liquid into a large mixing bowl, discarding any residue in the bottom of the pan. Put the bowl in the refrigerator and leave until the butter has solidified.

Remove from the refrigerator and beat or whisk the butter until it is creamy and white. Add the icing sugar, a little at a time, and continue beating. Now add the flour, a little at a time, and continue to mix until the mixture is stiff. Collect the dough up and knead it by hand until it forms a ball and becomes pliable. Leave to rest in the bowl for about 10 minutes.

Shape the mixture into walnut-sized balls. On a clean surface roll one into a sausage and join the ends to form a circle. Place on a baking tray and lightly press a halved almond over the join. Continue until you have used up all the mixture, placing the ghorayebah about 2.5cm (1in) apart.

Place in the oven preheated to 150C (300F) gas 2 and cook for about 20 minutes or until the almonds are a *very* light golden, but the biscuits are still white. Do not let the biscuits change colour because it will alter the flavour. Set aside to cool and then store in an airtight tin.

Makes about 18-20

ghoriba mughrabi

moroccan pastry balls

This is yet another version, this time making use of fine semolina. It also keeps well.

225g (½ lb) unsalted butter, melted and any white sediment discarded
110g (4 oz) icing sugar, sifted
350g (12 oz) fine semolina (or plain flour)

Garnish
icing sugar

In a large bowl mix together the melted butter, icing sugar and semolina. Knead together until it forms a ball and then leave for 2-3 hours.

Knead vigorously until the mixture becomes soft. Take a walnut-sized ball of the mixture and pass it from one palm to the other until it becomes very soft. Place on a buttered baking tray. Continue until you have used up all the mixture. Place in an oven preheated to 180C (350F) gas 4 and bake for 10-15 minutes or until golden. Remove and leave to cool. Cover generously with sifted icing sugar and store in an airtight tin.

Makes about 30

kourabiethes

greek shortbread

The Greeks – not to be outdone – have a pastry similar to ghorayebah called *kourabiethes* and, for the sake of one-upmanship they add a little brandy or ouzo (taboo with Muslims). Kourabiethes, amongst those of the Orthodox Christian faith (Greeks, Armenians, Assyrians) are traditionally made both for the New Year celebrations and for Christmas. It is claimed that St John Chrysostom even mentioned this sweet during one of his sermons. It is a custom, therefore, to stick a clove into each shortbread symbolising the three wise men who brought spices to Bethlehem that auspicious night.

225g (½ lb) unsalted butter, melted
3 tablespoons icing sugar, sifted
1 egg yolk
1 tablespoon ouzo or brandy
50g (2 oz) blanched almonds, toasted and then very finely chopped
275g (10 oz) plain flour, sifted
1 teaspoon baking powder
whole cloves
175g (6 oz) icing sugar

Pour the melted butter into a large bowl, discarding any milky sediment at the bottom of the pan, and leave until it has solidified. Add the 3 tablespoons icing sugar and whisk the mixture until white. Add the egg yolk and ouzo or brandy and beat well. Stir in the chopped almonds and then the flour and baking powder. Gather up the mixture into a ball and knead by hand until it is really soft and smooth.

Break off walnut-sized lumps and shape into balls. Flatten one slightly and then pinch the top twice making 4 indentations. Press a clove into the top and place on a baking sheet. Continue with the remaining balls of pastry.

Place in an oven preheated to 160C (325F) gas 3 and cook for 15-20 minutes or until lightly golden. Do not allow to brown or the flavour will change. Leave to cool on the trays for 10 minutes. Sift some of the icing sugar over some greaseproof paper and place the warm shortbread on it. Sift more icing sugar generously over the tops. When cold store in a container and sift any remaining icing sugar over them. Will keep for several days in an airtight tin.

Makes about 20

'Squeezing my hand
She whispered three words to me,
the most precious things I had all day;
"Tomorrow we'll meet",
And disappeared in the distance.

'I shaved twice,
Shone my shoes twice,
Borrowed a friend's suit – and two liras
To buy her sweets and white coffee.

'I sit alone
While lovers smile
And something tells me
We too shall smile.'
Mahmud Darwish

The *ghiraybeh* of Kuwait and Bahrain are very similar to the *ghorayebah* of Iraq, Palestine, Egypt and Jordan. It seems that the Arab's love of romance and chivalry has been stamped on all the cuisines of the region. For love transcends all and the yearning for love (*gharyb*) was a solace to the nomad in his endless wanderings through the desert.

'Ah when will our long parting cease?
And shall I ever win to peace,
that I may pour into thine ear
My anguished tale of yearning drear?

'I pray God grant us such a day
When I may chant my passion's lay –'
Ibn Zaidun 1003-1071 – quoted from
Aspects of Islamic Civilisation

maamoul

easter pastries

A North Syrian recipe that was traditionally prepared during Easter week. Today it is sold all year round throughout Syria and Lebanon. The recipe below is a family one using dates, walnuts and almonds. You can use fine semolina instead of flour.

Filling
225g (½ lb) dates, stoned
225g (½ lb) walnuts, roughly chopped
110g (¼ lb) almonds, roughly chopped – you can use pistachio nuts instead
110g (¼ lb) sugar
1 heaped teaspoon ground cinnamon

Dough
450g (1 lb) plain flour
225g (½ lb) unsalted butter, melted
2 tablespoons rosewater
4-5 tablespoons milk

Garnish
icing sugar

First prepare the filling by chopping the dates and placing them in a saucepan with 150ml (¼ pint) water, the nuts, sugar and cinnamon. Cook over a low heat until the dates are soft and the water has been absorbed.

Sift the flour into a large bowl, add the melted butter and mix by hand. Add the rosewater and milk and knead the dough until it is soft and easy to mould. Divide the dough into walnut-sized lumps. Take one lump, roll it into a ball and then hollow it out with your thumb, pinching the sides up until they are thin and form a pot-shape. Fill with some of the date mixture and then press the dough back over the filling to enclose completely. Roll into a ball and then gently press with your palm to slightly flatten it or, if you have a wooden spoon with a deep, curved bowl, mould each pastry with that. Repeat until you have used up all the pastry and filling.

Arrange all the pastries on baking trays. Make interesting patterns with a fork on each one. The traditional one is to mark straight lines down the length of each pastry. Bake in an oven preheated to 150C (300F) gas 2 for 20-30 minutes. Do not let them change colour or the pastry will become hard. Remove from the oven and allow to cool. Roll in sieved icing sugar and store in an airtight container.

Makes 30-40

lokumia parayemista

nut-stuffed cypriot pastries

A more modest version of Maamoul making use of almonds and cinnamon. This recipe uses flour, but fine semolina is often substituted.

500g (18 oz) plain flour or semolina
250g (9 oz) unsalted butter, melted
5cm (2in) piece cinnamon stick
1 tablespoon orange blossom water

Filling
175g (6 oz) almonds, coarsely ground
50g (2 oz) caster sugar
1½ teaspoons ground cinnamon

Garnish
60ml (2 fl oz) orange blossom water
icing sugar

Sift the flour into a large bowl, add the melted butter and mix well. Cover and leave for 6-8 hours or overnight.

Put 250ml (8 fl oz) water and the cinnamon stick in a small saucepan and bring to the boil. Remove the cinnamon stick and pour the water into the flour and butter mixture. Add the orange blossom water and mix until well blended. When cool enough to handle gather into a ball and knead until smooth. If crumbly add a little more water. Mix the filling ingredients together in a small bowl.

Break off a piece of dough about the size of a large walnut and mould into an oval shape. Make a hole through the centre from one end and then enlarge the hole by turning the dough in one hand and working the finger around inside. Fill the hole with the nut mixture and then close the dough back over the filling. Roll between your palms to reform the oval shape. Place on a baking tray. Continue until you have used up all the dough and filling.

Bake in an oven preheated to 190C (375F) gas 5 for about 20 minutes or until a light golden. Remove from the oven and brush with orange blossom water. Sift icing sugar generously over some greaseproof paper and place the hot pastries on it. Sift more icing sugar over the top until the pastries are thickly coated. When cold store in an airtight container. To serve dust with more icing sugar.

Makes 16-18

karabij

stuffed pastries with natife

A speciality of Aleppo in Syria. These pastries are dipped in a cream called *natef* and then eaten. Natef is made from pieces of wood called *bois de Panama* which can be bought from good health food shops and Middle Eastern stores. It is often sold in powdered form, which makes its preparation simpler. Karabij is a unique pastry which is well worth making for a special occasion.

Cream
75g (3 oz) bois de Panama – also known as 'halva wood'
225g (½ lb) sugar
1 tablespoon lemon juice
2 tablespoons orange blossom water
4 egg whites

Filling
225g (½ lb) walnuts, finely chopped
110g (¼ lb) sugar
1 tablespoon ground cinnamon

Dough
450g (1 lb) plain flour
225g (½ lb) unsalted butter, melted

First prepare the cream by pulverising the pieces of wood. Place in a bowl with about 150ml (¼ pint) water and leave to soak for 4-5 hours. Transfer the contents of the bowl to a saucepan and bring to the boil. Lower the heat and simmer until the liquid has thickened. Strain the mixture through fine muslin and set the liquid aside.

Dissolve the sugar in 8 tablespoons water in a small saucepan, add the lemon juice and bring to the boil. Lower the heat and simmer until the syrup has thickened – about 10 minutes. Remove from the heat, stir in the orange blossom water and the hot bois de panama liquid and beat vigorously. Set aside to cool.

When the mixture is cold place the egg whites in a large bowl and whisk until very stiff. Gradually add the cold syrup mixture, beating continuously until the mixture froths and expands. Transfer to a serving dish and set aside. Mix the filling ingredients together in a bowl.

To prepare the dough sift the flour into a large bowl, add the butter and knead. Add 3-4 tablespoons water and continue kneading until the dough is soft and smooth. Divide the dough into walnut-sized lumps. Take one lump, roll into a ball and then hollow it out with your thumb, pinching the sides up until they are thin and form a pot-shape. Fill the hollow with a little of the nut mixture and then press the dough back over the filling to form a ball. Gently press between your palms to make an oval shape. Repeat until you have used up all the dough and filling.

Place the karabij on baking trays and cook in an oven preheated to 150C (300F) gas 2 and cook for 20-30 minutes. Remove before the pastry changes colour – it should still be white. Set aside to cool. To serve arrange the karabij on a large plate and offer a bowl of the natef cream. Dip the karabij into the cream and eat. The pastries will keep for a long time in an airtight container, but refrigerate the cream.

Makes 30-40

briouat

almond pastries in honey

'Look at her! Made of honey and butter!
Isn't it worth loving a face like this?
Her mouth is made for sugar,
Her cheek made to kiss.'
Nahapet Kuchak, 16th century poet

These are very sweet pastries whose nut filling is wrapped in filo, fried in oil and then soaked in honey. A North African favourite that is beloved of children. Eat with tea or coffee.

450ml (¾ pint) oil
225g (½ lb) blanched almonds
175g (6 oz) icing sugar
1 teaspoon ground cinnamon
2 small eggs
3 tablespoons orange blossom water
7-8 sheets filo pastry
25g (1 oz) butter, melted
450g (1 lb) honey

Heat 150ml (¼ pint) of the oil in a saucepan, add the almonds and fry until golden. Remove with a slotted spoon and drain on kitchen paper. When cool place the almonds in a blender and grind. Reheat the oil, add the ground almonds, sugar and cinnamon and mix well. Remove from the heat and, one at a time, drop in the eggs and blend well. Stir in the orange blossom water and set aside to cool.

Place the sheets of filo on top of each other and cut into oblongs about 15 X 10cm (6 X 4in). Stack on top of each other and cover with a cloth to prevent them drying. When the filling is cold take one rectangle of filo and lay it out with one of the short sides nearest you. Take 1 heaped teaspoon of the filling and place it on the filo near the end closest to you. Spread it out with the back of the spoon. Fold in the end nearest you and then the 2 long sides. Brush a little melted butter over the other short end and then fold the filling over. The end result should be a flat parcel shape. Continue with remaining pastry and filling.

Place the remaining 300ml (½ pint) oil in a large saucepan and heat. Place the honey in another pan and bring just to the boil. Turn off the heat. Drop a few of the briouats into the hot oil and fry for about 1 minute, turning once, until golden. Remove with a slotted spoon and drop into the honey. Leave for 2-3 minutes then remove with a slotted spoon and place on a serving dish. Continue to fry the briouats and soak them in the honey. Every now and then return the honey to the heat. Do not boil for too long or it will become too thick. Allow to cool and then serve.

Makes about 36

fenikiah

pistachio-coated pastries

These very popular orange-flavoured pastries, which are dipped in syrup and coated with ground pistachio nuts and icing sugar, are reputed to be of Venetian origin – hence the name.

350g (12 oz) plain flour
1 level tablespoon baking powder
2 tablespoons sugar
120ml (4 fl oz) vegetable oil
120ml (4 fl oz) fresh, strained orange juice
grated rind of 1 orange

Syrup
350g (12 oz) sugar
1 tablespoon lemon juice

Topping
110g (4 oz) pistachio nuts, ground
3 tablespoons icing sugar
½ teaspoon ground cinnamon

First prepare the syrup by placing the sugar, lemon juice and 250ml (8 fl oz) water in a pan and bringing to the boil. Simmer for 5-10 minutes or until the syrup coats a spoon. Mix the ground pistachio nuts, icing sugar and cinnamon together in a small bowl and set aside.

To prepare the dough mix the flour, baking powder and sugar together in a bowl. Add the oil and rub in with your fingers until crumblike. Gradually add the orange juice and mix until you have a soft, smooth dough. Break off walnut-sized lumps and roll into balls. Take one ball and flatten between your palms until it is a round about 6cm (2½ in) in diameter. Roll it up into a finger and place on a baking tray with the seam underneath. Repeat with the remaining balls of dough.

Bake in an oven preheated to 190C (375F) gas 5 for about 10-12 minutes or until golden. Remove from the oven and drop the fenikiahs, a few at a time, into the warm syrup. Leave for 2-3 minutes, turning once, to absorb as much syrup as possible. Lift out with a slotted spoon and roll in the pistachio mixture. Arrange on a large serving place in a pyramid and sprinkle with any remaining topping mixture. Delicious with tea or coffee.

A Greek version 'Finikia' uses fine semolina instead of flour and includes 1 teaspoon ground cinnamon and ½ teaspoon ground cloves. The dough is shaped into ovals and the ends pinched to form a torpedo-shape. The topping is either chopped walnuts or toasted sesame seeds.

Makes about 20

anoush borek

sweet puff pastries

Borek are savoury pastries filled with cheese, meat, spinach and other vegetables. One of the glories of the Ottoman cuisine, these pastries are usually cooked in the oven and traditionally served on a *mezzeh* table as appetisers or as a main dish with a salad. Anoush borek are pastries filled with a nut and sugar mixture, or fruit or custard. They are soaked in syrup or covered with icing sugar and then served hot or cold. Sometimes baklava filo is used, but more often than not each recipe has its special dough.

These pastries are called *sambusak* in Arabic and were highly popular in the days of the caliphs when court poets and musicians soaked them with praise –

'After pastry of tardina
Follows sanbusaj well-fried;
Eggs vermillioned after boiling
Lie with olives side by side.'
Mahmud-Ibn Al-Husain Kushajim (poet and astrologer) 910-971 ad

Incidentally the Indo-Pakistan samosa pastries derive their origin and name from the acclaimed dishes of Baghdad.

I have below noted a recipe for nut borek and then given the basic ingredients for some others. The preparation and cooking methods are the same for all.

khoritzov borek

sweet borek with nut filling

Dough
225g (8 oz) plain flour
110g (4 oz) butter or margarine, cut into small pieces
3 egg yolks
2 tablespoons yoghurt or a little more

Filling
3 egg whites
1 teaspoon almond essence
2 tablespoons icing sugar
225g (8 oz) mixed chopped nuts – almonds, pistachios and walnuts

Garnish
50g (2 oz) icing sugar sifted with ½ teaspoon ground
cinnamon and ¼ teaspoon ground cardamom

Sift the flour into a bowl, add the pieces of butter or margarine and rub in until the mixture resembles fine breadcrumbs. In a small bowl beat the egg yolks and yoghurt together thoroughly. Add this to the flour mixture and knead for several minutes until the dough is soft and smooth. It may be necessary to add a little more yoghurt. Divide the dough into about 20 small balls, arrange on a baking tray, cover and refrigerate for 20 minutes.

Meanwhile prepare the filling by first beating the egg whites together. Stir in the almond essence, sifted icing sugar and nuts. Sprinkle a work top with a little flour, take one of the balls of dough and roll it out to form a circle about 3mm ($\frac{1}{8}$ in) thick and 7.5cm (3in) in diameter. Repeat with all the remaining balls. Put 1-2 teaspoons of the nut filling in one half of one of the circles and then fold over and pleat the edges with your fingers or seal with a fork. Repeat with all the remaining balls and filling. Place on lightly greased baking trays about 1 cm ($\frac{1}{2}$ in) apart. Bake in an oven preheated to 200C (400F) gas 6 for 20-30 minutes or until the borek are golden. Remove from the oven, leave to cool a little and then sprinkle with the icing sugar mixture. Serve as a dessert or with tea or coffee.

Makes about 20

elmali borek

apple borek

Dough
see Khoritzov borek

Filling
4-6 apples, peeled, cored and thinly sliced
2 tablespoons chopped pistachio nuts or hazelnuts
½ teaspoon ground cinnamon
50-75g (2-3 oz) caster sugar

Garnish
50g (2 oz) sifted icing sugar

Prepare the dough as above. Mix all the filling ingredients together. Continue as with the recipe above and when serving sprinkle with the icing sugar.

Makes about 20

salori borek

prune-filled pastries

Dough
see Khoritzov borek

Filling
**225g (½ lb) prunes
2 thin slices orange
25g (1 oz) chopped walnuts
juice of ½ lemon
grated rind of 1 lemon
50g (2 oz) sugar
25g (1 oz) raisins
½ teaspoon ground cinnamon**

Place the prunes and orange slices in a saucepan with enough water to cover and simmer until the prunes are tender and the water absorbed. When cool enough to handle remove the prune stones and then chop the flesh and orange slices. Transfer to a bowl and add the remaining ingredients. Mix well and leave to cool.

Proceed as with Khoritzov borek (page 76-7). You can eat these pastries as they are or sprinkle with icing sugar or steep in syrup.

Makes about 20

sambusik

date-filled pastries

A recipe from Jordan making use of dates and mahleb. This is perhaps the self-same dessert whose praises the poet sang. Serve warm and cold. Can be kept for a few days.

Dough
**275g (10 oz) plain flour
½ teaspoon ground mahleb
40g (1½ oz) melted butter
90ml (3 fl oz) milk
50g (2 oz) sugar
60ml (2 fl oz) oil**

Filling
225g (8 oz) dates, chopped

50g (2 oz) butter
1 tablespoon rosewater

Sift the flour into a large bowl, add the mahleb and butter and rub into the flour. Heat the milk and sugar in a small pan until the sugar has dissolved and then cool until lukewarm. Pour the milk and the oil into the flour and mix to a soft dough. Gather up into a ball and knead until smooth.

Prepare the filling by placing the chopped dates and butter in a small pan and cooking over a medium heat, stirring constantly, until the mixture is thick and paste-like. Remove from the heat and stir in the rosewater.

Lightly flour a work top and roll out the pastry until ½cm (¼in) thick. Cut into 5cm (2in) rounds with a plain pastry cutter. Put a teaspoon of the filling into the centre of each round and fold over to form a semi-circle. Seal the edges with your fingers or the prongs of a fork. Place on ungreased baking trays and bake in an oven preheated to 180C (350F) gas 4 for 20-25 minutes. Cool and store in an airtight container when cold.

A variation called 'Sambusik-bil-Loz' (almond-filled borek), again from Jordan, has a filling of 110g (4 oz) ground almonds mixed with 110g (4 oz) sugar, 1 tablespoon orange blossom water and 1 tablespoon rosewater. Prepare as for Sambusik. These can be cooked in the oven or deep-fried and then coated with icing sugar or dropped into syrup for about 30 seconds and then removed with a slotted spoon.

Makes 15-20

sambusik halawah

triangular borek

In the Gulf region of the Middle East (Bahrain, Kuwait, United Arab Emirates) a particularly well known dessert called *sambusik halawah* is prepared with baklava filo filled with cashew nuts and walnuts. Cashew nuts are much used in this area and they are imported from the Indian subcontinent. This sweet keeps well when stored in an airtight container.

about 10 sheets filo pastry
oil for frying

Filling
110g (4 oz) cashew nuts, coarsely ground or finely chopped
50g (2 oz) walnuts, coarsely ground or finely chopped
110g (4 oz) caster sugar
1 teaspoon ground cardamom

Place the nuts, sugar and cardamom in a small bowl and add 3-4 teaspoons water to form a paste. Take one sheet of filo and lay it out flat. Keep the others covered. Cut a strip widthways from the sheet of filo about 3.5cm (1½in) in width. Place a teaspoon of the filling on one end of the strip. Fold the pastry diagonally over the filling forming a triangle, then a straight fold up, followed by another diagonal fold in the opposite direction to the first fold. Continue folding to the end of the strip. Moisten the end of the pastry with water to seal. If you are successful making this first sweet cut the remaining sheets of filo into the same sized strips. If you found the first one rather difficult to make and the filling hard to contain, then cut the remaining strips about 5cm (2in) wide. As you make the pastries place them on a clean tea towel.

Heat enough oil in a large saucepan to deep fry, add a few pastries and fry for 2-3 minutes, turning once, until a deep golden. Do not cook too quickly or the inside layers of pastry will not be cooked. Remove with a slotted spoon and drain on kitchen paper. Serve cold.

Makes about 45-50

serov hatzi kadaif
bread cooked with honey

A highly sophisticated dessert using kaymak, but a simpler method is to use whipped or clotted cream. This dish was the creation of a great chef Tokatlian of Istanbul who, in the 19th century, developed and 'haute cuisinified' many once peasant dishes of the Ottoman Empire. I have also included a simpler sweet, Ekmek Kadayifi, which is perhaps the original of the above sweet – barring, of course, the brandy.

600ml (1 pint) double cream – if you are going to make kaymak
1 round loaf white or brown bread, e.g. Italian or Greek
about 75ml (2½ fl oz) milk
300ml (½ pint) clear honey
juice of 1-2 lemons

To serve
If not preparing kaymak you will need whipped or clotted cream

To prepare the kaymak, first pour the cream into a deep saucepan and bring just to the boil over a low heat. With a ladle lift out some cream and pour it back into the pan until bubbles start rising. Repeat this process for about 30 minutes or more – the more time spent the bigger and softer the bubbles will be. Switch off the heat and leave the pan in a warm place for 2 hours. Refrigerate for 6-8 hours. Run the point of a knife around the edge of the pan to loosen the cream and then remove with a palette knife to a large plate. Roll up the cream and slice.

Slice the loaf in half horizontally and use only the bottom half. Slice off the bottom crust leaving a thick slice of bread about 3cm (1¼in) thick. Place in an oven preheated to 180C (350F) gas 4 and leave until toasted, golden and crisp. Remove the bread, sprinkle on both sides with the milk and wrap in a tea towel until the milk is absorbed.

Mix the honey and lemon juice in a small saucepan and bring to the boil. Place the bread in a round ovenproof dish just large enough to hold it and spoon the honey evenly over it. Bake in an oven preheated to 180C (350F) gas 4 for about 30 minutes or until most of the honey has been absorbed and the bread is golden. Cut into pieces and top with the cream.

Serves 4

ekmek kadayifi
bread pudding

6 thick slices bread, crusts removed
4 eggs
110g (4 oz) sugar
1 teaspoon vanilla essence
2 tablespoons brandy
1 teaspoon grated lemon rind
600ml (1 pint) milk, scalded
50g (2 oz) raisins
50g (2 oz) cherries, stoned and quartered

Garnish
fresh cream
pomegranate syrup

Cut the bread into cubes, place on a baking tray and put into an oven preheated to 180C (350F) gas 4 until toasted and golden. Place the eggs in a bowl, add the sugar and beat until frothy. Stir in the vanilla essence, brandy, lemon rind, hot milk, raisins and cherries. Finally stir in the toasted bread cubes.

Generously butter a 1.8 litre (3 pint) ovenproof dish and pour in the bread mixture. Stand the dish in a pan of cold water and place in an oven preheated to 190C (375F) gas 5 and bake for about 1 hour or until set. To serve first cool, decorate with fresh cream and then dribble lightly with pomegranate syrup.

Serves 6-8

milk and rice puddings

'May you be worthy of your mother's milk.'
A Blessing

Milk has always been the most important drink of all nomads, whether Aryan, Mongolian-Turk or Arab. The Aryan tribes kept a little milk – *giv*, the produce of the living cow – in a saucer during their ceremonies and used it for sprinkling the sacred twigs for mixing with the holy-water (*Zohar*). Mongols and Turks literally lived on mares' milk; the Romans and Byzantines bathed in asses' milk. Assyrians lived on goats' milk, but Caliph Harun-al-Rashid preferred gazelles' milk! You and I were brought up on our mothers' milk so –

'May your mother's milk ever flow
May the snowcaps never melt
waters run
sun ever shine,
but above all
May your mother's milk never dry.'

The whiteness, purity and life-giving symbolism of milk is coupled with the fecundity of rice – the end product being a large selection of milk and rice dishes of which the Middle East is truely propitious. One of the simplest of such puddings is the one below from Iran with a 'heavenly' name.

yakh dar behesht

ice in paradise

50g (2 oz) rice flour or ground rice
900ml (1½ pints) milk
150g (5 oz) sugar
25g (1 oz) cornflour

Garnish
2 tablespoons chopped pistachios

Place the rice flour in a bowl and gradually pour in the milk, mixing constantly so that the mixture is smooth. Stir in the sugar. Place the cornflour in a small bowl and stir in 300ml (½ pint) water. Strain the mixture through muslin into the rice-milk mixture. Transfer the mixture to a saucepan and cook over a low heat until it thickens. Pour into a bowl or individual dishes and leave to cool. Garnish with the pistachio nuts and chill until ready to serve.

Serves 6-8

The traditional rice pudding of Iran is called 'Shir Berenji'. Another – 'Shol-e-Zard' – is usually prepared for the annual observance of the Martyrdom of Imam Hussein (Arba'een). The pudding is made yellow 'zard' with saffron because the holy man's death was regarded as a 'yellow death'. On the festive day the pudding is presented to one's family, friends, the poor and the orphans.

shol-e zard

saffron pudding

175g (6 oz) round-grain rice
350g (12 oz) sugar
½ teaspoon ground saffron dissolved in 2 tablespoons hot water
25g (1 oz) butter
2 tablespoons rosewater

Garnish
1 teaspoon ground cinnamon
2 tablespoons slivered, blanched almonds
1 tablespoon chopped pistachio nuts

Rinse the rice under cold running water until the water runs clear and then place in a saucepan with 1.2 litres (2 pints) water. Bring to the boil, lower the heat and simmer for about 20 minutes or until the rice is very tender. Add a little more water if necessary.

Stir in the sugar, dissolved saffron, butter and rosewater and continue to simmer until the mixture is quite thick. Pour the mixture into a greased baking dish and cook in an oven preheated to 180C (350F) gas 4 for about 30 minutes.

You can either leave the pudding in the dish or transfer to individual dishes. Cool, refrigerate until ready to serve and then decorate with the various garnishes.

Serves 4-6

Hussein was the son of Ali and the grandson of the Prophet (Mohammad). He was killed in a skirmish between government troops and a small body of supporters who were accompanying him to Kufa in Iraq. His grave, 60 miles south of Baghdad, immediately became a goal for pilgrims. A streak of fanaticism embedded in the psyche of Iranian tribes took over and the rituals as well as the doctrines of Shiite Islam were developed.

On the first of Muharram when the festival proper begins mourning clothes are donned, people refrain from bathing. Groups of men, their bodies dyed black and red, tour the streets pulling their hair, beating their chests, inflicting sword wounds upon themselves or dragging chains behind them. There are particular dishes served at this time of the year – a rice-flour halva distributed to all, as well as *shole zard* and another pudding *meshkoofi* which is made of cornflour, saffron and rosewater.

In Turkey a similar pudding called *Zarda* is prepared by the Alouites – followers of Ali. This pudding also appears during the Christian Christmas and New Year festivities. *Zarda* is usually made with honey or grape syrup (*bekmez*). In fact the most satisfying method is to use half grape syrup and half honey. You can also substitute 2-3 tablespoons of desiccated coconut for the pomegranate seeds if they are not available.

zarda

rice in honey and saffron

The recipe I have chosen below actually uses a sugar syrup rather than honey or *bekmez*, but if you wish you can use either 225g (8 oz) honey or *bekmez* or a mixture of the two instead of the sugar. A delightful sweet, in which the grains of rice are suspended in a delicately flavoured jelly.

75g (3 oz) round grain rice, washed thoroughly under cold water
450g (1 lb) sugar
3 tablespoons arrowroot soaked in 3 tablespoons water
½ teaspoon saffron dissolved in 2 tablespoons hot water
1 teaspoon ground cinnamon
2 tablespoons rosewater

Garnish
2 tablespoons sultanas, soaked in cold water for 1 hour
2 tablespoons pine kernels
1 pomegranate, peeled and seeded or 2-3 tablespoons desiccated coconut

Bring 1.8 litres (3 pints) water to the boil in a large saucepan, lower the heat, add the rice and simmer for about 20 minutes or until the grains are tender. Add the sugar, raise the heat and boil vigorously for 5 minutes.

Add the arrowroot, saffron, cinnamon and rosewater, stir well and simmer for 5 minutes. Remove from the heat and leave to cool for 10 minutes. Pour into a serving bowl and chill. Before serving decorate with the various garnishes.

Serves 6-8

kishk-el-fukhara

poor man's sweet

Although this is claimed to be a poor man's sweet it is, in fact, more like a rich man's pudding, since ground almonds, pistachios and mastic are often beyond the means of the poor! It is a simple recipe and perhaps that is the reason for the name. It has a beautiful flavour and aroma and is popular throughout Turkey, Syria, Jordan and Lebanon.

225g (½ lb) ground almonds
1.2 litres (2 pints) milk
75g (3 oz) ground rice
1 tablespoon rosewater
1 tablespoon orange blossom water
1 teaspoon powdered mastic tied in a small muslin bag
150g (5 oz) sugar

Garnish
50g (2 oz) slivered pistachio nuts

Put the ground almonds in a muslin bag and add about 90ml (3 fl oz) of the milk. Squeeze the mixture over a bowl until all the liquid is extracted. Add another 90ml (3 fl oz) of milk and squeeze out more almond juice. Repeat the process once more squeezing hard to extract every drop of liquid.

Place the ground rice in a small bowl and dissolve in 150ml (¼ pint) water. Bring the remaining milk to the boil in a medium saucepan and lower the heat. Stir in the dissolved rice, almond juice, rosewater, orange blossom water, bag of mastic and the sugar. Cook over the low heat, stirring constantly, until the mixture thickens. Remove from the heat and discard the muslin bag. When cold pour into a serving bowl and chill. When ready to serve decorate with the pistachio nuts.

Serves 6-8

meghli

aniseed rice pudding

A Lebanese recipe usually made in large quantities and traditionally served on the birth of a son. The desire for the first-born to be a son is very strong amongst Middle Easterners. At the time of confinement the pregnant woman's eyebrows are blackened so that if a person dressed in bright clothes enters the room no harm will come to mother or child. Incense is burned about the head of the woman in labour to speed delivery. Often the husband is called into the room, water is poured into the skirt of his long coat, up his sleeve and upon his feet. He stoops to drink some of that water.

If the baby born is a girl the mother repeats over and over again that she has 'given birth to a black baby' – she is ashamed that her child is not a boy. On the third day the new mother is given three dates to eat – so that the next child will be a boy. 'Later on she will take her baby to the bath on the same day that another woman with a little son is to be present. These 2 women will then throw some of their milk over each other so that their next children may be sons.' *The Wild Rue*

110g (¼ lb) ground rice
8 tablespoons sugar
1 teaspoon caraway seeds
1 teaspoon fennel seeds
1 teaspoon aniseed
1 teaspoon ground cinnamon

Garnish
chopped pistachios, pine kernels, almonds, walnuts

Place the ground rice in a bowl and slowly stir in about 150ml (¼ pint) water until you have a smooth paste. Now stir in the sugar, caraway seeds, fennel seeds, aniseed and cinnamon. Bring 1 litre (1¾ pints) water to the boil in a medium saucepan. Add a little to the rice mixture to thin it out and then pour it into the saucepan, stirring constantly.

Simmer for a few minutes, stirring all the time, until the mixture thickens. Allow to cool a little and then pour into a serving dish and chill. Before serving decorate with nuts of your choice.

Serves 6-8

gatnabour
armenian rice pudding

The Armenian rice pudding gatnabour is also served to visitors and well-wishers on the birth of a son. This is a very refined pudding, creamy and delicious.

75g (3 oz) round grain rice, washed thoroughly under cold water
1.2 litres (2 pints) milk
rind of 1 lemon
110g (4 oz) sultanas
110g (4 oz) sugar
2 teaspoons vanilla essence
50g (2 oz) split almonds, toasted under a hot grill until golden
white rum or any other favourite flavouring, to taste

Place the rice in a medium saucepan with 600ml (1 pint) of the milk and the lemon rind. Bring to the boil, lower the heat and then simmer very gently until the rice is tender and the milk absorbed. You may need to add a little more milk and stir occasionally to prevent sticking. Stir in the sultanas and simmer for a few more minutes. Remove from the heat and stir in the sugar, vanilla essence and almonds. If the mixture is very thick stir in a little more milk. Refrigerate.

When ready to serve, remove the lemon rind, add more milk to make a creamy consistency and then flavour with the rum. Pour into a serving bowl.

Serves 6-8

aşure

anatolian vegetable and rice pudding

A classic from Central Anatolia (Turkey) in which literally everything that is handy is used. It is one of the oldest dishes known to us – according to folk tradition, on the last day on the Ark Noah's female folk used all the remaining food in a large pot and Aşure was born! You may well wonder (as I often have) what Noah has got in common with the Turks.

Today the pudding is made in large quantities and served at parties, weddings and especially during the month of Aşure which was the Day of Atonement of early Muslims, but was later associated with the Tenth of Muharram – the first month of the Muslim year.

Some people like to purée the rice after it has been cooked and often the water is replaced by milk – in which case the dish is known as 'Beyaz Aşure' – white Aşure.

50g (2 oz) haricot beans, soaked overnight in cold water
50g (2 oz) chickpeas, soaked overnight in cold water
50g (2 oz) large burghul
50g (2 oz) long grain rice
150ml (¼ pint) milk
225g (8 oz) sugar
50g (2 oz) sultanas
4 dried figs, chopped
4 dried apricots, chopped
2 tablespoons rosewater
40g (1½ oz) walnuts, coarsely chopped
25g (1 oz) pine kernels
25g (1 oz) pistachio nuts, halved
25g (1 oz) butter

Place the haricot beans and chickpeas in separate pans with their soaking water, bring each to the boil and then simmer until tender. Add more boiling water if necessary. The chickpeas will probably take longer than the beans.

Rinse the burghul and rice thoroughly and place in a saucepan with 900ml (1½ pints) water. Bring to the boil, lower the heat and simmer for 20-30 minutes. When tender strain the beans and chickpeas and add to the rice pan together with the milk and simmer for a further 10 minutes. Add the sugar, sultanas, figs, apricots and rosewater, stir thoroughly and simmer for another 10 minutes. Stir in the nuts and butter. By now the mixture should resemble thick porridge. If you think it is still a little thin then simmer for a few more minutes, stirring frequently.

Pour the Aşure into individual bowls or a decorative serving dish and decorate, forming patterns with some combination of the following: sultanas, cinnamon, pomegranate seeds, chopped blanched almonds or halved walnuts.

Serves 8-10

muhallabieh

middle eastern rice pudding

I have labelled this pudding Middle Eastern for the simple reason that it is by far the most common and popular throughout the region. Muhallabieh, 'made with milk', is always served chilled and decorated with chopped pistachios, almonds or with a syrup of honey and water scented with ½-1 teaspoon orange blossom water. The recipe below is a standard one, a family favourite of ours. The pomegranate seeds give the pudding a pungent taste, but are optional.

110g (4 oz) ground rice
2 level tablespoons cornflour
1.2 litres (2 pints) milk
8 tablespoons sugar
2 tablespoons orange blossom water or rosewater or a mixture of the two
¼ teaspoon grated nutmeg
110g (4 oz) ground almonds

Garnish
1 small pomegranate, seeded
2 tablespoons chopped pistachio nuts

In a bowl mix together the ground rice and cornflour. Add about 10 tablespoons of the cold milk and stir until you have a smooth paste. Bring the rest of the milk to the boil in a medium saucepan. Lower the heat, add the sugar and stir until it has dissolved. Slowly pour the hot milk on to the rice paste, stirring constantly. Pour the mixture back into the saucepan and cook over a low heat, stirring constantly, until the mixture thickens. Stir in the orange blossom water or rosewater and the nutmeg and cook for a further 3-4 minutes, stirring constantly. Remove from the heat and stir in the almonds.

When cool pour into a serving bowl and refrigerate. Before serving decorate with the pomegranate seeds and nuts.

Serves 6-8

kahveli muhallebi

coffee rice pudding

A favourite variation of muhallabieh is Kahveli muhallebi which is popular in Turkey and is served in the Lokantas, restaurants and cafés. Light brown in colour with a delicate flavour, this pudding incorporates coffee, although sometimes cocoa is substituted.

1 tablespoon ground coffee
50g (2 oz) ground rice
25g (1 oz) cornflour
1.2 litres (2 pints) milk
110g (4 oz) icing sugar

Garnish
cream

Place the coffee in a small bowl and pour a little hot water over it. Set aside. Mix the ground rice and cornflour together in a bowl and mix to a smooth paste with a little of the cold milk. Bring the rest of the milk to the boil in a medium saucepan. Add the icing sugar, stir until dissolved and simmer for 2-3 minutes.

Pour some of the hot milk over the rice paste, stirring constantly. Pour back into the rest of the milk and simmer over a low heat for 3-4 minutes, still stirring constantly until the mixture thickens. Strain the coffee liquid (not necessary if using instant coffee) into the pan, stir thoroughly and simmer for a further minute. When cool pour into a decorative bowl or individual dishes and chill. Pour a little fresh cream over the pudding before serving.

Serves 6-8

portukhal muhallabieh

orange custard

Finally a milk pudding from Lebanon made with oranges.

3 eggs
4 tablespoons caster sugar
¼ teaspoon salt
450ml (¾ pint) milk, scalded
1 teaspoon vanilla essence
4 oranges
50g (2 oz) granulated sugar

Garnish
1 teaspoon ground cinnamon
1 tablespoon pistachio nuts, finely chopped

Beat the eggs and mix with the caster sugar in the top of a double saucepan or in a bowl which will fit over a saucepan. Gradually stir in the salt and scalded milk. Now put the pan or bowl over a pan of boiling water and, stirring constantly, cook for 10-15 minutes or until the custard thickens. Remove the pan or bowl containing the custard and place in a bowl containing cold water to cool. Stir in the vanilla essence.

Meanwhile peel the oranges and slice crossways into slices ½cm (¼in) thick. Arrange the slices over the base of a shallow glass serving dish. When the custard is cold beat it well with a wooden spoon and pour over the orange slices. Heat the granulated sugar in a small saucepan until it melts, add 2 tablespoons hot water, stir well and cook for about 2 minutes and then immediately pour over the custard. Sprinkle with the cinnamon and pistachio nuts and serve.

Serves 6-8

haytaliah
floating scented pudding

One of the most beautiful puddings in the world. Small squares of cornflour pudding float in a heavenly, scented syrup surrounded by raisins, almonds, pistachio nuts and rose petals. This is an Arab recipe which is popular throughout the Mediterranean lands, especially in Syria and Lebanon where one sees huge gilt bowls of haytaliah during the Muslim festivities.

To prepare this sweet you must first make the cornflour pudding. This is called Balouza and is equally famed amongst Arabs who often eat it on its own, chilled and garnished with chopped pistachios.

Balouza
110g (4 oz) cornflour
175g (6 oz) sugar
120ml (4 fl oz) orange blossom water or rosewater
50g (2 oz) chopped pistachios or blanched almonds

Garnish
1 teaspoon ground cinnamon

Syrup
110g (4 oz) sugar
6 tablespoons rosewater – or more according to taste
110g (4 oz) raisins
2 tablespoons halved pistachio nuts
seeds of 1 small pomegranate
a few rose petals, washed and dried carefully
ice cubes
ice cream of choice (optional)

Place the cornflour in a large saucepan and add about 300ml (½ pint) water, stirring constantly until you have a smooth paste. Stir in 1.5 litres (2½ pints) water and the sugar and stir over a low heat until the sugar dissolves. Bring to the boil, stirring constantly, and then lower the heat to a minimum and simmer for about 5-10 minutes or until the mixture thickens and coats the back of a spoon. Stir frequently to prevent sticking but do not scrape the bottom – the slight scorching of the bottom of the pan gives the pudding its unique flavour. Stir in the orange blossom water and cook for a further minute. Add the chopped nuts and stir thoroughly. Remove from the heat and leave to cool for 2 minutes. If you are going to serve it by itself then pour into individual bowls and chill. Before serving sprinkle with a little cinnamon and, if liked, a few chopped pistachio nuts.

If making haytaliah pour the balouza into a square or rectangular baking tin moistened with

cold water and even it out with the back of a spoon. The balouza should not be more than 2.5cm (1in) thick. Pour a little cold water over the top to give the pudding its crinkled appearance. Cool for 15 minutes and then refrigerate for several hours. Remove from the fridge and cut into 2.5cm (1in) squares.

Now prepare the syrup by mixing 1.2 litres (2 pints) water and the sugar in a large saucepan over a low heat stirring until the sugar dissolves. Bring to the boil, simmer for 10 minutes and then set aside to cool. Add the rosewater, raisins, pistachio nuts and pomegranate seeds and stir well. Pour into a decorative serving bowl, add a few rose petals and drop in the squares of balouza and some ice cubes.

Serves about 10

antep keşkul
cream and nut pudding

A recipe from Antep in Turkey where some of the most exciting 'Turkish' dishes originate. These dishes are, in reality, not Turkish at all, but more akin to Syrian-Arab, Armenian, Assyrian and sometimes Kurdish dishes. This multi-racial admixture has, as in other cases, produced a unique style – often labelled 'Antep-style'. A rich, creamy pudding reminiscent of balouza, but much more sophisticated.

600ml (1 pint) single cream
600ml (1 pint) milk
2 tablespoons ground rice
175g (6 oz) sugar
110g (4 oz) bitter almonds, ground or use blanched almonds instead
50g (2 oz) pistachio nuts, ground

Garnish
a selection from: pine kernels, desiccated coconut, pomegranate seeds, finely chopped pistachio nuts

Place the cream and milk in a medium saucepan and bring slowly to the boil. Meanwhile place the ground rice in a small bowl and add enough cold water to mix to a smooth paste. Pour a little of the hot milk into it and stir well. Return the mixture to the saucepan and stir constantly until the mixture comes to the boil. Add the sugar and ground almonds and pistachios and simmer over a low heat, stirring constantly until the mixture thickens. Remove from the heat and leave to cool for a few minutes. Pour into a serving bowl and chill for several hours.

Before serving use some of the suggested garnishes to decorate the top of the pudding. Icing sugar is sometimes dusted over the top.

Serves 6-8

fruit, nut and vegetable sweets

'A sweet dish after the main meal is Sunna.'

Allah has been kind to the Middle East, bestowing on it a climate suitable for growing most fruits, nuts and vegetables. We read from ancient chroniclers that fruit was eaten at the table either before or after the main meal[1]. Amongst those can be included apples, grapes, pomegranates, melons, citrus fruits, peaches, bananas, apricots etc. All these were first cultivated by the Assyrians, Hittites, Babylonians and Egyptians. The very first orchards and vineyards were planted in the Nile, Euphrates and Tigris valleys. Iraq and Syria produced many excellent fruits and the horticulture of Syria in particular (for centuries the granary of Imperial Rome) was highly specialised. 'Syrian apples' were proverbial and many fruits were exported to other parts of the Middle East. The pomegranates of Sirjar, Qumis and Tabaristan[2] were famed, while the favourite fruit of the Baghdadis was melon and the sweetest variety was called 'baranj'. The rich favoured pistachios, quinces, water melons, figs and sugar cane washed with rosewater; the poor classes, i.e. the mass of the people, preferred fruit having stones, such as olives, peaches and apricots, and also all forms of dried fruits.

Honey as a sweetener was much used although the rich preferred sugar (sukkar), which was introduced via India to Iran and hence to the rest of the Middle East. Apart from these two syrup (dibs) was usually made from grapes or carob. Sugar cane – the best came from Ahwaz in Iran – was chewed for its juice and the remains were used as fuel. Honey from Armenia and particularly from Isfahan in Iran was highly prized.

But the fruit that dominated the economic, social and culinary culture of the entire populace was, and in many respects still is, the date. The fresh dates of Iraq and Iran enjoyed great celebrity with Basra as the centre of palm tree cultivation where, it is reported, 300 varieties were produced. Love of the palm tree and its fruit is proverbial. It has, over the centuries, entered the very psyche of the nomad who has woven mystical and mythical powers around it which are almost supernatural in concept. The date dominates the regional cuisines of southern Iraq and the Gulf. It is used as a syrup – 'marees', it is baked, used in sweet and savoury dishes, is dried and exported.

A very simple way of preparing a date sweet is the recipe which opens our chapter on fruit, nut and vegetable sweets.

---

1   Al-Sabi Hilal B. Muhassin *al-Wuzard* ed. A. S. A. Farraj 1958.
    Abu'l-Qasim Ibn Hawqal *Surat al-Ard* ed. J. H. Krausers. Leiden 1938.
2   *The Apples of Damascus* H. Zayyat. Mashriq 1937.

halawah-temar

iraqi date sweet

A popular recipe from Iraq which makes use of dried dates.

450g (1 lb) dried dates, stoned and chopped
225g (½ lb) walnuts, coarsely chopped
225g (½ lb) almonds, coarsely chopped
2 tablespoons sesame seeds, toasted under a grill until golden (optional)
icing sugar

Mix the dates, nuts and sesame seeds together in a large bowl. Knead until smooth. Lightly dust a board with icing sugar. Place the ball of dates and nuts on the board and, with a rolling pin dusted with icing sugar, roll it out into a square about 1-2cm (½-¾ in) thick. With a sharp knife cut into 2.5cm (1in) squares.

Dust a serving plate with icing sugar, arrange the squares over it and then dust with a little more icing sugar. Delicious with coffee. Will keep well if wrapped in waxed paper and stored in an airtight tin.

Makes 24-30

ranghina

fresh date sweet

When fresh dates are available I suggest you try this simple but exotic sweet from Abu-Dhabi in the Gulf States.

450g (1 lb) fresh dates, stoned
50g (2 oz) butter or ghee
75g (3 oz) plain flour, sifted
1 teaspoon ground cardamom
1 tablespoon chopped walnuts
1 tablespoon raisins

Arrange the dates in 6 individual dishes. Melt the butter or ghee in a saucepan and slowly stir in the flour. Cook over a low heat, stirring constantly until the flour is golden. Remove the pan from the heat and stir in the cardamom, walnuts and raisins. Allow to cool for a few minutes, stirring occasionally, and then spoon over the dates. Serve at room temperature.

Serves 6

halwa ditzmar

libyan date slices

A speciality popular throughout North Africa, this date and nuts mixture is sliced and eaten with tea. It will keep for about 1 week. Use fresh fruit for this sweet.

450g (1 lb) dates, stoned
450g (1 lb) figs, peeled and mashed
225g (½ lb) walnuts, coarsely chopped
50g (2 oz) coarsely grated chocolate (optional)
½ teaspoon aniseed
3 tablespoons honey

Place all the ingredients in a large bowl and mix well. Pack the mixture firmly into a 15 X 15cm (6 X 6 in) cake tin, cover and store. Cut with a sharp knife and serve the slices with tea or coffee.

Makes 20-30

al-bathith

date cake

This spicy sweet from Iraq and Saudi Arabia is really a sweetmeat and is similar to some halvas. Simple and quick to prepare, it will keep for several days in an airtight container.

110g (4 oz) wholemeal flour
25g (1 oz) butter or ghee
1 bruised cardamom pod
110g (4 oz) chopped dates
½ teaspoon ground ginger

Garnish
icing sugar

Place the flour in a saucepan and cook over a medium heat, stirring constantly, until it is golden. Meanwhile melt the ghee or butter in a small saucepan with the cardamom pod. Keep over a low heat for about 5 minutes and then set aside. Add the dates to the flour and cook for 2-3 minutes, stirring constantly, until the dates soften. Remove and discard the cardamom pod and add the ghee and the ginger to the date mixture. Stir well and then remove from the heat.

When cool enough to handle take a tablespoonful of the mixture and knead by passing it from one hand to the other. When the mixture holds together, squeeze it into a smooth oval shape and leave to cool. Repeat with the remaining mixture. Serve sprinkled generously with icing sugar.

Makes 10-12

mishlachat ha negev

date rolls stuffed with nuts

An Israeli chef Roger Dabasque created these date rolls stuffed with nuts in honour of the Negev Expedition. It is however more of a variation than a creation since there are similar date sweets in North Africa – whence, I understand, he originates – and in Iran e.g. *khorma-yeh-porshodeh-ba-gerdou*. That having been said Mishlachat ha Negev is a very tasty and attractive sweet. It is perfect for parties and family get-togethers. These sweets will keep well in an airtight tin.

4 eggs
90ml (3 fl oz) double cream
600ml (1 pint) milk
10 tablespoons sugar
green food colouring
200g (7 oz) butter
150g (5 oz) plain flour
40 dates, stoned
150g (5 oz) shelled hazelnuts
250g (9 oz) roasted almonds, chopped
1 tablespoon vanilla essence
1 tablespoon almond essence

Garnish
40 almond or walnut halves

Separate the eggs and reserve the whites for another recipe. Mix the yolks in a small bowl with the cream. Bring the milk to the boil in a saucepan, add the sugar and a drop or two of the colouring until you have a light green. In another saucepan melt the butter, add the flour and stir constantly over a low heat until the flour begins to fry. Add the boiled milk gradually, stirring constantly to ensure it is smooth and free from lumps. When the mixture becomes thick and even, stir in the egg yolk mixture. Place in the refrigerator to cool.

Stuff each date with 3 whole hazelnuts. When the dough mixture is cool place it on a work top and knead until pliable. Add the chopped almonds, vanilla and almond essences and knead a little more. Flatten the dough and cut into strips 6 X 1cm (2$\frac{1}{2}$ X $\frac{1}{2}$in). You need 40 strips. Fold a strip of dough lengthways around each date and continue until all the dates have been wrapped in dough. Decorate each sweet with $\frac{1}{2}$ an almond or walnut. Particularly delicious with Turkish coffee or with tea.

Makes 40

A brief glimpse into the psyche of the Medieval Levantine – the passage is taken from *The Tale of the Eighth Captain* from the incomparable *The book of 1001 Nights*, full of love, hate, passions, soaked in romance and covered with a thick layer of mystery; all finger-lickingly good!

'The clarinet player's son stayed lonely on the top of the mountain, so far from the world that even the ants might not have found him, until he began to feel hunger and thirst, then he scrambled down, gnawing his hand for rage. In a day and a night he reached the middle height of Kaf and, on the morning of the second day came upon two date palms bowed with their abundance of ripe fruit. One of them bore red dates, the other yellow. The boy plucked a branch of each and, as he preferred yellow dates, swallowed one of them with great delight. But hardly had it passed his lips when he had an itching of his scalp and, carrying his hand to the place, felt a horn rapidly growing out of his head. This horn wound itself round one of the palms and the unfortunate youth found himself a prisoner.*

'"If I am doomed" he said to himself, "I would rather die fed than fasting." And he fell upon the red dates. But, no sooner had he eaten one of them than the horn writhed away from about the palm and, leaving him free, grew small and disappeared.*

'He ate the red dates until his hunger was satisfied and then, after filling his pockets with fruit of each colour, went on walking so vigorously that, by the end of 2 months, he had come back to the palace of the wrestling princess. He strode beneath the windows crying "Dates, early dates, oh, dates! Girl's fingers, oh, dates!"'*

Next he schemes to poison the beautiful princess, only to dash into the palace of the 1001 concubines, or is it Turkish delights! and proceeds to cure her with his red dates and – and they live happily ever after. For all I know they still are! All successful relationships are based on good dates!

narinchanoush

oranges in liqueur and syrup

A family favourite which is simple to prepare, delicious to eat and very attractive to the eye! Makes a delightful finish to a rich meal. The orange peel can be made in large quantities and stored in a sealed jar for future use. You can use sliced pistachios or chopped walnuts instead of the almonds.

900g (2 lb) oranges, peeled; reserve the flesh and the rind
900g (2 lb) sugar
1 tablespoon lemon juice
3 tablespoons orange blossom water

Garnish
3 tablespoons blanched slivered almonds, toasted
2 tablespoons orange liqueur, e.g. filfar or curaçao

Half fill a large saucepan with water, bring to the boil and drop in the pieces of peel. Simmer for about 30 minutes or until the peel is soft. Remove from the heat and drain. When cool enough to handle take a sharp knife and carefully slice off as much of the white pith as possible. Slice the peel into strips less than 3mm (⅛in) thick if possible.

Place the sugar, lemon juice and 900ml (1½ pints) water in a large saucepan, bring to the boil and simmer for 5 minutes. Add the sliced orange peel and simmer until the syrup thickens and coats the back of a spoon. Remove from the heat, stir in the orange blossom water and set aside to cool completely.

To prepare the sweet for serving cut the oranges crossways into ½cm (¼in) thick slices. In a shallow dish arrange the slices, overlapping, around the edge leaving a gap in the centre. Spoon some of the orange peel evenly over the slices and pile a little more into the centre. Pour some of the syrup evenly over the slices and then sprinkle with the toasted almonds and the liqueur. Chill before serving.

Serves 6-8

nuranoush

pomegranate sweet

The pomegranate – from the Latin meaning a multi-seeded apple – has a thin, tough rind, is red-fleshed and is indigenous to the Mediterranean. It is oft quoted in the holy books – Bible, Koran and Talmud. It was (and still is) the symbol of rejuvenation in Egyptian and later Christian art. It is also a symbol of fertility and immortality, hence the numerous Renaissance paintings of 'Madonna of the Pomegranates'.

Pomegranates are best exploited in the Caucasian and Iranian cuisines where numerous soups, salads, main dishes, syrups and sweets are prepared. One of the sweets is the recipe below made of pomegranates, and yoghurt with syrup. Nuranoush has a fascinating flavour and brilliant colour. It is simple to prepare.

2 large pomegranates
2 medium pomegranates
2 tablespoons coarse, dry breadcrumbs or crushed cream crackers
120ml (4 fl oz) yoghurt
2 tablespoons double or clotted cream

Syrup
175g (6 oz) sugar
1 teaspoon lemon juice
2 tablespoons rosewater

Garnish
2 tablespoons chopped pistachio nuts

First prepare the syrup. Place the sugar, lemon juice and 300ml (½ pint) water in a small saucepan and bring to the boil. Lower the heat and simmer for 10-15 minutes or until the syrup forms a film over a spoon. Stir in the rosewater and set aside.

Meanwhile cut the pomegranates in half and remove the seeds. Retain the halved shells of the large pomegranates and remove any pith remaining in them. Put the seeds and breadcrumbs or crushed biscuits in a bowl, mix and then mash. Spoon the mixture into the pomegranate shells and pack tightly. Pour the syrup slowly over the mixture giving it time to soak through. Place in the refrigerator and chill for 2-4 hours.

Whisk the yoghurt and cream together and spoon over the pomegranates. Sprinkle the chopped nuts over the top and serve immediately.

Serves 4

banana beersheba
fried bananas

An Israeli speciality in honour of the new (but old) city of Beersheba 'And Abraham took sheep and oxen, and gave them to Abimelechi; and both of them made a covenant.... Wherefore he called that place Beer Sheba, because there they sware both of them.' (*Genesis* XXI 27-31)

Beersheba has, after centuries of sleep, re-awakened to life –hence the dedication.

6 ripe bananas

Marinade
pinch of salt
pinch of black pepper
pinch of ground nutmeg
1 tablespoon lime or lemon juice
2 teaspoons rosewater
50g (2 oz) butter

Garnish
3 tablespoons sugar
1 tablespoon crushed walnuts
1 tablespoon crushed pine kernels

Peel the bananas, cut in half lengthways and arrange in a shallow dish. Mix the marinade ingredients together, sprinkle over the bananas and refrigerate for 1 hour. Heat half the butter in a large frying pan, add a few of the halved bananas and sauté for several minutes, turning at least once. Remove carefully and arrange on a large serving plate. Fry the remaining halves in the same way, adding more butter if necessary. Mix the garnishes together and sprinkle over the bananas. Serve warm or cold.

Serves 6

tefah wa banana bil louz

apple and banana dessert

A North African speciality which is also popular throughout the Arab world. The apples should be tart and the bananas hard and fresh. Serve cold but not necessarily chilled. Serve with cream.

4 large cooking apples, peeled and cored
75g (3 oz) blanched almonds, toasted until golden
2 teaspoons ground cinnamon
50g (2 oz) butter
rind 1 lemon cut into very thin strips
175g (6 oz) sugar
juice of 1 lemon
4 medium sized bananas, peeled and sliced
2 tablespoons orange blossom water

Cut the apples into 3mm (⅛in) thick slices and place in a bowl. Grind the toasted almonds and add to the bowl together with the cinnamon. Melt the butter in a saucepan, add the apple-almond mixture, slices of lemon rind, sugar, lemon juice and 120ml (4 fl oz) water and mix thoroughly. Cook gently over a low heat until the sugar dissolves and then add the banana slices. Simmer, stirring occasionally, until the mixture is fairly dry. Remove from the heat, stir in the orange blossom water and set aside to cool. Serve with cream.

Serves 6

Apricot is to the Armenians what the date is to the Arabs. The national fruit *Prunus Armeniaca* was introduced to Europe during the reign of Alexander of Macedonia. The fruit is a cross between the peach and the plum, having the tender but not fuzzy skin of the peach, but a smooth stone thickened at the edge and firm, sweet flesh deep pink in colour.

The apricot is extensively used in the Caucasus – particularly in the Armenian cuisine where soups, salads, main dishes and desserts exploit all its potential. The recipe below for stuffed apricots with almonds is a typical one from the region of Mount Ararat.

letzvadze dziran

apricots stuffed with almonds

450g (1 lb) fresh apricots
2 teaspoons lemon juice
sugar

75g (3 oz) ground almonds
1 tablespoon rosewater
1 tablespoon sugar

Place the apricots in a large saucepan with just enough water to cover, add the lemon juice, bring to the boil and simmer for just 1 minute. Strain off the liquid and reserve. Make a slit in the top of each apricot just large enough to remove the stones. Measure the liquid in a jug and then return to the saucepan, add an equal amount of sugar and bring to the boil. Simmer for about 15-20 minutes or until the syrup thickens. For the last 5 minutes of the cooking time return the apricots to the pan and cook in the syrup. Remove the apricots with a slotted spoon and cool and then refrigerate the syrup.

Mix the filling ingredients together in a small bowl to form a paste. When the apricots are cool enough to handle, fill with the paste and then refrigerate. Serve cold with the syrup poured over them and, if you wish, topped with cream.

Serves 4

kaymakli kayisi

apricots with cream

450g (1 lb) large, whole dried apricots, soaked overnight in cold water
225g (8 oz) sugar
4 tablespoons ground almonds
toasted blanched almonds

Garnish
150ml (¼ pint) kaymak or clotted cream or whipped double cream
2 tablespoons ground pistachio nuts

Drain the soaked apricots, place in a saucepan, add enough water to cover and cook over a low heat for 15 minutes. Remove with a slotted spoon. Add the sugar to the saucepan and stir constantly until it has dissolved. Simmer for about 15 minutes or until a heavy syrup has formed and then return the apricots to the pan and simmer for a further 5 minutes. Remove the apricots with a slotted spoon and place on a plate with their cut sides uppermost.

When cool enough to handle, spoon a little ground almond into each apricot and press in one toasted almond. Arrange in a shallow bowl and spoon the syrup evenly over the apricots. Cool and refrigerate. Either put a dab of cream on each apricot or serve separately and then sprinkle the apricots with the pistachio nuts.

Serves 4-6

zardalu-sarshir-desserdeh
apricot dessert

An Iranian speciality from Tabriz. You can also prepare this tasty sweet with figs or dried prunes.

175g (6 oz) dried apricots, soaked overnight in cold water and then drained
50g (2 oz) sugar
grated rind of 1 lemon
1 teaspoon grated orange rind

Garnish
150ml (¼ pint) whipped cream
2 tablespoons finely chopped pistachio nuts

Place all the ingredients in a large saucepan with 300ml (½ pint) water and mix thoroughly. Bring to a quick boil, stirring constantly until the sugar has dissolved. Then lower the heat and simmer for about 20 minutes or until the mixture is soft. Remove from the heat and leave to cool for 10-15 minutes and then purée the mixture either in a blender or by rubbing through a sieve. Pour the mixture into individual bowls or a serving dish and refrigerate. Spoon the cream over the top and sprinkle with the nuts.

Serves 4-6

halawah bil-mish-mish il lubnani
lebanese apricot dessert

A Lebanese version making use of rum and eggs has a touch of France about it, but it is nevertheless very delicious.

175g (6 oz) dried apricots, soaked overnight in cold water
150ml (¼ pint) double cream
50g (2 oz) sugar
1 tablespoon lemon juice
1 tablespoon rum
2 egg whites
pinch of salt

Garnish
1 tablespoon finely chopped almonds or pistachio nuts

Drain the apricots and place in a saucepan with enough water to cover. Bring to the boil and then simmer for 5 minutes. Remove from the heat, drain and cool. Reduce to a pulp by blending or rubbing through a sieve. Refrigerate for 2-3 hours.

Place the cream in a bowl and whisk until stiff and then fold in the apricot purée. Gently stir in the sugar, lemon juice and rum. Place the egg whites in another bowl with the salt and whisk until stiff. Fold into the apricot mixture until well blended. Pour into individual bowls or into a serving dish and chill before sprinkling with the nuts.

Serves 4-6

zardalu toush-porshodeh
stuffed apricot balls

450g (1 lb) large, soft dried apricots
3 tablespoons ground pistachio nuts
4 tablespoons icing sugar
2 tablespoons orange blossom water
½ teaspoon ground cardamom

Filling
2 tablespoons ground almonds
2 tablespoons sugar
½ teaspoon ground cinnamon

Garnish
sifted icing sugar

Wipe the apricots with a slightly damp cloth and then chop very finely or pass through a mincer. Place in a large bowl and add the pistachio nuts, icing sugar, orange blossom water and cardamom. Wet your hands and knead vigorously until you have a smooth paste. Wet your hands again and shape the mixture into marble-sized balls.

Mix the ground almonds, sugar and cinnamon together. Take one ball, hollow out and fill with a little of the nut mixture. Close the hole, roll the ball between your palms and then roll generously in the icing sugar. Repeat with the remaining balls. If wrapped in waxed paper and stored in an airtight tin these balls will keep for several weeks.

Makes 20-30

maadan hasultan

almond mousse topped with apricot sauce

From Israel this is a new dessert created by chef Roger Debasque. As with many of his recipes there is the flavour of France in it. Is very attractive to look at and equally delicious.

Custard
3 egg yolks
2 tablespoons sugar
300ml (½ pint) milk

Mousse (sultan's delight)
50g (2 oz) toasted almonds, ground
½ teaspoon vanilla essence
½ teaspoon almond essence
3 teaspoons gelatine
3 egg whites
2 tablespoons sugar
150ml (¼ pint) cream

Apricot sauce
225g (½ lb) fresh, ripe apricots, stoned or 110g (¼ lb) dried apricots,
soaked overnight
lemon juice
sugar

Garnish
6-8 cherries or fresh strawberries

Place the egg yolks in a small bowl, add the sugar and mix well. Bring the milk to the boil in a small saucepan. Pour a little of the milk into the egg mixture, stir and then pour it back into the rest of the milk in the pan. Stir well and lower the heat. Fill a large saucepan or bowl with cold water and, at the first sign of the milk boiling, remove the mixture from the heat, dip the pan into the cold water and leave to cool.

When the custard is cool prepare the mousse by first putting the ground almonds, vanilla and almond essences and the custard into a large bowl and mixing thoroughly. Place the gelatine in a small bowl with a few tablespoons of water, place over a pan of simmering water and stir until the gelatine has dissolved. Stir the gelatine into the almond mixture. Whisk the egg whites until stiff and fold in the sugar. Whisk the cream until thick. Fold the egg whites and cream into the almond mixture and stir carefully with a metal spoon until well blended.

Either spoon the mixture into a decorative glass dish or divide between 6-8 individual dessert glasses. Do not fill more than three-quarters of each glass. Leave in the refrigerator to set and prepare the apricot sauce. Blend the apricots with a little water to form a purée about the consistency of double cream. Add lemon juice and sugar to taste. When set pour the sauce over the top. Decorate with cherries or strawberries and serve chilled.

Serves 6-8

holu-e desserdeh

peach dessert

The peach – *Prunus Persica* – is the fruit of Iran. Although first cultivated in China it arrived in Europe via ancient Persia where it is still regarded (next to the melons of Ahwaz and pomegranates of Tabaristan) as the Iranian national fruit. It has a furrowed stone, yellow or red-flushed flesh and a thin but fuzzy skin. This dish is very simple and easy to prepare. You can cook other fruits in the same way, e.g. apples, pears and apricots.

110g (4 oz) sugar
4 large, firm peaches, blanched, peeled and sliced
2 teaspoons rosewater
½ teaspoon crushed cardamom

Place the sugar and 180ml (6 fl oz) water in a saucepan and bring to the boil. Add the peach slices and simmer for 5 minutes. Remove from the heat and leave to cool for 10 minutes. Then gently stir in the rosewater and cardamom. Delicious served with cream or ice cream.

Serves 4

salori litzkanoush

stuffed prunes

An Armenian delicacy also popular throughout Turkey and Greece. A very refined sweet that should be served cold. Serve with tea or coffee.

450g (1 lb) prunes, stoned if possible, soaked for a few hours in water if necessary
2 tablespoons sugar
rind of 1 lemon

Filling
110g (¼ lb) thick honey
25g (1 oz) blanched almonds, coarsely chopped
25g (1 oz) walnuts, coarsely chopped
25g (1 oz) pistachio nuts or hazelnuts, halved
3 tablespoons whipped double cream
50g (2 oz) digestive biscuits, crushed

Garnish
icing sugar

Place the prunes in a saucepan with enough water to cover. Add the sugar and lemon rind and bring to the boil. Lower the heat and simmer for about 15 minutes or until just tender. Remove from the heat and leave to cool.

Meanwhile place the honey and nuts in a bowl and mix until the honey is soft. Add the whipped cream and whisk until the mixture is frothy. Stir in the biscuit crumbs and place the filling in the refrigerator until the prunes are cool enough to handle.

If necessary remove the stones from the prunes by making a small slit down one side. Place 1 teaspoon of the filling in each prune and then roll each stuffed prune in the icing sugar. Arrange on a serving plate and refrigerate for a few hours. Ideal with tea or coffee.

Makes about 60

alani

dried peaches stuffed with walnuts

A classic from the Caucasus, beloved of Armenians and Georgians and named after the latter's ancestors – the war-like Alans. Alani will keep for a long time, so I suggest you prepare it in large quantities when peaches are in season.

2.25kg (about 5 lb) large peaches

Filling
225g (½ lb) walnuts, finely chopped or ground
110g (¼ lb) sugar
½ teaspoon ground cinnamon
¼ teaspoon ground cardamom

Place the filling ingredients in a bowl and mix well. Blanch and peel each peach. Place them on baking trays and place in an oven heated to the lowest heat for about 30 minutes. Remove from the oven and if, by luck, it is a sunny day leave the peaches to dry out in the sun, turning occasionally. Otherwise put in a warm place, such as the airing cupboard or in a cool oven. When dry (takes 36-48 hours) remove the stones with the point of a sharp knife.

Fill each hole with some of the walnut mixture. Now gently press each peach between your palms to flatten slightly. Thread on to a string with the openings upwards and then dry under the sun, or in an airing cupboard, for 3-4 days. Store in waxed paper and in an airtight container. Excellent with tea or coffee.

Makes about 20

kharpouzeh-ve-holu makhlut

melon and peach dessert

From Tehran this beautiful dessert is often served on Fridays (Muslim Sunday) after lunch. Simple to prepare, beautiful to look at and absolutely delicious.

1 large, ripe honeydew melon
1 ripe cantaloupe melon
50g (2 oz) caster sugar
½ teaspoon salt
4 firm, ripe peaches
60ml (2 fl oz) lemon juice
2-3 tablespoons rosewater

Garnish
crushed ice

Halve the melons. Place a sieve over a bowl and scoop the seeds into it. Let the juice drip into the bowl and then discard the seeds. Holding the halves over the bowl scoop the flesh out in neat balls using a melon scoop, letting the juices fall into the bowl with the melon balls. Add the sugar and salt and stir gently.

Blanch and peel the peaches. Place the lemon juice in a bowl. Halve and slice the peaches and add to the bowl. As you add each peach stir gently to coat with the lemon juice. When finished, add the peach slices and lemon juice to the melon balls. Stir gently and add rosewater to taste. Cover and chill for several hours. Pile into a serving bowl and decorate with crushed ice. Serve immediately.

Serves 8

Saidi said –

'Once when I was young I wished to fast. I was aware that I had to undergo certain cleansing rituals, but since I did not know how to do these I consulted our village holy man. "My son" he said "you have come to the right man. I am experienced in such matters. I shall lead you into the right path. Firstly, you whisper 'In the name of God'. Next you wash your mouth and nose using your little finger so. Do you understand? This ensures that your nostrils are clean. Then rub your front teeth with your forefinger so. Next you splash your face 3 times with clean water, covering all your face, forehead down to the chin, so. Next you wash your hands and arms up to the elbows, reciting aloud for all to hear 'God is mighty. God is great'. After which you wipe your head and wash your feet. Finally you whisper (as you began) 'In the name of God'. And that's it. As I said before I, a holy man, know all. When in doubt call me."

'Just then the Mukhtar (head man) of the village walked slowly past the front door. "Decrepit senile fool" muttered the holy man.'
Adapted from *Bustan*

meghrov khentzor

stuffed apples in honey

A beautiful dessert dish from Armenia. It can be served hot or cold. You can prepare quinces or firm un-ripe pears in the same way.

4 cooking apples, peeled and cored

Syrup
75g (3 oz) sugar
120ml (4 fl oz) honey
1 teaspoon lemon juice
5cm (2in) stick cinnamon
2 tablespoons orange blossom water

Filling
2 tablespoons walnuts or pistachios, chopped
2 tablespoons sultanas
¼ teaspoon ground cinnamon
¼ teaspoon crushed cardamom
1 tablespoon icing sugar

Garnish
kaymak or whipped cream

Place the sugar, honey and 250ml (8 fl oz) water in a saucepan and heat, stirring constantly, until the sugar dissolves. Add the lemon juice, cinnamon stick and orange blossom water and stir well. Set aside.

Place the filling ingredients in a bowl and mix well. With a teaspoon fill each apple with the mixture. Carefully arrange the apples side by side in the saucepan and baste with the syrup. Bring to the boil, lower the heat, cover and simmer for 12-15 minutes or until the apples are just tender. Baste every now and then. With a slotted spoon remove the apples from the pan and place in a serving dish. Pour the syrup evenly over them and serve hot or cold.

Serves 4

appithia se krassi

pears in wine

This is a Cypriot speciality and, for once, not of Arab-Turkish origin but Greek. I must explain that most so-called Cypriot food is in reality second or third hand Arab, Turkish or Armenian in origin. This is a beautiful dessert in which the dark red pears are coated in a thick syrup. You can prepare quinces and large cooking apples in the same way.

4 large, firm pears, peeled but with the stems left on
600ml (1 pint) dry red wine
175g (6 oz) sugar
2 cinnamon sticks
4 cloves
rind of 1 lemon

Pour the wine into a medium-sized saucepan and bring to the boil. Add the sugar, cinnamon sticks, cloves and lemon rind and simmer for 3-4 minutes. Carefully arrange the pears side by side in the saucepan with their stems upwards. Simmer gently, basting the pears regularly, until they are tender. Remove from the pan with a slotted spoon and arrange in a glass bowl.

Raise the heat a little and continue to cook the syrup until it thickens and coats a spoon. Pour this thick syrup over the pears and then refrigerate.

Serves 4

tapouichim veh mango de-crème

apples and mangoes in cream

An Israeli recipe that combines apples and mangoes – the latter is a new addition to the Middle Eastern cuisine, and to date is not widely known. It is successfully being cultivated on Israeli kibbutzim. Decorated with fresh fruit this sweet makes a very beautiful dessert.

1kg (2 lb) cooking apples (or firm pears) peeled and thickly sliced
75g (3 oz) sugar
juice of 1 lemon
1 teaspoon ground cinnamon
½ teaspoon ground nutmeg
225g (½ lb) digestive biscuits, crushed
300ml (½ pint) kaymak or whipped cream
50g (2 oz) pine kernels
450g (1 lb) mangoes, peeled and sliced

Garnish
fresh cherries, tangerine slices, mulberries etc.

Place the apple slices, sugar, lemon juice and 120ml (4 fl oz) water in a large saucepan and cook over a low heat until the apple slices are just tender. Do not overcook or they will break up. Remove from the heat, cool and refrigerate for 1-2 hours.

Remove from the refrigerator and carefully lift out and arrange the apple slices on a serving dish. Sprinkle with the cinnamon and nutmeg and then cover with half the biscuit crumbs. Now cover with half the cream. Sprinkle with the pine kernels and then arrange sliced mangoes over the top. Sprinkle the remaining biscuit crumbs over the top and then spread with the remaining cream. Decorate with fresh fruit.

Serves 8

'And in the autumn when you gather the grapes of your vineyards for the winepress; say in your heart:
I too am a vineyard, and my fruit shall be gathered for the winepress.
And like new wine I shall be kept in eternal vessels.
And in winter, when you draw the wine, let
there be in your heart a song for each cup;
And let there be in the song a remembrance for the autumn days,
And for the vineyards and for the winepress.'
from *The Prophet* K. Gibran

The grape vine *vitis vinifera* is one of the oldest plants cultivated by man. Its natural habitat was the Caucasus, whence it spread east and west. It was cultivated by the Ancient Egyptians, Hittites and Urartians. In the first book of Moses (Genesis) we are told how Noah began 'to be an husbandman' and planted a vineyard: 'And he drank of the wine, and was drunken'. The whole of the Song of Solomon is full of allusions to this delightful fruit.

There are basically 4 categories of grape cultivation: dessert or table grapes, wine grapes, grapes that are dried for raisins and grapes that are converted into juice. Though normally eaten fresh, grapes are often used to prepare desserts. One of the simplest methods is to frost them – as with the recipe below which is popular in Greece and Turkey.

staphilia zaharomena

frosted grapes

Make sure you are using fresh, firm and seedless grapes.

1kg (2 lb) seedless white grapes
250g (9 oz) icing sugar
1 teaspoon ground cinnamon (optional)
2 egg whites

Wash the grapes thoroughly under cold running water. Drain and then dry with kitchen paper. Break the bunches up into smaller, attractive clusters. Place the egg whites in a bowl and whisk until frothy but not stiff. Now, using a pastry brush, thoroughly coat each grape with egg white. Spread some foil over a cake rack and arrange the clusters of grapes over it. Sieve the icing sugar – and cinnamon if using it – over the grapes, turning them several times until well coated. Refrigerate for several hours and then serve with pastries.

orojig

grape juice and walnuts

This sweet is also known as 'sweet soujouk', but in Eastern Turkey and Armenia where it originated it is better known as *orojig* or *reojig* meaning 'round balls'. Basically it is halved walnuts dipped in a grape juice and sugar syrup. There is an equally popular sweet called 'goshdig' meaning 'crooked one'. Here the halved walnuts are alternated with blanched almonds –this gives a more irregular appearance. Sometimes other fruit juices are used, but in my opinion nothing beats the original version given below. Needless to say this sweet should be dried under the sun, but you can improvise by using a radiator or airing cupboard.

350g (12 oz) plain flour, sifted
450g (1 lb) sugar
110g (4 oz) cornflour
3.6 litres (6 pints) grape juice
about 40 walnut halves
icing sugar, sifted

Mix the flour, sugar and cornflour together in a large bowl. Add a little of the grape juice and mix to a smooth paste. Little by little add the rest of the juice, stirring all the time.

Take a length of string and a strong needle and thread the first 2 walnut halves back to back into the middle of the string. Thread the rest of the nuts. The nuts on either side of the 2 centre nuts should face the same way as those 2 nuts.

Tie the 2 ends of the string to a stick, leaving a gap of at least 7.5cm (3in) between the ends so that the nuts do not touch.

Pour half the grape juice mixture into a large saucepan and gradually bring to the boil, stirring constantly. Lower the heat and simmer, still stirring, until the mixture thickens. Dip the strung nuts into this juice 4-5 times, or until they have picked up most of the liquid. Hang to dry overnight above something in which to catch the drips. The next day dip the nuts again, using the remaining juice, but this time leave to dry for several days.

When completely dry cut into 15cm (6 in) lengths, roll in icing sugar and store in an airtight container.

Makes 6-8 lengths

basdegh

fruit paste

This is a thin, dry paste traditionally made from grape juice, sugar and cornflour. The word derives from the Armenian *basdar* meaning 'fine linen' because the thin syrup was spread over a fine cloth to dry. The classic basdegh is called 'Khagoghi basdegh'.

During the Christian Christmas a very special sweet called Yerangyoun Basdegh is often prepared. I remember going visiting on Christmas day (6th January according to the calendar of the Apostolic Armenian Church) and at relations' houses, near and far, I was inevitably given a few pence, some sweets and basdegh.

khagoghi basdegh

grape paste

150g (5 oz) plain flour, sifted
110g (4 oz) cornflour
250ml (8 fl oz) honey or corn syrup
5 litres (about 4 quarts) grape juice*
800g (1¾ lb) sugar
2 teaspoons ground mahleb

*First prepare the grape juice by removing the stems from about 2.7kg (6 lb) grapes. Place the grapes in a large saucepan with 2.5 litres (4 pints) water. Bring to the boil and then simmer for 15 minutes. Pass through a colander, pushing through as much of the pulp as possible. Discard what remains in the colander and place the pulp and juice in a cloth bag or jelly bag and leave it suspended over a large bowl, preferably overnight, until the last drop of moisture has been obtained. Measure the juice you have collected and make it up to 5 litres (4 quarts) with water if necessary.

Mix the flour and cornflour together in a large saucepan and then gradually stir in 600ml (1 pint) cold water and mix until the mixture is smooth. Set aside. In another large pan bring the honey, sugar and grape juice gently to the boil. Spoon a little of the grape juice mixture into the flour mixture and stir thoroughly. Repeat this several times until the mixture has thinned out. Slowly pour in the remaining grape juice, stirring constantly, and then bring to the boil. Now soak the mahleb in 2 tablespoons water for about 5 minutes and then strain the liquid into the basdegh. The mixture should be as thick as double cream. If you think it is a little too thin then mix 2-3 tablespoons of cornflour with a few tablespoons of the hot basdegh to form a smooth paste. Add a little more basdegh to thin out the paste and then stir back into the basdegh and simmer for a few more minutes.

The basdegh is now ready to be dried. Cut a fine cotton cloth, e.g. muslin, into a rectangle about 75 X 125cm (30 X 50in) and spread it out flat on a large table. Pour the hot basdegh slowly over the cloth, smoothing it out in an even layer about 3mm (⅛in) thick. Use the back of a wooden spoon. Leave to dry. This will probably take about 2 days in the summer and 4 days in the winter.

When it is dry turn the basdegh over and peel off the cloth. To facilitate this soak a cloth in cold water and then rub it over the basdegh cloth until it is thoroughly wet. Now leave it for a few minutes and then try lifting 1 corner of the cloth. If it comes away easily then peel it off completely.

Sprinkle a little cornflour through a sieve evenly over the damp surface of the basdegh to remove any moisture. Cut the sheet of basdegh into rectangles 12.5 X 15cm (5 X 6in) and then fold each one in half, floured side inside. If going to make Yerangyoun Basdegh described on page 114 then cut the sheet into 7.5 X 30cm (3 X 12in) strips. Spread over the table and leave for 2-3 hours. Wrap the pieces in waxed paper and store in an airtight container. Serve by itself or make omelettes or soup with it.

Makes about 50 pieces

yerangyoun basdegh

nut-filled grape paste

Khagoghi basdegh (page 113) cut into 7.5 X 30cm (3 X 12in) strips
a little honey

Filling
225g (½ lb) chopped walnuts or almonds or pistachios or a mixture
4 tablespoons sugar
½ teaspoon ground cinnamon

Mix the filling ingredients together in a bowl. Fold over one short end of the strip to form a triangle and then fold again. Place 1 tablespoon of the filling into the open side of the triangle. Continue rolling into triangles until you reach the end of the strip. Spread a little honey along the inside edge of the strip to stick the end in place. Store in waxed paper or in an airtight tin.

Makes about 40

amardin

apricot basdegh

The finest apricot paste came from Syria – or so I thought until I found one labelled 'Amardin produced in South Africa'. I suspect there lurks an enterprising Lebanese behind the product. The recipe below is for Amardin prepared in trays and then cut into squares or lozenges. If you wish to make the thinner version, follow the instructions for khagoghi basdegh, page 113.

1kg (about 2 lb) dried apricots
560g (1¼ lb) sugar

Place the apricots in a large saucepan, add just enough water to cover and bring gently to the boil. Lower the heat and simmer for about 30 minutes or until the apricots are plumped up and the water has been absorbed. Cool, transfer the mixture to a blender and blend to a smooth purée. Add a little water if necessary. Return the purée to the saucepan and stir in the sugar. Cook over a low heat until the mixture is reduced to a thick, stiff consistency and comes away from the sides of the pan. Stir frequently to prevent the mixture sticking and burning.

Wet 2 shallow baking tins, pour half the mixture into each and spread evenly with the back of a spoon. It should not be more than ½cm (¼in) thick. Set aside until the top is dry. Cut into 7.5cm (3in) strips, carefully turn the strips over and leave to dry in the same way. Do not over dry. Stack the strips with layers of greaseproof paper in between. This sweet can be eaten on its own, diluted to form a delicious drink or cut into smaller strips and cooked in stews, omelettes etc.

Makes 16-20

Similarly in Anatolia and Greece a delightful basdegh is made with quinces. It is called *ayve pasteli* in Turkish and *kythonopasto* in Greek. All these pastes will keep for a long time when stored at room temperature. They are the main attraction during Christmas celebrations when the dinner table is laden with all kinds of nuts, fruits, puddings and basdeghs. An old folk song sings

'Tomorrow's Christmas,
The year's at an end
Soon it will end. Tomorrow's Christmas
Alleluia.
Orojig, basdegh, dry fruits, gaghant
Open your aprons, sing the praises of
Alleluia.
Home and stable are filled with hope
Happy Christmas. Praise be the Son
Alleluia.
Open your aprons, sing the praise of
Give in palmfuls, eat in joy,
Alleluia.'

ayve pesteli
quince basdegh

This paste is usually served with iced drinks or with coffee.

6 large quinces, peeled, quartered and cored
175g (6 oz) sugar
1 tablespoon lemon juice
50g (2 oz) walnuts or blanched almonds, ground
blanched whole almonds
caster sugar

Place the prepared quinces in a saucepan with 150ml (¼ pint) water and simmer for 20-30 minutes, stirring frequently until reduced to a pulp. When cool enough, place the contents of the pan in a blender and liquidise until smooth. Alternatively pass the pulp through a sieve. Return the purée to the saucepan, add the sugar and lemon juice and cook over a low heat for 20-30 minutes, stirring very frequently to prevent burning. Remove from the heat and leave to cool for 2 minutes.

Wet a shallow baking tin and spread half the mixture over the base so that it is about ½cm (¼in) thick. Sprinkle the ground nuts evenly over the surface. Spread the remaining purée evenly over the top. Mark the surface into diamond or square shapes and press one blanched almond into the centre of each shape. Cover the tin with a cloth and leave to dry for 3 days.

With an oiled knife cut the paste into the required shapes. Dip each piece into caster sugar and then wrap the paste in greaseproof paper and store in an airtight container.

Makes 20-24

The quince is the fruit of a small tree *cydonia oblonga* and is related to the pear and apple. Its natural habitat is the Caucasus and Asia Minor and has been cultivated for over 3,000 years in the Middle East. It was a particular favourite of Babylonians, Assyrians and Persians. It was introduced to Europe via Rome, but never really caught on, though it was better known in the days of 'Merrie England' than it is today.

However, in the Middle East it is still highly popular and is widely used, not just for its marvellous qualities for jam-making but as a basic ingredient of great flavour. The recipe below from North Africa (where the quince is regarded as having almost magical qualities) makes a delightful spread and is often eaten for breakfast, especially with mint tea.

safarjal

quince with honey

1kg (about 2 lb) quinces
6 tablespoons honey – or more according to taste
1 teaspoon ground cinnamon
¼ teaspoon ground nutmeg
2 tablespoons ground almonds
1 teaspoon oil

Garnish
1 tablespoon finely chopped walnuts or pistachios

Half fill a large saucepan with water and bring to the boil. Quarter the quinces without peeling or coring them and drop them into the water. Simmer for 5-10 minutes or until the fruit is tender. Remove the pieces with a slotted spoon and set aside to cool. Place in a sieve set over a bowl and rub through with a wooden spoon. Add the remaining ingredients to the pulp and mix well. Transfer to a serving plate, sprinkle with the chopped nuts and set aside to cool.

Makes about 450g (1 lb)

engouyzov sergevil

quinces filled with walnuts

'I have plenty of apples and pears, bur my heart yearns for quinces.'
Armenian saying

6 large quinces, washed
25g (1 oz) butter

Filling

110g (4 oz) walnuts or hazelnuts or a mixture of the two, chopped
50g (2 oz) caster sugar
1 teaspoon ground cinnamon

Slice the tops off the quinces and reserve. With a corer remove the core and seeds of each quince. Mix the filling ingredients together in a bowl. Place the quinces side by side in a greased baking dish and fill each quince with the nut mixture. Place a knob of butter on each and then replace the reserved caps. Place in an oven preheated to 180C (350F) gas 4 and bake for 20-30 minutes or until the quinces are tender. Do not overcook or the skins will split. Remove from the oven, leave to cool and then refrigerate. Serve with cream.

Serves 6

tetumi anoush

pumpkin in syrup

This is a very old dish popular with Turks, Armenians and Kurds. The humble pumpkin, which has almost disappeared from the cuisine of the West is still highly prized in the East and maximum use is made of this versatile vegetable. It is used in jams, soups, stews and as a sweet. Shredded coconut or ground pistachios are often used instead of walnuts.

225g (8 oz) sugar
450g (1 lb) pumpkin, peeled and seeded
4 tablespoons finely chopped walnuts or half a walnut per pumpkin slice
1 large teaspoon ground cinnamon

Garnish

double cream or kaymak

Put the sugar and 150ml (¼ pint) water in a medium-sized saucepan, bring to the boil, lower the heat and simmer until the syrup lightly coats the back of a spoon. Meanwhile cut the pumpkin flesh into slices about 5 X 2cm (2 X ¾in). Add the pumpkin pieces to the syrup and simmer for about 30 minutes until most of the syrup has been absorbed and the pumpkin is thick and soft.

Carefully remove the pumpkin slices with a slotted spoon and arrange on a large serving dish. Sprinkle generously with the nuts and cinnamon or alternatively put half a walnut on each piece of pumpkin. Serve with cream.

Serves 4

As a variation on this sweet, keep the sliced pumpkin in lime water for about 6 hours before cooking – this gives the pumpkin a snow-white and translucent appearance. This version is better known as Antep Kabak Lokmasi.

melon haroun el rashid

melon filled with strawberries and almond mousse

The greatest of all Arab caliphs was Haroun al Rashid. He was much loved by his people and his name and fame have become legends in Arabic literature. This recipe, created by chef Roger Debasque, is in honour of a great leader under whose rule all people, especially Jews, were well treated.

  This sweet is better if prepared the day before it is to be eaten. It is spectacular in appearance and makes an ideal dessert for a dinner party.

3 round, ripe melons, e.g. cantaloupe or ogen
450g (1 lb) strawberries

Custard
3 egg yolks
2 tablespoons sugar
300ml (½ pint) milk

Mousse
50g (2 oz) unroasted pistachio nuts
½ teaspoon vanilla essence
½ teaspoon almond essence
3 teaspoons gelatine
3 egg whites
2 tablespoons sugar
150ml (¼ pint) double cream

Place the egg yolks in a small bowl, add the sugar and mix well. Bring the milk to the boil in a small saucepan. Pour a little of the milk into the egg mixture, stir and then pour it back into the rest of the milk in the pan. Stir well and lower the heat. Fill a large saucepan or bowl with cold water and at the first sign of the milk boiling remove the mixture from the heat, dip the pan into the cold water and leave to cool.

  When the custard is cool prepare the mousse. First put the pistachio nuts, vanilla and almond essences and the custard into a large bowl and mix thoroughly. Place the gelatine in a small bowl with a few tablespoons of water, place over a pan of simmering water and stir until the gelatine has dissolved. Stir the gelatine into the custard mixture. Whisk the egg whites until stiff and fold in the sugar. Whisk the cream until stiff. Fold the egg whites and cream into the custard and stir carefully with a metal spoon until well blended.

  Cut a thin slice, about ½cm (¼in) thick, off either end of each melon. Scoop a small hole in the top of each melon and remove and discard the seeds. Rinse with cold water, turn upside down and leave to drain. Half fill each melon with mousse. Place some of the strawberries in each, retaining a few for decoration; then continue to add mousse until each melon is full. Refrigerate until the mousse has set.

  When ready to serve, cut each melon in half crossways. Place each half in an individual bowl and decorate with strawberries.

Serves 6

talebi ba gelatin
melon-fruit mousse

A recipe from Tehran which has been rather updated in imitation of European mousses. This method of fruit preparation has, in recent years, become very popular with middle class Iranians and the cuisine already has several interesting recipes such as strawberry gelatin and cherry gelatin.

1 large eating apple, peeled and cut into small pieces
10 cherries, halved and stoned
10 strawberries, sliced
175g (6 oz) icing sugar
15g (½ oz) gelatine
150ml (¼ pint) double cream
1 large cantaloupe or ogen melon, halved crossways and seeded

Garnish
2 tablespoons finely chopped pistachio nuts

Place the prepared fruit in a bowl, sprinkle with the icing sugar and mix well. Place the gelatine in a small bowl and sprinkle with 2 tablespoons cold water. Add 250ml (8 fl oz) boiling water and stir until dissolved. Then leave to cool.

Whisk the cream until stiff. When the gelatine is cool whisk it into the cream. Fold in the fruit and icing sugar and set aside until the mixture begins to set. Pile into the melon halves and chill. Just before serving halve each half and sprinkle with the chopped pistachio nuts.

Serves 4

gouyava im tahina
guavas with tahina

In recent years guavas have been introduced to Israel and have already entered the cuisine. This is a fascinating sweet making use of figs, coconut, pine kernels, grapes and walnuts. Well worth trying.

1kg (about 2 lb) guavas
5 tablespoons prepared tahina
110g (¼ lb) figs, coarsely chopped
2 tablespoons shredded coconut
2 tablespoons pine kernels
2 tablespoons chopped walnuts

small bunch of grapes
2 tangerines, peeled and segmented

Cut the guavas in half. With a sharp knife hollow out the insides leaving a shell about 1cm (½ in) thick. Discard the pulp. Put the prepared tahina in a bowl and mix in 150ml (¼ pint) water. Add the remaining ingredients and mix well. Fill the guavas with this mixture. Chill for a few hours then arrange in a dish, garnish with the grapes and tangerine segments and serve.

Serves 4-6

halawat-el-teen

dry figs with aniseed

Figs are usually eaten fresh or dried. This Syrian recipe makes use of dried figs flavoured with mastic and aniseed. It is a highly flavoured sweet which often includes leaves of fresh witchweed. You can replace the latter with other fragrant leaves. It has a marvellous aroma. Serve while still warm.

225g (½ lb) sugar
1 tablespoon lemon juice
3 bay leaves or borage leaves or balm leaves or any other fresh, scented leaves
450g (1 lb) dried figs, halved
1 tablespoon sesame seeds, roasted under the grill until golden
½ teaspoon aniseed
¼ teaspoon ground mastic

Place the sugar, lemon juice and 450ml (¾ pint) water in a large saucepan and bring to the boil. Add the leaves, lower the heat and simmer for 10 minutes. Remove the leaves, add the figs and simmer for a further 15 minutes or until the syrup has thickened and coats a spoon. Remove from the heat, add the sesame seeds, aniseed and mastic and mix thoroughly.

When cool enough, pour the halawat into a serving bowl and serve. Delicious with cream.

Serves 6

fruit salads

Naturally the Middle Easterner usually gets his fresh fruit 'straight from the tree' – as the saying goes. But in certain regions western influences have crept in – particularly in Lebanon, Israel and Western Turkey whence this salad originates. The fruits can vary depending on availability. Some people like to add dry white wine, others 1 tablespoon of jam – usually strawberry or cherry. My own preference is for 1-2 tablespoons rose petal jam.

Serve with cream.

istanbul meyva salatase

istanbul fruit salad

1 large orange, peeled and with each segment cut into 2-3 pieces
1 peach, peeled and thinly sliced
1 pear, peeled and thinly sliced
2 dessert plums, flesh chopped
1 small ripe honeydew or ogen melon, flesh cut into 1cm (½in) pieces
1 tangerine, peeled and segmented
1 small pomegranate, seeded
225g (½ 1b) grapes, seedless and rinsed

Juice
50g (2 oz) sugar
120ml (4 fl oz) orange juice
1 tablespoon lemon juice
1 tablespoon rosewater

Place the sugar and 3 tablespoons water in a small saucepan and heat, stirring constantly, until the sugar dissolves. Simmer for 3 minutes, add the orange juice, lemon juice and rosewater, stir well and simmer for a further 2 minutes. Leave to cool a little.

Put all the prepared fruits except the pomegranate seeds and grapes in a glass serving bowl and pour the warm syrup over them. Set aside to cool for 1 hour. Just before serving stir in the pomegranate seeds and grapes.

Serves 6-8

salata fawakeh

lebanese fruit salad

A delightful Lebanese fruit salad making use of all local fruits. Naturally, fresh figs and dates will produce a more authentic result, but dried fruits are equally successful.

60ml (2 fl oz) mulberry syrup, orange syrup, Filfar, Kirsch or Cointreau
90ml (3 fl oz) clear honey
2 tablespoons rosewater
8 dried figs (stalks removed), cut into 1cm (½in) pieces
about 15 dried dates, stoned and halved
2 tablespoons whole, unblanched hazelnuts
1 tablespoon whole, unblanched almonds
1 tablespoon pistachio nuts
2 tablespoons raisins or sultanas
1 melon, honeydew or ogen

Garnish
2 tablespoons finely chopped pistachio nuts

In a bowl mix together the syrup or liqueur, honey, rosewater and 300ml (½ pint) lukewarm water.

Add the figs, dates, hazelnuts, almonds, pistachio nuts and raisins or sultanas. Stir well and refrigerate for at least 2 hours.

Cut the melon in half and discard the seeds. Either use a melon scoop to scoop out as much of the flesh as possible or remove the flesh and chop into 2.5cm (1in) pieces. Add the flesh to the fruit salad and mix well. Chill for at least 1 hour. Serve garnished with the nuts.

Serves 6

desser-e miveh

fresh fruit dessert

This is a popular fruit salad from Tehran, Iran, where large bowls of mixed fruits are topped with cream and served at banquets and at expensive restaurants. It is very decorative and tasty and will make a fine finish to a meal.

1 ripe but firm honeydew melon
6 strawberries, halved
8 Morello-type cherries, stoned
1 apricot, sliced

1 tangerine, peeled and segmented
8 seedless grapes, halved
6 tablespoons icing sugar
1 tablespoon orange blossom water
150ml (¼ pint) double cream
1 teaspoon vanilla essence

Garnish
1 small pomegranate, seeded
2 tablespoons finely chopped pistachio nuts

Cut the melon in half and carefully remove and discard the seeds. Remove as much of the flesh as possible using a melon scoop. Place the melon balls in a glass serving dish with the remaining fruit and toss gently. Sprinkle half the icing sugar and the orange blossom water over the fruit and again toss gently. Refrigerate for 2-3 hours.

Just before serving whip the cream until stiff and fold in the remaining icing sugar and the vanilla essence. Pile half of the cream on to the fruit and serve the rest in a separate bowl. Sprinkle the pomegranate seeds and pistachio nuts over the top and serve.

Serves 4

kaghtsradz mirk

candied fruit

One of the oldest methods of preserving fruit known to the ancients was the cooking and covering of it with a thick, sugary syrup. Today, most people in the West and the Middle East buy their candied fruit from shops but, as with most things, 'home-made is best'. In the Middle East many kinds of fruit are prepared, e.g. peaches, apricots, pears, plums, cherries. The candied fruits of Istanbul, Damascus, Yerevan and Isphahan are famous with, in my opinion, the very best coming from Damascus.

A few points to note:
a) make sure the fruit is firm and fresh
b) do not prepare fruit in large quantities
c) large fruits, e.g. peaches or apricots, should be peeled and halved or quartered
d) small fruits need only be stoned
e) candy each fruit individually, this will produce better results.

Below is a simple recipe for preparing candied fruit.

1kg (about 2 lb) fruit of your choice
750g (1 lb 10 oz) sugar
2 tablespoons orange blossom water

Garnish
sugar

Place the fruit in a large saucepan, cover with 600ml (1 pint) water and bring to the boil. Lower the heat and simmer until the fruit is just tender, but do not overcook or the fruit will lose its shape. Drain the fruit and reserve the cooking water.

Make the syrup by dissolving 350g (³/₄ lb) sugar in the cooking water, bringing it slowly to the boil. Simmer for about 10 minutes or until a thin syrup is formed.

Arrange the fruit in a shallow dish, pour the syrup over it (the fruit should be covered) and set aside for 24 hours.

For the next 3 days – every day drain the syrup off into a saucepan, add 50g (2 oz) sugar each time and bring to the boil. Pour the syrup back over the fruit each time. On the 5th day drain the syrup into a saucepan, add 110g (4 oz) sugar and bring to the boil. Stir in the orange blossom water, pour over the fruit and set aside for 2 days. Repeat the directions for the 5th day (excluding the orange blossom water), but this time set aside for 4 days.

With a slotted spoon lift out the fruit and place on clean, dry baking sheets. Set the oven at its lowest temperature and leave the fruit in it to dry, turning occasionally so that it dries on all sides. The fruit is ready when it is really dry and not at all sticky. To store pack in a wax or cardboard box with each layer separated by waxed or greaseproof paper. The container must not be airtight or the fruit may go mouldy.

kompostolar
fruits cooked in syrup

Wherever one eats in Turkey, at the end of a meal one is inevitably offered a Komposto - be it of quinces, apples, pears, apricots, peaches, strawberries, oranges or tangerines. The fruits are cooked in syrup until tender and then chilled and served with kaymak, double cream or natural yoghurt. The syrups are often flavoured with cinnamon, rosewater or orange blossom water. Dried fruits can be prepared in the same way. As most kompostolar are similar I have given the recipe for Armut Kompostosu – pears in syrup – in full and then noted the basic ingredients for a variety of fresh kompostolar.

armut kompostosu
pears in syrup

1 kg (about 2 lb) fresh, firm pears, peeled, quartered and cored
½ lemon
350g (12 oz) sugar
3 cloves

Rub the pear quarters all over with the ½ lemon - this will give them a glistening white appearance.

Place the pears in a saucepan with 600ml (1 pint) water, bring to the boil and simmer for 5 minutes. Add the sugar and cloves and simmer for 10-15 minutes, basting occasionally, until the pears are tender. Remove from the heat and allow to cool.

Place in a glass bowl or individual dishes and serve with kaymak, cream or yoghurt.

Serves 4-6

ayva kompostosu

quinces in syrup

**1kg (about 2 lb) quinces, peeled, cored and quartered or cut into smaller pieces
450g (1 lb) sugar**

Place the quinces in a saucepan with 900ml (1½ pints) water, bring to the boil and simmer for 5 minutes. Add the sugar, raise the heat and bring to the boil. Lower the heat and simmer for 20-30 minutes or until the fruit is tender. Do not overcook or the fruit will lose its shape. Continue as with the recipe above.

Serves 4-6

taze kayisi kompostosu

fresh firm apricots in syrup

**675g (1½ lb) fresh apricots
250g (9 oz) sugar**

Drop the apricots into a pan of boiling water for 30 seconds. Remove and peel. Cut the apricots in half, remove the stones and reserve. Place the sugar and 450ml (¾ pint) water in a saucepan and bring to the boil. Lower the heat and simmer for 5 minutes. Add the halved apricots and simmer for a further 10 minutes or until the fruit is tender.

Continue as for Armut kompostosu, opposite.

You can drop the apricot stones into boiling water for 2 minutes and then remove. Crack them open, remove the kernels, halve them and use to decorate the kompostosu.

Serves 4

şeftali kompostosu

peaches in syrup

1 kg (about 2 lb) fresh, firm peaches
275g (10 oz) sugar

Drop the peaches into a pan of boiling water for about 1 minute. Remove and peel. Halve the peaches and remove the stones. Place the sugar and 600ml (1 pint) water in a saucepan and bring to the boil. Add the halved peaches and simmer for about 10 minutes or until the fruit is tender.
Proceed as for Armut kompostosu, page 124.

Serves 4-6

vişne kompostosu

black cherries in syrup

250g (9 oz) sugar
675g (1½ lb) black cherries, washed

Place the sugar and 450ml (¾ pint) water in a saucepan and bring to the boil. Lower the heat and simmer for 3 minutes. Add the cherries and simmer in the syrup for 4-5 minutes. Remove from the heat and leave to cool. Serve with cream or yoghurt.

Serves 4

çilek kompostosu

strawberries in syrup

350g (¾ lb) sugar
juice of 1 lemon
1kg (about 2 lb) fresh, firm strawberries, washed and drained
8 tablespoons fresh strawberry juice (optional)

Place the sugar, lemon juice and 600ml (1 pint) water in a saucepan and bring to the boil. Simmer for 10 minutes and then drop in the strawberries. Cook for about 3 minutes and then

remove from the heat. If using it, carefully stir in the strawberry juice. Allow the kompostosu to cool and then chill. Serve with cream or yoghurt.

Serves 4-6

portakal kompostosu
oranges in syrup

4 medium-sized oranges, peeled
175g (6 oz) sugar
2 tablespoons orange blossom water

To remove as much of the white pith as possible drop the oranges into a pan of boiling water for 1 minute. Segment the oranges. Place the sugar and 250ml (8 fl oz) water in a saucepan and bring to the boil. Simmer for 3 minutes. Add the orange segments and cook for 5 minutes. Add the orange blossom water, remove from the heat and cool. Chill and serve with cream or yoghurt.

Serves 4

kaymakli elma kompostosu
apples with cream

This is similar to the other Turkish favourite 'Kaymakli Kayisi' – apricots with cream. It is cheap and simple to prepare and makes an excellent after-dinner dessert.

225g (½ lb) sugar
1 teaspoon lemon juice
12 cloves
4 large cooking, or firm eating, apples, peeled and cored

Garnish
8 tablespoons kaymak or clotted cream or whipped cream will also do
2 tablespoons finely chopped pistachio nuts or walnuts

Place 250ml (8 fl oz) water, the sugar and lemon juice in a saucepan and bring to the boil. Insert 3 cloves around the top of each apple and then place the apples in the pan and baste with the syrup. Reduce the heat, cover the pan and simmer very gently, basting occasionally, until the apples are just tender. The time will vary according to the type of apple, but between 10-15 minutes is the normal time. Remove the pan from the heat and set aside to cool.

Transfer the apples to individual serving dishes and spoon the cream into the centre of each apple. Pour a little syrup over each apple and sprinkle with the nuts. Chill until ready to serve.

Serves 4

izmir kompostosu

dried figs in syrup

This is a speciality of Izmir which is famed for her wonderful figs. You need to use dried figs for this recipe. It is simple and quick to prepare. I suggest you serve with cream as this will enhance the flavour and control the sweetness.

110g (4 oz) sugar
juice of 1 lemon
450g (1 lb) dried figs, any hard stems discarded

Garnish
50g (2 oz) finely chopped hazelnuts or pistachio nuts

Place the sugar, lemon juice and 600ml (1 pint) water in a saucepan and bring to the boil. Lower the heat and simmer for 5 minutes. Arrange the figs in the syrup and simmer gently until the figs begin to 'plump up' and to take on something of their original shape. Remove the figs with a slotted spoon and arrange in a serving dish. Sprinkle with the nuts and serve.

Serves 4

mirkabour

dried fruit sweet

A traditional, festive sweet from the mountains where, during the summer and autumn, all kinds of fruit were dried under the sun and stored for winter use. The mixed fruit should include prunes, apricots, raisins, dates, figs etc. The larger fruit can be chopped.

225g (½ lb) mixed dried fruit
5cm (2in) piece of cinnamon stick
75g (3 oz) sugar
1 tablespoon lemon juice

150ml (¼ pint) double cream
3 tablespoons slivered, blanched almonds, toasted
1 tablespoon finely ground pistachio nuts

Place the mixed fruit, cinnamon stick and 900ml (1½ pints) water in a saucepan and bring to the boil. Boil quickly for 2 minutes and then lower the heat and simmer for about 25 minutes or until the fruit is tender. Remove the pan from the heat and discard the cinnamon stick. Leave to cool.

When cool lift the fruit out of the pan with a slotted spoon and transfer to a blender and reduce to a purée. Add the sugar to the juice in the pan, stir in the lemon juice and keep over a low heat until the sugar dissolves. Return the purée to the pan, stir well and cook for 2-3 minutes. Remove from the heat and leave to cool. Spoon into dessert glasses and chill. Just before serving top with cream and sprinkle with the nuts.

Serves 4-6

khushab

dried fruit compote

Named after an historic region of Armenia and famed for her impregnable castles. Another sweet eaten during the winter months when fresh fruit is not available.

225g (½ lb) dried apricots, soaked overnight in cold water
225g (½ lb) prunes, stoned, soaked overnight in cold water
225g (½ lb) dried peaches or pears, soaked overnight in cold water
110g (4 oz) sultanas, soaked overnight in cold water
75g (3 oz) honey
rind of 1 lemon in one piece
½ teaspoon ground nutmeg
1 stick cinnamon about 5cm (2in) long
2 tablespoons pine kernels
2 tablespoons brandy

Drain the dried fruit and reserve about 300ml (½ pint) of the soaking water. Place the fruit and soaking water in a large saucepan and add the honey, lemon rind, nutmeg and cinnamon. Bring to the boil then lower the heat and simmer for 20-30 minutes or until the fruits are soft and tender. Remove from the heat and discard the lemon rind and cinnamon stick. Add the pine kernels and stir gently. Cool to room temperature and then stir in the brandy. Transfer to a serving bowl or individual dishes and refrigerate.

Serves 8

hadig

wheat dessert

This dessert is one of the oldest in the Greek and Armenian Orthodox tradition. It is called *Kolyva* in Greek and *Hadig* in Armenian and was evolved into its present form during the Byzantine era, though like most dishes of the Middle East, its origins go much further back in time. Hadig is served when a baby's first tooth appears, 40 days after the death of a member of the family and – amongst people of the Greek Orthodox tradition, Cypriots, Greeks and Orthodox Arabs – on the anniversary of a death.

The recipe below is a family one since there is no standard one accepted by all. A colourful and rich dessert.

75g (3 oz) chickpeas, cleaned and soaked in cold water for 1 hour
275g (10 oz) whole wheat, cleaned of impurities, washed and drained 3 times
1 tablespoon ground cinnamon
1 teaspoon aniseed
5-6 tablespoons (or more to taste) sugar
2 tablespoons chopped, blanched almonds
2 tablespoons chopped walnuts
2 tablespoons chopped pistachios
3 teaspoons caraway seeds, toasted under the grill for 2 minutes
2 tablespoons 'hundreds and thousands'
about 15 sugared almonds
seeds of 1 large pomegranate

Drain the chickpeas and rinse under cold water for several minutes. Drain and place in a saucepan with 300ml (½ pint) water. Bring to the boil and then simmer over a low heat for about 25 minutes or until most of the water is absorbed. Add 1.8 litres (3 pints) boiling water and the wheat and simmer for about 2 hours until the wheat is soft and all the water is absorbed. Remove from the heat, cover and leave to stand for 10 minutes.

Transfer the mixture to a large bowl, add all the remaining ingredients and mix thoroughly. Refrigerate for 2-3 hours. Serve piled into a serving dish or in individual bowls.

Serves 8-10

hatzi anoush

bread pudding with fruits

This recipe is from Anatolia (Turkey) and is as old as the hills. Although often, for the sake of economy and time, the housewives use their left-over stale bread, a special dough –called *kalip ekmegi* in Turkish – should be prepared. I have included its recipe below if you wish to prepare it.

Kalip Ekmegi
**15g (½ oz) fresh yeast
210ml (7 fl oz) milk
450g (1 lb) plain flour
1 teaspoon salt
50g (2 oz) icing sugar
50g (2 oz) unsalted butter
3 egg yolks**

Dissolve the yeast in a cup with a few tablespoons of the milk, warmed, and set aside for about 10 minutes or until the mixture begins to froth. Sift the flour, salt and icing sugar into a large bowl. Add the butter and rub it in until it resembles fine breadcrumbs. Make a well in the centre and add the yeast mixture and egg yolks and mix with a wooden spoon. Add the milk, little by little and, after thoroughly mixing knead for about 10-15 minutes until the dough is smooth and elastic. Cover with a cloth and leave in a warm place for 30 minutes.

Lightly sprinkle a work top with flour and divide the dough into equal portions. Take one ball and roll out until ½cm (¼in) thick. Cut into rounds with a 7.5cm (3in) pastry cutter. Gather up the scraps, roll out again and cut into more rounds. Repeat with the other ball of dough. Place the rounds on greased baking trays and bake in an oven preheated to 130C (150F) gas ½ for 30 minutes. Remove and leave for 4-5 hours. The rounds are now ready to be used in a bread pudding. The ones you do not need can be stored in an airtight tin.

Serves 4

visneli ekmek tatlisi

bread pudding with cherries

This is the most popular bread pudding in Turkey. You can use tinned cherries, but if they are sweetened then omit the sugar and water and use the tinned syrup, made up to 300ml (½ pint) with water if necessary.

**8 portions of Kalip ekmegi or 8 thin slices stale white bread
75g (3 oz) unsalted butter
450g (1 lb) morello cherries, stoned or any other kind in season
or tinned cherries
225g (½ lb) icing sugar**

Spread the slices of bread generously with butter, trimming off any crusts. Arrange the slices in a large shallow ovenproof dish and bake in an oven preheated to 180C (350F) gas 4 until lightly golden. Meanwhile place the cherries, icing sugar and 250ml (8 fl oz) water in a saucepan, mix well and bring to the boil. Boil vigorously for 2 minutes and then lower the heat and simmer for about 10 minutes or until the syrup becomes sticky and coats the back of a spoon. If using tinned syrup boil for about 4-5 minutes.

Remove the bread from the oven, pour the cherries and syrup over it and then bake in the oven until most of the syrup has been absorbed. Remove from the oven and serve with kaymak or whipped cream.

Serves 4

dzirani hatzi-anoush
apricot bread pudding

This is an Armenian favourite.

8 portions of Kalip ekmegi or 8 thin slices stale white bread
75g (3 oz) unsalted butter
225g (½ lb) icing sugar
1kg (about 2 lb) firm apricots, halved and with stones discarded

Spread the bread generously with butter, trimming off any crusts. Arrange the slices in a large shallow ovenproof dish and bake in an oven preheated to 180C (350F) gas 4 until lightly golden. Meanwhile place the icing sugar and 250ml (8 fl oz) water in a saucepan and bring to the boil. Add the halved apricots and simmer, stirring occasionally, until the apricots are just tender and the syrup has thickened and will coat the back of a spoon.

Remove the bread from the oven, pour the apricots and syrup evenly over it and then bake in the oven until most of the syrup has been absorbed. Remove from the oven and serve with kaymak or whipped cream.

Serves 4

yoghurt and cheese sweets

An essential ingredient in the Middle Eastern cuisine, yoghurt is always home-made. The preparation is very simple and no mechanical help is needed. It is quite often used in desserts and I strongly recommend that you make your own as it will always be superior to commercial products. Below is the basic recipe for yoghurt.

yoghurt

1.1 litres (2 pints) milk
1 tablespoon live yoghurt – this is known as the 'starter'. It can be bought from many food stores. You can also use some from the previous batch you have made

Bring the milk to the boil in a large saucepan. As the froth rises turn off the heat. Allow the milk to cool to the point where you can keep your finger in for a count of 15. Place the tablespoon of 'starter' in a teacup and add 2-3 tablespoons warm milk. Beat until smooth and then stir back into the milk. Pour into a bowl, cover the bowl with a large plate and then wrap a towel around it. Place in a warm place, e.g. near a radiator or in an airing cupboard, and leave undisturbed for about 8 hours or overnight. Then refrigerate.

Yoghurt will keep for up to a week in the refrigerator before it begins to turn sour. When the yoghurt is nearly finished use a little of it as a 'starter' for a fresh batch.

Makes 1.1 litres (2 pints)

A favourite way of mine with yoghurt is to add a few teaspoons of sugar, stir and eat as a dessert. In the Anatolian and Iranian villages sweetened natural yoghurt is still a favourite while, for over 2000 years, the Yogis of India have eaten a mixture of yoghurt and honey for breakfast. Indeed yoghurt with honey is an exceedingly tasty way of achieving health and longevity. The recipe below from Cyprus is a sophisticated version of the Yogi's 'Yoghurt with honey' meal. Ideal for breakfast time it is also a beautiful accompaniment to desserts and makes an unusual alternative to cream.

yaourti me meli

yoghurt with honey

150ml (¼ pint) clear honey
1 teaspoon grated lemon rind
1 teaspoon grated orange rind
1 teaspoon orange juice
½ teaspoon lemon juice
750ml (1¼ pints) yoghurt

Pour the honey into a mixing bowl, add the lemon and orange rind and beat until smooth. Add the juices and whisk until frothy. Add the yoghurt and stir until well blended. Chill before serving.

Serves 4-6

moz-bi-laban

bananas with yoghurt

This Lebanese and Palestinian favourite makes a charming dessert.

600ml (1 pint) yoghurt
4 ripe bananas
sugar to taste

Garnish
1 teaspoon ground cinnamon

Pour the yoghurt into a bowl and beat until creamy. Slice the bananas thinly and stir gently into the yoghurt. Stir in a little sugar at a time until it suits your taste. Spoon into a serving bowl or individual dishes, sprinkle with the cinnamon and serve.

Serves 4

touz madznov

figs in yoghurt

The finest figs in the world come from the Izmir region of Turkey where they grow as roses would in the Gardens of Paradise. For generations the peasants of Greece and Anatolia have served their honoured guests this simple but extremely delicious dessert. Use fresh figs.

12 fresh figs
150ml (¼ pint) kaymak or clotted cream
300ml (½ pint) Yaourti me meli (see page 135)

Garnish
½-1 teaspoon ground cinnamon

Drop the figs into a bowl of hot water, leave for 2-3 minutes and then drain. Peel off the skins and quarter the figs. Whisk the cream a little and add to the yoghurt sauce. Spoon a little of the sauce into 4 or 6 serving dishes. Divide the figs between the dishes and then spoon the remaining yoghurt mixture over the top. Sprinkle with the cinnamon and chill.

Serves 4-6

From figs to apricots, from a simple dish to one rather sophisticated,
from Turkey to Armenia!

armeniaca

apricot souffle with yoghurt

450g (1 lb) fresh apricots, halved and stoned
150ml (¼ pint) apricot brandy
50g (2 oz) butter
225g (8 oz) caster sugar
4 eggs, separated
150ml (¼ pint) yoghurt
75ml (2½ fl oz) double cream
2 tablespoons finely chopped pistachio nuts

Place the apricots, apricot brandy and 600ml (1 pint) water in a large saucepan and cook over a moderate heat until the apricots are nearly tender, but still firm. Remove with a slotted spoon and place in an ovenproof dish. Dot with the butter and bake in an oven preheated to 180C (350F) gas 4 for about 10 minutes.

Meanwhile add the sugar to the liquid in the pan and boil for about 10 minutes or until the juice is reduced and thickened. Pour this sauce over the apricots and bake for a further 10-15 minutes. Remove from the oven and set aside for 10 minutes. Beat the egg yolks until fluid and pour over the apricots. Whisk the egg whites until stiff, fold into the apricots and return to the oven for a further 12-15 minutes. Remove and bring to the table immediately. Beat the yoghurt, cream and pistachio nuts together, pour over the sweet and serve.

Serves 4-6

madznov gerass

cherries in yoghurt

Some of the most memorable and pleasant moments of my childhood were spent in the villages of Syria where we went every summer on vacation and where we were treated to some of the loveliest fresh fruits and other goodies such as kaymak, orojig, thin Arab bread etc. One of the most pleasant sweets – utterly simple in its conception – was Madznov Gerass which the peasant farmers ate for breakfast or as a dessert after a hearty evening meal. The recipe below is the nearest I have come to equalling that delicious dish of my childhood.

450g (1 lb) fresh black cherries; if not available use tinned morello cherries
110g (4 oz) soft brown sugar
½ teaspoon ground ginger
1 teaspoon rosewater
450ml (¾ pint) yoghurt

Garnish
1 tablespoon finely chopped pistachio nuts

Place the cherries and sugar in a saucepan and cook over a low heat, stirring frequently, until the sugar has dissolved. Stir in the ginger and rosewater, cover the pan and cook for 8-10 minutes or until the cherries are soft, but still retain their shape. Remove the pan from the heat and leave to cool. Pour into a serving dish and refrigerate.

Just before serving stir in the yoghurt and sprinkle with the pistachio nuts.

Serves 4-6

kuntig

walnut-filled yoghurt balls

This traditional recipe comes from the Caucasus. It keeps well in an airtight container. Usually served with tea or coffee.

2 egg yolks
90ml (3 fl oz) yoghurt
1 teaspoon bicarbonate soda
50g (6 oz) unsalted butter, melted
225g (½ lb) plain flour, sifted

Filling
110g (4 oz) sugar

1 teaspoon vanilla essence
175g (2 oz) walnuts, finely chopped
1 teaspoon ground cinnamon
½ teaspoon ground cardamom

Garnish
icing sugar

In a mixing bowl beat the egg yolk and yoghurt together. Add the bicarbonate of soda and the butter and mix well. Gradually add the sifted flour and mix until a dough is formed. Gather up and knead for several minutes until soft and malleable. Place in a clean bowl, cover with a damp cloth and set aside for an hour.

Mix all the filling ingredients together in a bowl.

When ready roll the dough out on a lightly floured surface until about 3mm ($\frac{1}{8}$ in) thick. Cut the dough into 6cm (2½in) squares. Place 1 teaspoon of the filling in the centre of each square. Dampen the edges, gather up and press to seal. Roll between your palms to obtain a round ball. Repeat until all the ingredients are used up.

Place the balls on lightly greased baking trays and bake in an oven preheated to 180C (350F) gas 4 for 15-20 minutes or until golden. Remove and leave to cool.

Roll in icing sugar and store when cold.

Makes about 35-40

madznov katah

yoghurt spice cake

A moist yoghurt-based cake with a delicious crunchy top. Armenians are perhaps the finest exponents of yoghurt, particularly when using it in desserts and sweets. No other Middle Eastern cuisine can match the rich imaginative yoghurt desserts of the children of Haig.

225g (½ lb) plain flour
1½ teaspoons ground cinnamon
½ teaspoon ground cloves
½ teaspoon ground nutmeg
2 teaspoons baking powder
½ teaspoon salt
1 teaspoon bicarbonate of soda
3 large eggs
250g (9 oz) brown sugar
1 teaspoon vanilla essence
6 tablespoons clarified butter, melted (page 194)
250ml (8 fl oz) yoghurt

Topping
50g (2 oz) desiccated coconut

50g (2 oz) finely chopped walnuts
110g (4 oz) brown sugar
60ml (2 fl oz) double cream
3 tablespoons clarified butter, melted (page 194)

Sift the flour, cinnamon, cloves, nutmeg, baking powder, salt and soda into a large mixing bowl. Break the eggs into a large bowl, add the sugar and whisk well. Add the vanilla essence, melted butter and the yoghurt and beat until well blended. Pour this mixture into the flour and mix well. Spoon this mixture into a greased and floured cake tin about 21cm (8½in) in diameter. Bake in an oven preheated to 160C (325F) gas 3 for about 40 minutes or until cooked. Remove and set aside to cool.

Meanwhile mix all the topping ingredients together in a bowl. When the cake is cool spread the topping thickly over it. Place the cake under a hot grill for 2-3 minutes or until the topping is golden. Take care not to burn. Leave to cool on a rack and store when cold.

Makes 1 large cake

yogurtlu mouz tatlisi

yoghurt banana cake

A cake from Istanbul, Turkey, that reflects the European influence. Bananas, of course, were a luxury in the 19th century when this particular sweet evolved. They were imported at great expense from Lebanon (sweet but small) and Somalia (large and delicious). It is said that the latter variety were much sought after in the Ottoman harems – for their versatility!

110g (4 oz) unsalted butter
225g (8 oz) sugar
2 eggs
120ml (4 fl oz) yoghurt
225g (8 oz) plain flour
½ teaspoon baking powder
1 teaspoon bicarbonate of soda
pinch of salt
2 ripe bananas, mashed

Decoration
150ml (¼ pint) whipped cream
2 tablespoons coarsely ground walnuts
2 tablespoons coarsely ground pistachios
1 large banana – because it will discolour quickly, even if tossed in lemon juice, I suggest you only decorate with banana if you feel the whole cake will be eaten in 1 sitting!

Place the butter in a mixing bowl and beat until light and creamy. Add the sugar and beat a little longer. Add the eggs and yoghurt and whisk until smooth.

Sift in the flour, baking powder, soda and salt and fold in with a metal spoon.

Add the mashed bananas and fold in until evenly blended. Spoon into a greased and floured 18.5cm (7½in) round cake tin and smooth over the surface. Bake in an oven preheated to 180C (350F) gas 4 for about 40 minutes or until the cake is cooked. Cool for 10 minutes, turn on to a rack and leave until cold.

Slice the cake in half crossways and spread half the whipped cream evenly over the bottom half. Sprinkle the nuts evenly over the cream and then replace the top of the cake. Spread the remaining cream over the top of the cake and, if you wish, decorate with sliced bananas added at the last minute before serving.

Makes 1 large cake

madznov sankatah

yoghurt pancakes

Delightful pancakes which are simple to prepare. They are usually eaten with a little honey but I have included several other serving suggestions below. My particular favourite being fine strips of basdegh topped with a little extra icing sugar.

2 eggs, separated
3 tablespoons sifted icing sugar
150ml (¼ pint) yoghurt
25g (1 oz) butter, melted
50g (2 oz) plain flour
1 teaspoon baking powder
½ teaspoon bicarbonate of soda
pinch of salt

Put the egg yolks into a large bowl, add the icing sugar, yoghurt and melted butter and beat briskly with a wooden spoon. Sift the flour, baking powder, soda and salt into a small bowl and then gradually add this to the yoghurt mixture, stirring constantly until soft and smooth.

Put the egg whites into a bowl and whisk until stiff and standing in peaks. Fold gently into the batter with a metal spoon. Melt a little butter in a small frying pan 15-17.5cm (6-7in) in diameter and swirl it around to coat the sides. Pour off the excess. Drop 1-2 tablespoons of the batter into the hot pan and tilt the pan around to allow the batter to spread. Fry gently until the underside is golden and the mixture is just set. Turn with a palette knife and brown the other side. Remove and keep warm while you cook the remaining pancakes.

Serve warm with:
a)   maple syrup
b)   grape syrup (*bekmez*) or carob juice
c)   mixture of yoghurt and sugar
d)   mixture of yoghurt and sweetened fresh fruit

e) mixture of yoghurt and honey
f) honey and a little lemon juice
g) spread with a little melted butter and a jam of your choice
h) strips of any basdegh (grape, apricot, quince, apple etc) scattered over the pancake, folded and dusted with icing sugar.

Makes 8-10

yogurtlu çicolata kek
yoghurt chocolate cake

A popular cake from Istanbul where it is often sold in delicatessens and restaurants. Excellent with tea or coffee.

110g (4 oz) unsalted butter
250g (9 oz) caster sugar
2 eggs
150g (5 oz) dark bitter chocolate
150ml (¼ pint) yoghurt
225g (½ lb) plain flour
1 teaspoon baking powder
1 teaspoon bicarbonate of soda
¼ teaspoon ground nutmeg

Filling
apricot or cherry jam

Topping
coconut-walnut topping used for Madznov Katah (see page 138-9)

Beat the butter and sugar together in a large bowl until light and creamy. Add the eggs and whisk until smooth. Break up the chocolate, place in a bowl over a saucepan of hot water and stir until the chocolate has melted. Leave to cool a little and then add to the cake mixture and stir until well blended. Stir in the yoghurt.

Sift the flour, baking powder, soda and nutmeg into the bowl and fold in well with a metal spoon. Pour into a greased and floured 21cm (8½in) round cake tin and bake in an oven preheated to 180C (350F) gas 4 for about 40 minutes or until cooked.

Cool for a few minutes and then turn out on to a wire rack and leave until cold. Slice in half crossways and sandwich together with jam. Prepare the coconut-walnut topping as described in Madznov Katah, spread over the top of the cake and place under a hot grill until golden. Take care not to burn. Serve cold with tea or coffee.

Makes 1 large cake

Chocolate –
to see . . . . good living, good health
to eat . . . . good luck
to buy . . . . good news
to give or sell to someone . . . . . to lose other people's
friendship or to waste one's
time with fruitless deeds.
The Book Of Dreams

In every town there is a bazaar – dark and labyrinthine. Almost all were constructed hundreds of years ago in the heyday of the Ottomans, or even further back during the Byzantine and Arab rules. The bazaar is the heart of the Oriental town. It is there that all traditional business is carried out. Goods are bought and sold. Silversmiths vie with each other. Carpet dealers, goldsmiths, sellers of herbs, clothing and pots and pans clutter the small arched shop units.

'Trade is a game, and it is played as a rule with great good humour. The seller names his price and you name yours. Then you begin the compromise between them, and many harrowing details of poverty and impending ruin are rehearsed before the final sum is adjusted. Or perhaps the deal comes to an impasse; then you change the subject and buy other things to win the dealer's favour, while he plies you with coffee and cigarettes to win yours. Then you, or he, or both of you, revert to the original subject; and so the day goes on.'
from *Damascus To Palmyra* John Kelman

When a child of 7 or 8 I remember going to the 'Big Bazaar' behind the famed Citadel of Aleppo that soared up from the desert lands to the sky; an enormous battlement of stone built thousands of years before by the mighty Hittites. Well before dawn Syrian peasants scurried to the bazaar laden with their goods. In one of the dark corners were found the *Labanjis* – milk and yoghurt sellers who displayed their wares in large wooden containers. My uncle performed all the rituals of trading as described by J. Kelman and when a deal was struck, off we went home chatting and munching a sweet or two while the *hamal* (porter), laden with 2 large barrels of yoghurt, followed us. Sometimes I used to sneak behind him and, dipping my fingers into a barrel, lick a little yoghurt. It was fresh with a flavour of the countryside, cool, tingling and wholesome. My uncle would give me one of his classic fierce looks – eyebrows squashing eyes semi-closed as the moustache sharpened at the edges like a poisoned arrow. Intimidated, I would hurry to join my cousins. My uncle had a large family and my aunt could not possibly prepare all her own yoghurt – it was not practicable. Next to bread, yoghurt was the most important ingredient in their diet –as indeed it still is with most Middle Eastern families.

Out of this great dependence on yoghurt was created the following cake made with creamed cheese (drained yoghurt) and soaked in syrup. This recipe, from the region of Adana and Gazi-Antep (the birthplace of my uncle) in southern Turkey, is one that I adore and I am delighted to include it in this book.

yogurt tatlisi
yoghurt sweet

A light sponge soaked in syrup. Before this sweet is prepared you need to make the *labna*. To do this you need either a colander lined with a piece of muslin (or even a cotton tea towel) or a muslin bag with a drawstring top.

300ml (½ pint) yoghurt – this will give you about 110g (¼ lb) *labna*
110g (4 oz) sugar
1 teaspoon bicarbonate of soda
3 eggs, beaten
175g (6 oz) plain flour, sifted

Syrup
350g (¾ lb) sugar
1 tablespoon lemon juice

First prepare the *labna* by pouring the yoghurt into the lined colander or muslin bag and leave to drain in the sink (if using the colander) or suspended from a tap over the sink (if using the muslin bag) overnight. The thick cream left is the *labna*.

Prepare the syrup. Put the sugar, lemon juice and 450ml (¾ pint) water in a pan and bring to the boil. Lower the heat and simmer for 10 minutes. Set aside to cool. Place the *labna* in a large bowl, add the sugar and soda and stir for 2-3 minutes. Add the eggs and beat thoroughly. Add the flour, little by little, and mix thoroughly.

Grease and liberally flour a baking tin about 17.5 X 27.5cm (7 X 11in). Pour in the *labna* mixture and smooth over the surface with the back of a spoon. Bake in an oven preheated to 200C (400F) gas 6 for 20-25 minutes. Remove from the oven, cut in 5cm (2in) squares and pour the cool syrup evenly over the top. Set aside to cool.

Makes about 15 pieces

Labna is the glory of the Arab breakfast table – the bacon and eggs or cornflakes or croissants of Europe. If there is any *labna* left over after preparing the above sweet I suggest you serve it on a small plate, sprinkled with a pinch of dried mint and a drop or two of olive oil and eat if for breakfast with fresh bread –magnificent!

banirov mirk

fruits stuffed with cheese

An Armenian recipe which makes a quick and easy dessert in winter time when fresh fruits are difficult to find. They look especially attractive in small paper sweet cases. I have not given exact quantities as this is virtually impossible as the size and types of fruit used will vary greatly, but for a rough guide allow 110g (4 oz) *labna* for each 225g ($^1/_2$ lb) dried fruit.

Fruits (use one variety of dried fruit or a mixture depending on your preferences)
dates
apricots
figs
prunes

Filling
cream cheese, *labna* or cottage cheese
desiccated coconut – use half the quantity of cheese used
½ teaspoon ground cardamom for each 110g (4 oz) cheese used

Garnish
blanched almonds
caster sugar
***bekmez* – grape syrup or any syrup of your choice**

Wash the fruit and place in the top of a double saucepan over hot water or in a colander fitted over a saucepan of water. Simmer over a low heat for 15 minutes. Set aside and allow the steamed fruit to cool. When cool enough to handle make a slit in each piece of fruit and, if there are any, carefully remove the stones without spoiling the shape of the fruit.

In a small bowl mix together the cheese, coconut and cardamom. Place a little of the cheese mixture in each fruit. Decorate each fruit with a blanched almond. Arrange on a serving plate and sprinkle with caster sugar. If you wish dribble over a little syrup of your choice and serve immediately or chill first.

ugat gvina

cheesecake

To the Jews the whiteness of milk and cheese represents the purity of Mosaic Code, hence the traditional Jewish love for this dessert which is so well known today that I need not elaborate further – save for the simple fact that it has been rather difficult to choose one recipe out of the scores that are available and in use in Israel.

The Lebanese, Armenians and Turks have similar desserts, but it is the Jewish (hence Israeli) housewife who has perfected this delight. The recipe chosen is for the traditional Jewish cake in its simplest form. I believe it to be the best of all.

4 eggs, separated
175g (6 oz) caster sugar
150ml (¼ pint) soured cream
1 tablespoon plain flour
450g (1 lb) cottage cheese, sieved
1 tablespoon semolina
4 tablespoons sultanas
1 teaspoon vanilla essence
grated rind of 1 lemon
50g (2 oz) butter
6 tablespoons biscuit or dry sponge crumbs
½ teaspoon ground cinnamon

Place the egg yolks in a large bowl, add the sugar and beat until light and creamy. Add the cream, flour, cheese, semolina, sultanas, vanilla essence and lemon rind and beat or whisk for several minutes until well blended and smooth. In a separate bowl whisk the egg whites until stiff. Carefully fold them into the cheese mixture with a metal spoon.

Lightly grease a 21-22.5cm (8½-9in) round cake tin. Melt the butter in a small saucepan and stir in the crumbs and cinnamon. Press this crumb mixture evenly over the base of the tin. Pour the cheese mixture into the tin and smooth over the surface with a wooden spoon. Place in an oven preheated to 180C (350F) gas 4 and bake for 45 minutes. On no account open the oven door during this time. When the cooking time is up turn off the oven, but leave the cake inside to cook for a further 15 minutes. Remove from the oven and leave to cool.

Makes 1 large cheesecake

peynir tatlisi

cheese fingers in syrup

From the west coast of Turkey this is a regional speciality of white cheese mixed with butter, eggs and flour and then soaked in syrup. It is a recipe from the Ottoman period. To vary the flavour you can add the grated rind of 2 lemons or 3 tablespoons ground pistachios or 4 tablespoons desiccated coconut. Often served with kaymak or clotted cream.

Syrup
900g (2 lb) sugar
juice of 1 lemon

Dough
275g (10 oz) white cheese, preferably feta (otherwise Lancashire or Stilton),
soaked in tepid water for 2 hours
110g (4 oz) unsalted butter
50g (2 oz) caster sugar
2 teaspoons bicarbonate of soda
3 eggs
225g (½ lb) plain flour
75g (3 oz) cornflour

Prepare the syrup by placing the sugar, lemon juice and 1.2 litres (2 pints) water in a saucepan and bringing to the boil. Lower the heat and simmer for 10-15 minutes or until it forms a thin film on a spoon. Set aside.

Drain the soaked cheese and squeeze in a muslin bag or between kitchen paper to remove any liquid. The cheese must be dry and should now weigh about 225g (½ lb).

Place the butter, sugar and bicarbonate of soda in a large bowl and beat with a wooden spoon until smooth and creamy. Crumble the cheese and add to the mixture. Add the eggs and stir until the mixture is well blended. Sift in the flour and cornflour and mix in with a wooden spoon. Now knead with your hands until the mixture is smooth and forms a ball. It may be necessary to add a sprinkling of flour if the mixture is a little sticky.

Grease 2 large baking trays. Using a 2cm (¾in) nozzle, pipe fingers about 6cm (2½in) long on to the baking trays, placing them 2.5-3.5cm (1-1½in) apart. Place in an oven preheated to 160C (325F) gas 3 and bake for 15 minutes. Remove the trays from the oven, brush each cheese finger with hot water and then cover with a cloth for 3-4 minutes. Bring the syrup back to boiling point. Remove the cloth and pour the boiling syrup over the fingers and then return to the oven. Cook for about 30 minutes or until the fingers are a golden brown. While they are cooking turn them 2-3 times so that they absorb as much syrup as possible. Remove from the oven and leave to cool. Serve cold with a little of the syrup and some cream.

Makes 15-20 pieces

cakes and gateaux

The Middle East is not rich in cakes and gateaux as the terms are understood in the West. Cake – from medieval English *kake* was basically a sweetened composition of flour and other ingredients such as eggs, milk, dried fruit, nuts and flavourings; often having its surface partly or wholly iced. Gateau – from medieval French *gasteau* has the same meaning.

The Middle Eastern cakes and gateaux are very simple fare with no cream or icing. They are, generally, sweetened breads. Amongst Iranians, Arabs in general, Turks and Caucasians, gateaux as they are understood in Europe are virtually non-existent and what there are are undoubtedly of European influence and of recent vintage. A good test is to compare the gateaux and cakes of Israel – a Western orientated land – with those of Armenia and Turkey – still bedded in Oriental traditions. However all this does not mean that there are no exciting cake recipes to be found in the Middle East. Indeed there are, and below are some that are authentic enough to be included under this heading.

elmali kek

apple cake

This is a particular favourite of the Kurds of the Diyarbakir region in Turkey where some of the world's most beautiful and delicious apples are grown. It is a simple, peasant recipe, and perhaps because of this it is very tasty. Serve warm or cold – I prefer the former.

225g (½ lb) margarine or unsalted butter
175g (6 oz) sugar
1 egg
275g (10 oz) plain flour
1 tablespoon baking powder
6 medium cooking apples, peeled, cored and sliced
1 teaspoon ground cinnamon
4 tablespoons icing sugar

To serve
kaymak or double cream

Cream the margarine or butter and sugar in a large bowl until light and fluffy. Add the egg and beat until smooth. Sift in the flour and baking powder and mix until you have a soft, smooth dough. Divide the dough into 2 equal parts.

Grease a baking dish about 30 X 22.5cm (12 X 9in). Roll out each ball of dough on a lightly floured work top to the approximate size of the dish. Lay one layer of the dough into the bottom of the dish and press down gently. Arrange the apple slices over the dough and sprinkle evenly with the cinnamon and the icing sugar. Cover with the other sheets of dough and press the edges down gently. Bake in an oven preheated to 180C (350F) gas 4 for 25-30 minutes or until a light golden colour. Remove from the oven. Serve warm or cold cut into 5cm (2in) squares.

Makes about 18 squares

apples —

to see . . . . sadness
while still green and raw . . . . . . disorders in one's home
ripe . . . . happiness
to pick off a tree . . . . birth of a child
to eat . . . . profit
to take from someone . . . . good news
to cut down an apple tree. . . . . . relegation in one's career
The Book Of Dreams

gateau lubnani
lebanese date cake

This is a popular cake from Beirut where it has even been called the national gateau. It is naturally of European origin, but so much Middle Eastern in finish – note the use of nutmeg, local nuts and, of course, dates which do grow in Lebanon and are slightly different from the dried ones sold in shops here. The Lebanese dates are longer, dark red in colour and not quite as sweet as the more famed ones from Iraq. A lovely cake that will grace your tea table.

225g (½ lb) plain flour
2 teaspoons baking powder
1 teaspoon salt
175g (6 oz) sugar
110g (4 oz) unsalted butter
3 eggs, well beaten
180ml (6 fl oz) milk
175g (6 oz) dried dates, finely chopped
2 tablespoons pistachios, finely chopped
2 tablespoons raisins, chopped
½ teaspoon ground nutmeg
1 teaspoon vanilla essence

Sift the flour, baking powder and salt into a large bowl. Stir in the sugar. Add the butter and rub in with your fingertips until the mixture resembles fine breadcrumbs. Fold in the beaten eggs and the milk. Stir in the remaining ingredients and mix for 2-3 minutes until well blended.

Grease and flour a 18.5cm (7½in) round cake tin and pour in the cake mixture. Smooth over the surface with the back of a spoon. Bake in an oven preheated to 180C (350F) gas 4 for about 50-60 minutes or until the cake is cooked. Remove from the oven, cool in the tin and then turn out and leave on a rack until cold. Store in an airtight container.

Makes 1 large cake

ugat tapouze

orange cake

This cake, from Israel, makes use of another local product – oranges. It is a typical mixture of European and Middle Eastern cuisines.

1 orange, squeezed
110g (4 oz) currants
50g (2 oz) walnuts
225g (½ lb)
¼ teaspoon bicarbonate of soda
225g (½ lb) sugar
150g (5 oz) margarine
250ml (8 fl oz) milk
2 eggs
5 tablespoons orange juice
1 tablespoon lemon juice
1 teaspoon ground cinnamon

Cut the squeezed orange into pieces, place in a blender and reduce to a pulp. Scrape into a bowl. Now blend the currants, and then the nuts, and add both to the bowl. Mix them thoroughly.

Mix the flour, soda and 175g (6 oz) of the sugar together in a large bowl. Add the margarine and three quarters of the milk and cream together for about 2 minutes or until light and smooth. Add the eggs and remaining milk and beat for a further 2 minutes. Stir in the orange-nut mixture until evenly distributed.

Grease and flour a 18.5cm (7½in) round cake tin and pour in the cake mixture. Bake in an oven preheated to 180C (350F) gas 4 for about 50 minutes. Remove from the oven and immediately pour over the mixed orange and lemon juices. Mix the remaining sugar with the cinnamon and sprinkle it over the surface.

Leave until cold before serving.

Makes 1 large cake

ugat tsimukim

raisin cake

'As the apple tree among the trees of the wood,
So is my beloved among the sons.
I sat down under his shadow with great delight,
And his fruit was sweet to my taste.
He brought me to the tavern,
Bring me raisin-cakes, comfort me with apples;
For I am sick with love.
His left hand is under my head,
And his right hand doth embrace me.'
Song Of Songs. Chapter 2

Again this is a tart or flan rather than a cake. It comes from Israel and has a rich, nutty flavour.

175g (6 oz) plain flour
½ teaspoon salt
50g (2 oz) butter
150ml (¼ pint) milk

Filling
3 eggs
110g (4 oz) sugar
1 teaspoon vanilla essence
75g (3 oz) raisins
25g (1 oz) pine kernels
25g (1 oz) pistachios, halved

Sift the flour and salt into a bowl, add the butter and rub in with your fingertips until the mixture resembles fine breadcrumbs. Gradually add just enough of the milk to mix to a dough. Gather up and knead for several minutes until soft and malleable. Set aside for about 15 minutes.

Lightly grease a pie dish about 20cm (8 in) in diameter. Roll out the pastry on a lightly floured work top to a shape a little larger than that of the dish. Carefully transfer the pastry to the dish and press down. Trim off excess pastry around the edge of the dish.

In a bowl beat the eggs and fold in all the remaining ingredients. Pour into the pastry case. Place on the top shelf of an oven preheated to 190C (375F) gas 5 and bake for about 30-40 minutes or until the filling is golden and firm. Remove from the oven and serve warm or cold with cream.

Makes 1 large cake

noushi gargantag

almond cake

*'Her eyes were of almonds
The ears of cherries pink,
Cheeks of water-melon red
Lips of crimson mulberries.
Her hair gold like corn in our fields,
Nose a gherkin soft and sweet.'*
Assyrian Folk Song

This light, fatless cake is an Armenian recipe and makes a fine teatime treat. Some people like to add 1 teaspoon ground bitter almonds – as these are rather difficult to find I suggest either spiced apricot kernels, which are available from most good continental or health food shops or 1 teaspoon lemon juice.

4 eggs, separated
225g (½ lb) icing sugar
1 teaspoon vanilla essence
2 tablespoons sultanas
150g (5 oz) self-raising flour, sifted
75g (3 oz) blanched almonds, ground
½ teaspoon ground cinnamon

Place the egg yolks in a large bowl, sift in the icing sugar and whisk until pale and thick. Stir in the vanilla, sultanas, flour, 50g (2 oz) of the ground almonds and the cinnamon. Place the egg whites in a bowl and whisk until stiff. Carefully fold into the cake mixture with a metal spoon.

Grease and flour a 21cm (8½in) round cake tin. Pour in the cake mixture, sprinkle the remaining almonds evenly over the surface and press down *very* lightly.

Bake in an oven preheated to 180C (350F) gas 4 for 25-30 minutes or until the cake is cooked and lightly golden. Remove from the oven, leave for 10 minutes and then cool on a cake rack. Serve with tea or coffee.

Makes 1 large cake

ugat dvash

honey and spice cake

This cake is also known as *Lekach* amongst Jews in general. It is a must on the Sabbath. Cut into slices and store in an airtight tin. Before serving spread with a little butter.

40g (1½ oz) butter
150ml (¼ pint) clear honey
50g (2 oz) soft brown sugar
60ml (2 fl oz) milk
3 eggs
1 teaspoon bicarbonate of soda dissolved in 1 tablespoon milk
275g (10 oz) plain flour
1 teaspoon ground ginger
pinch of salt
1 teaspoon mixed spice
¼ teaspoon ground cloves

Garnish
50g (2 oz) flaked almonds

Place the butter, honey and sugar in a small saucepan and place over a low heat, stirring constantly, until the sugar has dissolved. Remove from the heat and set aside. Place the milk, eggs and soda mixture in a bowl and whisk until frothy. Sift the flour, ginger, salt, mixed spice and cloves into a large bowl. Make a well in the centre and pour in the honey mixture and the milk and egg mixture. Use a metal spoon to mix the liquids together, gradually drawing in the flour. When all the flour has been incorporated and the mixture is smooth, pour the batter into a greased and floured 20cm (8in) round cake tin. Sprinkle the flaked almonds evenly over the surface and press down very gently into the surface of the cake.

Bake in an oven preheated to 180C (350F) gas 4 for about 1 hour or until the cake is cooked. Remove from the oven and leave in the tin for 30 minutes. Turn out on to a wire rack and leave until completely cold before serving.

Makes 1 large cake

karithopita

walnut cake

Popular throughout Greece, Turkey and Armenia this is a cake of Byzantine origin where the rich walnuts of Anatolia are put to good use. This recipe – from Cyprus, hence the brandy – was given to me by a lady who hails from Famagusta. Omit the brandy or increase the quantity if you wish!

110g (4 oz) butter
75g (3 oz) sugar
4 eggs, separated
175g (6 oz) plain flour
4 teaspoons baking powder
1 teaspoon ground cinnamon
pinch of salt
175g (6 oz) walnuts, finely chopped

Syrup
175g (6 oz) sugar
2.5cm (1in) piece cinnamon stick
1 tablespoon lemon juice
1 tablespoon brandy (optional)

Place the butter and sugar in a large bowl and cream together until light and fluffy. Add the egg yolks and beat until smooth. Whisk the egg whites until stiff. Sift the flour, baking powder, cinnamon and salt into the bowl and fold into the mixture. Add about $1/3$ of the beaten egg white and fold in with a metal spoon. Now fold in the chopped walnuts and lastly the remaining egg whites. Do this as quickly and as gently as possible to trap as much air as possible in the mixture.

Grease and flour a baking tin about 30 X 22.5cm (12 X 9in) and spoon in the mixture. Smooth over the surface with the back of a spoon. Place in an oven preheated to 180C (350F) gas 4 and bake for 30-40 minutes or until cooked.

Meanwhile prepare the syrup. Place the sugar, cinnamon stick, lemon juice and 450ml ($3/4$ pint) water in a small saucepan and bring to the boil. Lower the heat and simmer for 10 minutes. Discard the cinnamon stick, stir in the brandy and set aside to cool. When the cake is cooked remove from the oven, pour the cool syrup evenly over the surface and leave in the tin until cold. Cut into squares or diamond-shaped pieces and serve with cream.

Makes about 15 pieces

khoritz

cake fillings

Khoritz is the name given to fillings that are used in making *katah* type cakes. Katah are dry cakes made with a sweet yeast mixture and the fillings usually include some combination of the following – flour or semolina, butter, nuts, dried fruit, spices and sugar. There are numerous such cakes and many are specialities of a particular town or village e.g. Stepanavani katah or Yerevan katah. The tops of the cakes usually have a pattern pressed into them using the prongs of a fork – straight lines or wavy lines or a lattice pattern.

Basic katah dough
15g (½ oz) fresh yeast or 8g (¼ oz) dried yeast
250ml (8 fl oz) tepid milk
50g (2 oz) sugar

110g (4 oz) butter, melted
400g (14 oz) plain flour, sifted
½ teaspoon salt

Filling
choose one from those described below

Garnish
25g (1 oz) butter, melted
1 egg, beaten

Place the yeast in a small bowl and add half the milk. Pour the remaining milk into a large mixing bowl, add the sugar and stir until dissolved. Add the melted butter to this mixture. When the yeast has softened pour the mixture into the mixing bowl and stir. Gradually stir in the flour and salt. When well blended transfer the dough to a well floured work top and knead for at least 10 minutes. Roll the dough into a ball, place in a clean bowl, cover with a cloth and set aside in a warm place until it has doubled in size. Remove the dough to a work top, punch down and knead for a few more minutes.

Now prepare the filling of your choice.

Divide the dough into 3 equal parts. Take one part and roll out on a floured surface until 3-5mm (⅛-¼in) thick. Brush the surface all over with melted butter. Fold the edges into the centre to make about a 12.5cm (5in) square. Place one-third of the filling in the centre of the square and bring the opposite corners of the square over to completely enclose the filling. Then gently roll the cake out until it is about 15cm (6in) square, taking care not to let the filling ooze out. Place on a greased baking tray.

Repeat with the remaining dough and filling. Brush the top of each with beaten egg and set aside in a warm place for a further 30 minutes. Place in an oven preheated to 200C (400F) gas 6 and bake for about 20 minutes or until risen and golden. Remove and cool on wire racks. Serve sliced with tea or coffee.

Makes 3 cakes, each to serve 8

fillings

A
110g (4 oz) butter
110g (4 oz) plain flour
4 tablespoons sugar

B
50g (2 oz) butter
110g (4 oz) plain flour

C
50g (2 oz) butter
110g (4 oz) flour
50g (2 oz) sugar
1 teaspoon ground cinnamon
2 tablespoons chopped walnuts

For the above fillings first melt the butter in a small pan, add the flour and fry, stirring constantly, until golden and then stir in any remaining ingredients.

D

25g (1 oz) butter
2 tablespoons raisins
2 tablespoons chopped walnuts
1 tablespoon brown sugar
1 tablespoon white sugar
1 teaspoon ground cinnamon
1 tablespoon sesame seeds

Melt the butter in a small pan and stir in all the remaining ingredients.

zadgva katah

easter cake

During Easter Armenians traditionally make this and many other dry cakes – sometimes with fillings and sometimes without. This cake is delicious with tea or coffee.

To prepare follow the instructions for the basic katah dough on the page opposite and use filling **D**.

Makes 3 cakes, each providing 8 slices

Sung on Easter Sunday:

'On the Sepulchre of the immortal that is risen,
On this day the heavenly holy angel cried aloud:
Christ did arise, Christ did awake
Out of the Virgin tomb, out of the tomb of light.

'The keepers did shake for fear,
For out of the new, virgin sepulchre
Christ did arise, Christ did awake
Out of the Virgin tomb, out of the tomb of light.

'By the holy stone sat the marvellous one and cried aloud,
And the oil-bearing women preached joyfully;
Christ did arise, Christ did awake,
Out of the new tomb, out of the Virgin tomb.'
Divine Liturgy

artzak katah

artzak semolina-filled cake

This cake from Artzak (Armenia) has a khoritz of semolina, almonds and cardamom and the inclusion of ground mastic in the dough gives it a marvellous aroma. Ideal with tea or coffee.

Dough
15g (½ oz) fresh yeast or 8g (¼ oz) dried yeast
1 teaspoon sugar
50g (2 oz) clarified butter, melted (page 194)
2 eggs
150ml (¼ pint) milk
75g (3 oz) sugar
½ teaspoon salt
1 teaspoon vanilla
½ teaspoon ground mastic
450g (1 lb) plain flour

Filling
175g (6 oz) clarified butter
110g (4 oz) fine semolina
110g (4 oz) ground almonds
¼ teaspoon ground cardamom
150g (5 oz) icing sugar

Garnish
25g (1 oz) butter, melted
1 egg, beaten

Mix the yeast, sugar and 2 tablespoons tepid water in a small bowl and set aside in a warm place until the mixture begins to froth. Meanwhile in a large bowl mix together the melted butter, eggs, milk, sugar, salt, vanilla and mastic. Add the yeast mixture and stir until well blended. Gradually sift in the flour, stirring all the time, until a dough is formed. Gather up and knead on a floured work top for about 7-10 minutes until the dough is soft and pliable. Place in a clean bowl, cover with a tea towel and put in a warm place until it has doubled in size.

Meanwhile prepare the filling by melting the butter in a medium saucepan, adding the semolina and frying until the semolina is lightly golden. Add the remaining ingredients and cook for a further 2 minutes, stirring all the time.

When it is ready punch down the dough, knead for 1-2 minutes and then divide into 3 equal parts. Take one portion and roll into a ball. Now roll it out on a lightly floured work top until it is ½cm (¼in) thick and as round as possible. Brush the surface with the melted butter and then spread one-third of the filling evenly over it to within 1cm (½in) of the edge. Fold the dough in half to make a semi-circle. Carefully roll it out to make it a little larger and shape it into a round about 1cm (½in) thick. Place on a greased baking tray. Repeat with the remaining dough and filling.

Press around the edge of each round with your fingertips to give a fluted appearance and then make a pattern on the top with the prongs of a fork. Brush the tops generously with the beaten egg and bake in an oven preheated to 180C (350F) gas 4 for about 30-40 minutes or until golden brown. Leave to cool on cake racks. Store in an airtight tin. Serve sliced with tea or coffee.

Makes 3 cakes, each providing 8 slices

ugat foukhyevesha
sponge cake

A standard cake recipe popular all over eastern Europe as well as Israel. People belonging to the Jewish faith eat this cake during Passover when no artificial leavening is used and so whisked egg whites are substituted. As ordinary flour cannot be used, ground nuts, matzo meal and potato flour are substituted. However the cake is equally successful if the potato flour is replaced by plain flour.

110g (4 oz) fine matzo meal
50g (2 oz) potato flour or plain flour
¼ teaspoon salt
175g (6 oz) caster sugar
6 eggs, separated
60ml (2 fl oz) oil
1 tablespoon lemon juice
60ml (2 fl oz) orange juice
1 tablespoon grated lemon rind

Filling
jam of your choice or fresh fruit and cream
icing sugar

In a large bowl mix together the matzo meal, flour, salt and 110g (4 oz) of the sugar. In another bowl mix together the egg yolks, oil, lemon and orange juice and the lemon rind. Pour this mixture into the matzo meal bowl and mix in thoroughly until smooth. In another bowl whisk the egg whites until stiff. Add the remaining sugar and whisk for a further minute. Fold 3 tablespoons of the egg white into the cake mixture until well blended and then add the remaining egg white and fold in with a metal spoon until the mixture is smooth.

Grease and flour a 21cm (8½in) round cake tin, pour the mixture in and smooth over with the back of a spoon. Bake in an oven preheated to 160C (325F) gas 3 for about 1 hour or until golden and firm. Remove from the oven, turn out onto a cake rack and set aside until cold. Slice the cake in half with a sharp knife and fill with a jam of your choice. I find apricot jam particularly delicious in this sponge. Filled with fresh fruit and cream this simple cake becomes a spectacular dessert. Dust the surface generously with icing sugar.

Makes 1 large cake

purim stollen

purim cake

Purim is the Feast of Lots and occurs exactly one month before Passover – 14th of Adar (February/March). During these festivities many cakes and desserts are prepared. Purim stollen is an age-old recipe. Below is a simplified method with a jam and nut filling.

Filling
grated rind of 1 lemon
2 tablespoons lemon juice
2 tablespoons sugar
5 tablespoons jam, e.g. apricot
3 tablespoons chopped hazelnuts or walnuts
50g (2 oz) poppy seeds

Dough
1 egg, beaten
5 tablespoons evaporated milk
110g (4 oz) sugar
110g (4 oz) ground digestive biscuit crumbs
225g (8 oz) plain flour, sifted
50g (2 oz) butter, melted

Put the filling ingredients into a small bowl and mix thoroughly. Place the egg, milk, sugar, biscuit crumbs, flour and 3 tablespoons of the melted butter into a large bowl and mix thoroughly to form a stiff dough. Flour a work top, turn out the dough and knead for a few minutes. Flour the work top again and roll the dough out into a rectangle about 25 X 37.5cm (10 X 15in). Brush the surface lightly with a little melted butter.

Spread the filling down one of the long sides of the rectangle, 2.5cm (1in) from the edge, so that one half of the rectangle is covered. Carefully fold the pastry over the filling and pinch the edges together to completely seal in the filling. Lightly grease a large baking tray and lift the stollen on to it. Brush the remaining melted butter over the stollen and bake in an oven preheated to 200C (400F) gas 6 for about 20-25 minutes or until nicely browned. Remove, cool a little then cut into slices – diagonally if you wish – and serve warm.

Makes 10-12 pieces

tea and coffee time

'Oh thou who asks me about my food, know that dry bread is the chief of all things.'
Egyptian Saying

Throughout the centuries bread has been the staple diet of the mass of people. It was made of millet, rice, barley or wheat – bread made of the latter was considered best of all. The predominance of wheat bread was one of the intrinsic characteristics of the Middle Eastern diet as compared with that of Europeans in the Middle Ages. (See E. Ashtor's article 'The Diet of Salaried Classes in the Medieval East' in the *Near East Journal of Asian History IV* 1970)

Bread, fresh as well as in a variety of dried forms, was highly popular. Indeed it was the custom for housewives to prepare unleavened bread *lavash* in large quantities in early autumn for storage throughout the severe winter months. Similarly many varieties of biscuit were prepared. A typical bread is Nazug. This is a delicious cinnamon-flavoured bread which is eaten either with cheese or with jams and preserves.

nazug
cinnamon bread

15g (½ oz) fresh yeast or 8g (¼ oz) dried yeast
60ml (2 fl oz) warm milk
2 eggs, lightly beaten
6 tablespoons melted butter
50g (2 oz) sugar
½ teaspoon salt
2 teaspoons ground cinnamon
1 teaspoon vanilla essence
350-400g (12-14 oz) plain flour

Garnish
beaten egg

Place the yeast in a large bowl, add the milk and stir until the yeast has dissolved. Add the eggs, cooled melted butter, sugar, salt, cinnamon and vanilla and stir well. Gradually sift in enough flour to make a soft dough. Transfer to a lightly floured surface and knead for about 10 minutes or until the dough is smooth and elastic. Wash and dry the mixing bowl and oil it lightly. Add the dough and roll it round the bowl until the surface is lightly greased. Cover the bowl with a cloth and set aside in a warm place for about 2 hours or until the dough has doubled in size.

Punch the dough down and knead for a few more minutes. Divide the dough into 4 portions. Roll or press each portion out into a round about 1cm (½in) thick. Place on greased baking trays about 5cm (2in) apart and set aside in a warm place for a further 30 minutes.

Brush the surface of each piece of dough with beaten egg and bake in an oven preheated to 190C (375F) gas 5 for 10-15 minutes or until golden and baked through.

Makes 4 small loaves

dziranov hatz
apricot and walnut bread

Although called a bread this is really more of a cake and it can be eaten on its own or with cheese or with jams. It is a delicious fruity and nutty loaf with the exquisite aroma of mahleb, which is a spice extracted from the kernel of the black cherry stone. Although difficult to find and quite expensive mahleb is a must with many yeast-breads and biscuits. You should be able to get it from good Middle Eastern stores. Grind it in a mortar. Mahleb will appear over and over again in this chapter, so it is best to acquire a little if possible.

110g (4 oz) dried apricots
175g (6 oz) sugar
2 tablespoons butter, softened
1 egg, beaten
120ml (4 fl oz) orange juice
225g (8 oz) plain flour
1 teaspoon salt
2 teaspoons baking powder
pinch of bicarbonate of soda
1 teaspoon ground mahleb
50g (2 oz) walnuts, chopped
2 tablespoons flour

Soak the apricots for 30 minutes in cold water and then drain and cut into small pieces. Place the sugar and butter in a large bowl and beat until creamy. Add the egg and beat until smooth and creamy. Stir in 60ml (2 fl oz) water and the orange juice. Sift the 225g (8 oz) flour, salt, baking powder and soda into the bowl and stir in with a metal spoon until well blended. Stir in the mahleb. Place the chopped apricots and walnuts in a small bowl, add 2 tablespoons flour and toss well. Add this to the cake mixture and stir until evenly distributed.

Lightly grease and flour a 900g (2 lb) loaf tin and pour in the mixture. Smooth over the top. Place in an oven preheated to 180C (350F) gas 4 and bake for about 1 hour. Cool on a wire rack and slice when cold.

Makes 1 large cake

blor keteh

flaked bread

'The mother is newly-made bread, still warm.
Whoever eats will be nourished
and filled.
The father is unwatered wine,
Whoever sips will be intoxicated.
The brother is the rising sun
that lights the valley
and the mountainside alike.'
Folk song from *Anthology Of Armenian Poetry*

This is a delicious flaky bread which is best eaten warm with jam, honey or cheese.

15g (½ oz) fresh yeast or 8g (¼ oz) dried yeast
1 teaspoon sugar
450g (1 lb) plain flour
180ml (6 fl oz) evaporated milk, warmed
1 egg, beaten
1 teaspoon salt
1 tablespoon caster sugar
40g (1½ oz) unsalted butter, melted

Garnish
75g (3 oz) unsalted butter, melted
1 small egg, beaten
sesame seeds or black cumin seeds

Place the yeast and teaspoon of sugar in a small bowl, add 120ml (4 fl oz) warm water, stir well and set aside in a warm place until the mixture begins to froth. Meanwhile sift the flour into a large bowl. Place all the remaining ingredients together in a bowl and stir until the sugar has dissolved.

Make a well in the centre of the flour and pour in the frothy yeast and the milk mixture and blend thoroughly until you have a soft dough. Remove to a work top and knead for at least 10 minutes until the dough is soft and satiny. Grease a clean bowl with a little butter, roll the dough around it to coat with the butter and then cover and leave in a warm place for 1-2 hours until the dough has doubled in size.

Punch down the dough, place on a floured work top and knead until smooth. Divide into 6 equal portions, roll each into a ball and cover with a cloth. Lightly flour a large work top, take a ball of dough and roll it out into a large thin circle about 30-35cm (12-14in) in diameter. Brush the surface of the circle with some of the 75g (3 oz) of melted butter. Roll up the circle to form a long rope. Hold each end gently and swing the pastry up and down, letting the dough hit the work top. This will double the length of the rope. Coil the pastry around and press the outside end on top of the outer coil. Now flatten with your hands or a rolling pin into a 15cm (6in) round. Place on a greased baking tray. Repeat with the remaining balls of dough. Leave the baking trays in a warm place for a further 30-45 minutes until the dough has risen.

Brush the tops of the rounds with beaten egg and sprinkle with the sesame seeds or cumin seeds. Bake in an oven preheated to 190C (375F) gas 5 for 12-15 minutes or until golden and cooked.

Makes 6 small loaves

choreg
festive dry biscuits

Choreg are dry breads (from the Armeno-Turkish words *chor* meaning dry, *ekmeg* meaning bread). Traditionally prepared for Christmas, Znunti choreg, and Easter, Zadgi choreg, celebrations. They are generally plaited and usually prepared in large quantities and stored in airtight tins. Excellent for breakfast or with tea or coffee, serve them plain or with cheese or jams.

The Greek Tsourekia, which is eaten at breakfast on Easter day, is related to the recipe below, which is a family favourite. I have described how to prepare two of the standard shapes, but feel free to create your own.

15g (½ oz) fresh yeast or 8g (¼ oz) dried yeast
1 teaspoon sugar
450g (1 lb) plain flour
pinch of salt
110g (4 oz) margarine or butter
1 teaspoon mahleb, crushed
1 tablespoon cooking oil

Topping
1 egg, beaten
sesame seeds

Place the yeast and sugar in a small bowl, add 250ml (8 fl oz) warm water, stir to dissolve and put in a warm place for about 10 minutes or until the mixture begins to froth. Meanwhile sieve the flour and salt into a large bowl. Add the margarine or butter and rub it in until the mixture resembles fine breadcrumbs. Stir in crushed mahleb. Make a well in the centre and pour in the yeast mixture. Blend until you have a stiff dough. Now add 120-250ml (4-8 fl oz) water a little at a time and knead until you have a soft dough. The amount of water you will add will vary because of the differing qualities of the various brands of flour. When the dough comes away easily from the sides of the bowl, remove to a clean work top and knead for about 10 minutes until it is elastic and pliable. Add the oil and knead it in. Roll the dough into a ball, place in a clean bowl, cover with a tea towel and leave it to rest in a warm place for 1-2 hours until it has doubled in size.

When the dough is ready heat the oven to 200C (400F) gas 6. Grease several baking trays with cooking oil. Place the beaten egg in a small bowl and pour some sesame seeds on to a plate. Punch down the dough a few times and then break off a piece about the size of a walnut. Roll between your palms to form a ball. Place on a clean work top and roll it to and fro with your palms until you have a long strip which is pencil thin and about 30cm (12in) long. These strips can then be made into many different shapes, which vary from family to family. The two described below were favoured by my mother.

The twisted circle
Bring one end of the strip over to meet the other, thus halving its original length. Lightly roll your palm over the loose ends 2 or 3 times to obtain a twisted strip. Bring the ends of the strip together and press the uncut end over the loose ends to form a circle.

The plait
Break off one-third of the strip and press one end of it half way along the remaining strip. Plait the 3 strips of dough together and then press the 3 loose ends together.

Place each choreg on a baking tray, leaving a little space between each one. Brush each one with beaten egg and then sprinkle with sesame seeds. Turn the oven off, place the baking trays inside and leave for 15-20 minutes to rise a little. Turn the oven up to 200C (400F) gas 6 again and cook for 12-15 minutes or until golden. As they become golden remove the trays from the oven and pile all the choreg on to 1 tray. When all are cooked, turn off the oven and return the tray to the oven. Leave for several hours until the biscuits have dried out. When cold store in an airtight container.

Makes 25-30

kimyonov choreg

cumin seed sticks

Dry bread sticks flavoured with cumin. They can be eaten by themselves, but are particularly delicious with cheese. Will keep for a long time in an airtight container.

15g (¹/₂ oz) fresh yeast or 8g (¹/₄ oz) dried yeast
1 teaspoon sugar
450g (1 lb) plain flour
¹/₂ teaspoon salt
50g (2 oz) butter, melted
60ml (2 fl oz) vegetable oil
1 teaspoon cumin seeds

Garnish
1 egg, beaten

Place the yeast and sugar in a small bowl, add 2 tablespoons warm water, stir to dissolve and leave in a warm place for about 10 minutes until it begins to froth. Meanwhile sift the flour and salt into a large bowl. Make a well in the centre and pour in the melted butter and oil. Rub in until the mixture resembles fine breadcrumbs. Make a well in the centre and add the yeast, cumin seeds and about 180ml (6 fl oz) water. Mix until a dough is formed. Remove to a clean work top and knead for about 10 minutes until the dough is soft. Place in a clean bowl, cover with a tea towel and leave in a warm place for 1-2 hours until the dough has doubled in size.

Heat the oven to 200C (400F) gas 6 and then grease 2 large baking trays. Return the dough to the work top, punch down and knead for a further minute or two. Break off a walnut-sized piece of dough and roll it into a ball. Place on the work top and roll it to and fro to form a stick about 15-17.5cm (6-7in) long and ¹/₂-1cm (¹/₄-¹/₂in) thick. Place on the baking tray. Repeat with the remaining dough, placing the finished sticks about 2.5cm (1in) apart on the baking trays. Brush with the egg. Turn off the oven and place the trays inside. After 15 minutes, during which time the sticks will have risen, return the oven to 200C (400F) gas 6 and cook the choreg for 12-15 minutes or until golden.

Remove from the oven and pile on to 1 tray. Turn off the oven and return the tray to the oven and leave for several hours to allow the choreg to dry. When cold store in an airtight container.

Makes about 30

simit

dry biscuits with sesame seeds

One of the most popular dry biscuits in the entire region, simit is usually sold by street vendors who run around the narrow streets laden with baskets full of these dry biscuits shouting 'Simit, ya, simit'. Simit is related to, but not the same as, choreg. They are eaten at breakfast or with tea or coffee with dried yoghurt, *labna*, or cheese or jam.

350g (12 oz) plain flour
½ teaspoon salt
1½ teaspoons baking powder
110g (4 oz) butter, melted
120ml (4 fl oz) olive oil
60ml (2 fl oz) milk
1 egg

Topping
milk or beaten egg
sesame seeds

Sieve the flour, salt and baking powder into a large bowl. Put the remaining ingredients into another bowl with 60ml (2 fl oz) water and mix well. Make a well in the centre of the flour mixture and pour in the liquid mixture. Gradually blend the flour into the liquid until you have a soft, slightly oily dough. Heat oven to 200C (400F) gas 6. Flour your hands and break off pieces of dough about the size of a walnut. Roll each one into a sausage about 20cm (8in) long and ½-1cm (¼-½in) thick. Fold the strip in half and twist it 3 or 4 times. Place each one on a greased baking tray about 2.5cm (1in) apart, either as they are or twisted into a circle with the 2 ends pressed together. Brush each with the milk or beaten egg and sprinkle with sesame seeds. Bake for 25-30 minutes or until golden. Cool on wire racks and store in an airtight container.

Makes 18-20

qirshalli

crisp kahks

Kahk is the Arabic name for choreg or simit, i.e. dry biscuits or bread. Qirshalli is a Lebanese speciality and in contrast to most of the similar recipes in this chapter it is cooked as a cake and then cut into fingers and dried out. These kahk emit the marvellous aroma of aniseed. There are many variations of this Arab biscuit. Some use fine semolina instead of flour; others add chopped walnuts or hazelnuts while others are shaped into bracelets.

275g (10 oz) plain flour
2 teaspoons baking powder
120ml (4 fl oz) oil
3 eggs
110g (4 oz) sugar
1 teaspoon vanilla
1 teaspoon aniseed
50g (2 oz) raisins

Garnish
1 egg yolk, beaten

Sift the flour and baking powder into a large bowl and make a well in the centre. Add the oil and rub it in with your fingers until the mixture resembles fine breadcrumbs. In another bowl beat together the eggs, sugar, vanilla and aniseed. Add to the flour mixture and mix thoroughly. Stir in the raisins. Cover the bowl with a cloth and set aside for 10-15 minutes.

Grease a baking tin about 30 X 22.5 X 5cm (12 X 9 X 2in) and spoon in the mixture. Smooth over the surface with the back of a spoon. The mixture should be about 1cm (½in) thick. Brush the surface generously with the beaten egg yolk. Bake in an oven preheated to 180C (350F) gas 4 for 30 minutes. Remove from the oven and leave to cool for 10 minutes. Turn out on to a work top and cut into fingers 7.5cm (3in) long and 1cm (½in) wide. Pile the fingers on to a large baking tray. Reduce the heat to 120C (250F) gas ½ and leave for about 20-30 minutes or until browned all over. Remove from the oven and leave to cool. When cold store in an airtight tin. Will keep for several weeks.

Makes about 30 fingers

*One day –
Saidi, while seated in the garden, told the tale of a famed king who
confronted a learned Arab doctor with the following question
'Tell me doctor, how much should I, daily, eat?'
'The weight of a hundred dirams,' the doctor replied.
'Will this give me sufficient strength?' asked the king.
'It will carry you,' replied the doctor. 'If you eat more you will have to carry it.'*
Bustan

urfa choregi
urfa-style choreg

A speciality from the town of Urfa (classical Edessa) in southern Turkey. It is one of the oldest towns in the Middle East. Legend has it that Abraham was slain there. It was once the centre of the Osrhoenic Kingdom whose kings took the title Abgar and of whom the 15th king Abgar Uchomo is famous for his legendary correspondence with Christ. In 1097, during the first crusade, it was seized by Baldwin who created the 'Countdome of Edessa'. The population throughout the ages has been Armenian and Jacobite with a smattering of Kurds. However, after the First World War when the Christians were massacred, Urfa shrank into a small, dirty, delapidated market town inhabited mainly by Kurds.

The reason for all this history is that Urfa was, and to some extent still is, one of the great culinary centres of the Middle East whence innumerable dishes spread to all corners of the Ottoman Empire. The recipe below is an example of that art. The choreg were made on festive days and are full of the exotic aromas of the Middle East.

450g (1 lb) plain flour
1 teaspoon mahleb, crushed
¾ teaspoon caraway seeds
½ teaspoon ground nutmeg
½ teaspoon ground cinnamon
½ teaspoon fennel seeds
110g (4 oz) sugar
175g (6 oz) butter, melted
1 tablespoon olive oil
15g (½ oz) fresh yeast or 8g (¼ oz) dried yeast
1 teaspoon sugar
120ml (4 fl oz) warm milk

Garnish
1 egg, beaten

In the morning of the day before baking, sift the flour into a large bowl and stir in the mahleb, caraway seeds, nutmeg, cinnamon, fennel seeds and sugar. Make a well in the centre and pour in the melted butter and oil. Rub with your fingertips until the mixture resembles sandy crumbs. Cover the bowl, wrap in a towel and leave in a warm place for 8-10 hours.

At night place the yeast and teaspoon of sugar in a small bowl. Add 45ml (1½ fl oz) warm water, stir to dissolve and leave in a warm place for about 10 minutes or until the mixture begins to froth. Uncover the flour bowl, make a well in the centre of the mixture and pour in the yeast liquid and the warm milk. Blend and then knead for 5-10 minutes until the dough is smooth and pliable. Cover the bowl and set aside overnight.

The next morning uncover the bowl and break off a walnut-sized lump of dough. Roll it out on a work top until about ½ cm (¼in) thick. Form into a circle, pressing one end over the other, or double the length of dough, twist 2 or 3 times and then form into a circle. Place on a greased baking tray. Repeat until you have used up all the dough.

Brush the tops with the beaten egg and bake in an oven preheated to 190C (375F) gas 5 for about 20-25 minutes or until golden. Remove and cool on a rack.

Makes 20-24

berazeh shami

damascus sesame biscuits

The most famous dry biscuit that hails from one of the oldest cities in the world, famed for her fresh fruits and ice creams.

Earlier in this century John Kelman wrote bewitchingly about this ancient city: 'Before entering the detailed life of the streets and bazaars of Damascus it is well to see it from afar as a whole – now clear, with wonderful illumination of sand, grass and rock by slanting sunset light; not dim and uniformly colourless, or swept by far-distant thunderclouds. But after all, the setting matters little compared with the jewel it holds. Surrounded by those gardens and orchards which Abana has created, the city lies, pearly white upon its carpet of green. Sometimes the pearl brightens to sharp-edged silver and the green is lustrous; sometimes it fades to opal, that seems to blend at all its edges with the mystic dark of a green that is felt rather than seen. But ever it lies there in the utter silence, dreaming through many moods – dreaming, dreaming.

'Yet is this wonderful city made up, like the rest of things, of individual details – so many and diverse are they, and no-where in this world does a guidebook list of sights seem more impertinent than here.

'Here, where (the sunlight) strikes upon shop-fronts; here is a glorious blaze of piled oranges; here the paler light of lemon reflected from some shopkeeper's silk robe. And the mid-street of the bazaar sparkles with ruby, diamond, emerald, amber and sapphire as the head-dresses and silken robes of passers-by come for a moment within the line of light.' (From *Damascus to Palmyra*.)

These beautiful biscuits of Damascus are exported throughout the Middle East. They are excellent with tea or coffee and will keep for a long time. Children will love them. I still do, but then I am still a child at heart – when it comes to Berazeh Shami!

15g (½ oz) fresh yeast or 8g (¼ oz) dried yeast
1 teaspoon sugar
450g (1 lb) plain flour
350g (¾ lb) caster sugar
175g (6 oz) butter
3 tablespoons coarsely chopped pistachio nuts

Topping
40g (1½ oz) butter, melted
175g (6 oz) sesame seeds spread over a large plate

Place the yeast and sugar in a small bowl with 150ml (¼ pint) warm water, stir to dissolve and set aside in a warm place until it begins to froth. Meanwhile sift the flour into a large bowl, add the butter cut into small pieces and rub in with your fingertips until the mixture resembles fine breadcrumbs. Stir in the chopped pistachio nuts. Make a well in the centre and pour in the yeast mixture. Mix thoroughly until you have a dough. Add a little more water if necessary. Remove to a work top and knead for about 10 minutes or until the dough is soft and pliable. Cover the bowl with a tea towel and leave in a warm place for 1-2 hours.

Remove the dough to a lightly floured work top and knead for 1-2 minutes. Divide it into 2 portions. Roll out one portion on the floured work top until about 3mm (⅛in) thick. Cut out as

many rounds as possible using a 10cm (4in) cutter. Repeat with the remaining portion of dough. Brush the surface of one biscuit with the melted butter and then place it, butter side down, on the sesame seeds. Shake off excess seeds and place on a greased baking tray. Repeat with remaining biscuits. Bake in an oven preheated to 160C (325F) gas 3 for 15-20 minutes or until golden. Remove and cool on racks. Store in an airtight tin when cold.

Makes about 24

dilber gozu
'pretty eyes' biscuits

'May I love your eyes' – an apology.

These delicious and attractive biscuits are from Turkey. They are a typical Turkish adaptation of European pastries. In recent years there have been far too many of these 'adaptations' taking place in Turkey – and to a lesser extent in Lebanon and, of course, Israel. The latter is more understandable due to the European origin of many of their people, but the former – in my opinion – almost unforgivable! However, as the saying goes 'I know it is wrong, but I like it', so here is the recipe and may your eyes be as pretty as these biscuits!

225g (½ lb) unsalted butter
110g (¼ lb) icing sugar
1 teaspoon vanilla essence
350g (¾ lb) plain flour, sifted

Filling
thick jam of your choice

Place the butter in a large bowl and beat until pale and creamy. Add the sugar and vanilla and continue to beat until well blended. Gradually mix in the flour and when the mixture becomes stiff knead with your hand until smooth. Divide into 2 portions.

Lightly flour a work top and roll out one portion of the pastry to a ½cm (¼in) thickness. Using a 5cm (2in) pastry cutter, decorative if you wish, cut out as many rounds as possible. Repeat with the remaining portion of pastry. Place half the biscuits on lightly greased baking trays. In the remaining biscuits make 3 holes about ½-1cm (¼-½in) in diameter using a piece of round wood or something similar. I used the top of a ballpoint pen. Place on greased baking trays. Bake in an oven preheated to 180C (350F) gas 4 for 10-15 minutes or until a light golden. Remove and place on racks. Sprinkle the biscuits with holes in with a little icing sugar. Leave the biscuits to cool.

Spread a little jam over the whole biscuits and top with the ones with holes. Press the tops down gently so that the jam oozes up the holes. Store in an airtight tin when cold. Delicious with tea or coffee.

Makes 20-24

mafish

pastry twists

I have included this recipe because these delicious little sugary pastries were a childhood favourite of mine. They are cheap and easy to prepare and will keep a long time if permitted to! If you wish you can use soured cream or a mixture of double cream and orange juice instead of the yoghurt.

15g (½ oz) fresh yeast or 8g (¼ oz) dried yeast
1 teaspoon sugar
175g (6 oz) butter, melted
150ml (¼ pint) yoghurt
1 egg
350g (¾ lb) plain flour, sifted
1 teaspoon lemon essence
110g (4 oz) sugar

Place the yeast and sugar in a small bowl with 60ml (2 fl oz) warm water, stir to dissolve and set aside in a warm place until the mixture begins to froth. Pour the butter into a large bowl and stir in the yoghurt and egg. Stir in the yeast mixture and the lemon essence. Gradually stir in the flour and mix until you have a soft dough. Add a little more flour if necessary. Knead for several minutes until smooth. Divide into 2 portions, wrap each in foil and refrigerate for several hours.

Remove from the fridge, unwrap and leave for 10 minutes. Take one portion and half the sugar. Sprinkle a little of the sugar over the work top and roll out the dough into a rectangle about 3mm (⅛in) thick. Sprinkle some of the sugar over the surface, fold in half and roll out to its original shape. Repeat this process twice more sprinkling the work top and the surface of the dough with a little sugar each time. Cut the final rectangle into strips 2 X 7.5cm (¾ X 3in). Using the thumb and forefinger of each hand pick up each strip and twist into a spiral. Place on greased baking trays about 1cm (½in) apart. Repeat with remaining ball of dough and portion of sugar. Bake in an oven preheated to 180C (350F) gas 4 for 15-20 minutes or until lightly golden. Cool on wire racks.

Makes 70-80

Almond tree –
to see . . . . newly born and happy love
to eat almonds . . . . increment of debts
bitter almonds . . . . steady and fruitful friendship
The Book of Dreams

The almond, perhaps more than any other, is the nut of the Middle Eastern confectioners. Neither walnuts nor pistachios – the two runners-up – can match its versatility. Almonds appear in most biscuit recipes and the ones below are only a small selection. This nut, to which women's eyes and skin are often compared and whose praises poets oft sang, is found all over the region although the finest ones come from Turkey and Jordan.

In the 'Tale of Judan' (*1001 Nights*) Sheherazade recommends 'sausages, stuffed vegetable marrow, stuffed mutton, stuffed ribs. Kataif with almonds, bee's honey mixed with sugar, pistachio fritters perfumed with amber and almond cakes.' While in Ecclesiastes the almond tree is represented as grey hairs. 'In the day when the keepers of the house (the hands) shall tremble, and the strong man (the legs) bow themselves, and the grinders (the teeth) cease because they are few, and those that look out of the windows (the eyes) be darkened . . . and the almond tree (grey hairs) shall flourish and the grasshoppers be a burden and desire shall fail . . .' (*Ecclesiastes* XII 3-5).

The versatile almond, which comes ground, chopped, roasted, flaked or sugared, perpetually appears in the Middle Eastern cuisine, as does love, honour and chivalry in her poetry and the Oud in her music.

kaab el-ghazal

gazelle horns

This North African pastry derives its name from its curved shape. They take quite a time to make, but the effort is well worth it.

Filling
225g (½ lb) ground almonds
175g (6 oz) icing sugar, sifted
1 teaspoon ground cinnamon
30-60ml (1-2 fl oz) orange blossom water

Pastry
225g (½ lb) plain flour
2 tablespoons melted butter
3 tablespoons orange blossom water

First prepare the filling by mixing the almonds, icing sugar and cinnamon together in a bowl. Add enough of the orange blossom water to bind the mixture together. Knead until smooth. Divide into 16 balls. Roll each ball into a sausage about 5cm (2in) long which is thicker in the middle and tapers at both ends. Set aside.

Sift the flour into a mixing bowl, make a well in the centre and add the butter and orange blossom water. Gradually fold in the flour and, little by little, add just enough cold water to form a dough. Place on a work top and knead for at least 20 minutes until the dough is very smooth and elastic. Divide into 2 balls. Take a ball of dough and roll it out into a strip about 10cm (4in) wide and at least 75cm (30in) long. You will find that you will be able to stretch the pastry by wrapping first one end of the pastry and then the other over the rolling pin and pulling gently.

Arrange 8 of the almond sausages on the pastry in a line about 3.5cm (1½in) in from the long edge nearest you, and leaving about 5cm (2in) between each sausage. Fold the pastry over the sausages to enclose completely. Cut down between each sausage. Taking 1 pastry at a time, press the edges together to seal in the filling. Trim the pastry edge to a semi-circle, but do not cut too close to the filling or the edges will be forced open during cooking and the filling will ooze out. Crimp the edges with the prongs of a fork or a pastry trimmer. Now pinch the pastry up to form a steep ridge and gently curve the ends around to form a crescent-shape. Repeat with the remaining pastries.

Place the pastries on greased baking trays and cook in an oven preheated to 180C (350F) gas 4 for 20-30 minutes or until pale golden. Cool on wire racks and store in an airtight tin when cold.

Makes 16

badem pare

almond rounds in syrup

There are several versions of this particular sweet which is really an almond-based biscuit dipped in syrup. The most famous one, sold throughout the length and breadth of Turkey, is probably badem pare. Popular throughout the Middle East, they are known as M'kroons in Lebanon and are the biscuits from which the western macaroon developed.

110g (4 oz) margarine
110g (4 oz) caster sugar
½ teaspoon bicarbonate of soda
pinch salt
275g (10 oz) plain flour, sifted
75g (3 oz) almonds, toasted under a grill and then ground
2 eggs

Syrup
225g (8 oz) sugar
1 tablespoon lemon juice

Topping
about 24 whole, blanched almonds

First prepare the syrup by placing the sugar, lemon juice and 450ml ($^3/_4$ pint) water in a saucepan and bringing to the boil. Simmer for about 10 minutes or until the syrup thinly coats a spoon. Set aside to cool. Place the margarine in a large bowl with the sugar, soda and salt and cream until smooth. Add the flour and ground almonds and mix in until the mixture resembles fine breadcrumbs. Break the eggs into a small bowl and beat well. Pour most of the egg into the mixture, retaining just enough to coat the tops of the rounds. Knead the eggs into the mixture until smooth and forming a ball. Cover with a damp cloth and set aside for 15 minutes.

Break off walnut-sized lumps of dough and roll into balls – about 24. Take a ball and press lightly between the palms. Place on a lightly greased baking tray. Repeat with the remaining balls, placing them about 2.5cm (1in) apart on the baking trays. Brush the top of each round with a little of the remaining egg. Press a whole, blanched almond in the centre of each.

Bake in an oven preheated to 180C (350F) gas 4 for about 20 minutes or until the biscuits are light golden. Remove from the oven and dip each one quickly in and out of the cold syrup. Set aside to cool.

Makes about 24

kahk-bil-loz

almond and pistachio fingers

Whenever a friend or relative comes to visit me they inevitably bring a box of *kahk-bil-loz*. It is my favourite sweet and I consider it one of the greatest in the whole Middle Eastern repertoire. These sweets are an Aleppan speciality and, for generations, were produced by one family – the Azraks (Arabic-speaking Armenians). They have kept their age-old recipe pretty close to their hearts. Plead as I did on several occasions for the recipe, I was merely confronted with an inscrutable smile and the brief comment 'Why bother to make your own when we can post it to you in England.'

The sweets are small fingers of ground pistachio nuts covered with ground almonds scented with rosewater and orange blossom water. Traditionally they are made in long 1cm (½in)-wide moulds and then cut into 5cm (2in) pieces. The recipe below is my adaptation of this wonderful sweet and, if I may say so, almost as good as that of the Azraks' – but not quite!

450g (1 lb) ground almonds
350g (¾ lb) icing sugar
6 tablespoons rosewater
1 egg white
225g (½ lb) ground pistachio nuts
3 tablespoons orange blossom water

Place the ground almonds, icing sugar and rosewater in a bowl and knead until you have a smooth paste. Beat the egg white until stiff and mix into the paste. Leave to rest for 5 minutes. Meanwhile in another bowl mix the ground pistachios and orange blossom water together and knead to a smooth paste.

Now spread half the almond paste over the base of a shallow baking tin until about ½cm (¼in) thick, making sure that every corner is filled and the surface is as even as possible. Spread the ground pistachio paste evenly over the top. Now top with the remaining almond paste, smoothing over the surface. Bake in an oven preheated to 180C (350F) gas 4 for 10 minutes. The fingers should not be overcooked or coloured. Remove from the oven and, using the prongs of a fork, mark horizontal lines evenly over the surface.

Place the tin under a hot grill for 2-3 minutes or until the surface is lightly browned. Remove and leave to rest. The sweet will become firm as it cools. When absolutely cold cut the sweet with a sharp knife into 1 X 5cm (½ X 2in) fingers. Store in waxed paper in an airtight tin.

Makes 40-45

tout shirini

mulberry-shaped sweets

A delicious Iranian sweet made with almonds, pistachios and sugar. Extremely attractive, they are very popular with children and also go well with coffee at the end of a meal. To add extra flavour and aroma add a piece of vanilla pod to the airtight container in which you store the sweets.

175g (6 oz) ground almonds
110g (4 oz) icing sugar, sifted
4 tablespoons rosewater
1 tablespoon vanilla essence
175g (6 oz) caster sugar
about 30 slivers of pistachios

Mix the almonds and icing sugar together in a bowl. Add the rosewater and vanilla essence and knead until the mixture holds together. Form into marble-sized balls. Take 1 ball and roll between your palms to lengthen a little to give a mulberry-shape. Repeat with all the remaining balls.

Spread the sugar out on a plate and roll each 'mulberry' in it until well coated. Stick a sliver of pistachio in the end of each to represent a stem. Store in an airtight container.

Makes about 30

sohan asali

almond and honey sweets

'My son, eat thou honey, because it is good; and the honeycomb,
which is sweet to thy taste.'
Proverbs 24-13

Sohan Asali is sold in all the confectionery stores of Iran's hundreds of bazaars, but the most famous ones come from the city of Qom, the home of the famous Ayatollahs. This is one of Iran's most famous sweets and children love them.

50g (2 oz) clarified butter (page 194)
2 tablespoons honey
175g (6 oz) sugar
175g (6 oz) slivered almonds
1 teaspoon powdered saffron dissolved in 2 tablespoons boiling water

Garnish
about 2 tablespoons halved pistachios

Melt the butter in a large saucepan, add the honey and sugar and stir until the sugar dissolves. Add the almonds and cook, stirring occasionally, until the almonds turn golden brown. Add the saffron mixture to the saucepan and mix well. Remove from the heat and set aside for 5 minutes.

Generously grease a 15 X 15cm (6 X 6in) dish. Pour in the mixture and spread evenly. Arrange halved pistachio nuts at 2.5cm (1in) intervals over the surface and then set aside until cold. Cut into 3.5cm (1Ðin) squares with a sharp knife and store in an airtight tin.

About 16 pieces

feqa'min zbib
raisin and almond biscuits

Feqa's are crispy little biscuits – more like titbits. The traditional feqa is a small $\frac{1}{2}$cm ($\frac{1}{4}$in) thick, dry biscuit made of flour, sugar, gum arabic (mastic) and orange blossom water. The recipe below is for feqa with raisins and almonds. Delicious to nibble with tea or coffee.

110g (4 oz) icing sugar
2 eggs
2 tablespoons melted butter
2 tablespoons corn oil
110g (4 oz) ground almonds
1 teaspoon vanilla essence
110g (4 oz) raisins
350g (¾ lb) plain flour, sifted

Sift the icing sugar into a large bowl, add the eggs and whisk until creamy and pale. Add the melted butter and oil and whisk for a further 2-3 minutes. Add the almonds, vanilla and raisins and mix well. Gradually stir in the flour, gather up into a ball and knead for a few minutes until smooth. Divide the dough into 5 balls and place on a lightly floured work top. Lightly flour your palms, take 1 ball and roll it into a sausage about 15-20cm (6-8in) long and 2.5-3.5cm (1-1½in) thick. Repeat with remaining balls.

Place on a lightly greased baking tray and bake in an oven preheated to 180C (350F) gas 4 for 12-15 minutes. Remove before the surface changes colour. Set aside until cold.

When completely cold cut the sausages crossways into thin slices about ½-1cm (¼-½in) thick. Spread the pieces over about 2 large baking trays and cook in an oven preheated to 180C (350F) gas 4 for a further 15-20 minutes or until golden, turning once. Remove and when completely cold store in an airtight tin.

Makes about 80-100 pieces

makroud-el-louze

algerian almond biscuits

These and similar biscuits are popular throughout North Africa. The almond biscuits are dipped in syrup and then rolled in icing sugar. Will keep well and are excellent with tea or coffee.

450g (1 lb) ground almonds
225g (½ lb) sugar
1 tablespoon finely grated lemon rind
2 eggs

Syrup
225g (½ lb) sugar
1 tablespoon lemon juice
1 tablespoon orange blossom water

Garnish
110g (4 oz) icing sugar

Prepare the syrup by boiling the sugar, lemon juice and 600ml (1 pint) water for about 10 minutes or until the syrup forms a slightly sticky film on a spoon. Stir in the orange blossom water and set aside to cool. Place the almonds, sugar and lemon rind in a bowl and mix well. Make a well in the centre, add the eggs and mix until the mixture is smooth and holds together. Divide the dough into 4 balls. Flour a work top and your palms and roll 1 of the balls into a sausage about 22.5cm (9in) long and 2.5cm (1 in) in diameter. Flatten the sausage slightly until it forms a 3.5cm (1½in) wide oblong. Cut the oblong diagonally into 3.5cm (1½in) pieces. Arrange on an ungreased baking tray. Repeat with the remaining balls of dough.

Bake in an oven preheated to 180C (350F) gas 4 for 15-20 minutes or until the biscuits are just beginning to change colour. Remove and leave to cool. When cool dip each biscuit into the syrup, remove with a slotted spoon and then drop into a bowl containing the icing sugar. Toss to coat generously and arrange on a large plate. Shake any remaining icing sugar generously over the biscuits. Store when completely cold.

Makes 20-24

Along with the almond, sesame (*Sesamum Indicum*) from the family of *Pedaliaceae* is widely used in Middle Eastern cooking in general and desserts in particular. The use of its seeds and the oil extracted from it are of ancient vintage. Indeed the ancient Egyptians were well versed in it. They prepared breads, sauces and soups with it. In ancient Mesopotamia sesame was of such importance in the daily diet of the people that King Hammurabi in his *Code**, before 2000BC, had passed the following laws: 'if a man has received silver from a trader, and has given to the trader a cornfield or a sesame field saying "I shall plant the field with corn or sesame; take and reap whatever there is", then when the cultivator has grown corn or sesame, whatever is upon

The Hammurabi Code. Chilperic Edwards. Watts and Co 1904

the field at the harvest; he shall give to the trader corn for the silver he has received from the trader – if an already planted field, or a field already planted with sesame, has been given; the lord of the field shall take the corn or sesame which is in the field and he shall render silver and interest to the trader. If he has not silver to pay back, he shall give to the trader sesame according to the value of the silver he has received.' Acts 49-52

I have selected a few recipes where sesame seeds and tahina (sesame cream) are used.

ma'akaroneh

arab sesame-aniseed biscuits

These are Lebanese biscuits with a wonderful aroma emanating from the mixture of mahleb and aniseed. Ideal at any time, but I particularly like them for breakfast with cheese.

225g (8 oz) plain flour
1 teaspoon baking powder
50g (2 oz) sugar
50g (2 oz) sesame seeds
2 teaspoons ground mahleb
2 teaspoons ground aniseed
120ml (4 fl oz) vegetable oil

Sift the flour and baking powder into a large bowl and stir in the sugar, sesame seeds, mahleb and aniseed. Add the vegetable oil and rub in with your fingers until the mixture is crumbly. Now add 2-3 tablespoons cold water and mix to form a soft dough – add just a little more water if necessary. Knead for a few minutes until smooth.

Lightly flour a work top and roll the dough out to a ½cm (¼in) thickness. Cut out as many rounds as possible using a 5cm (2in) pastry cutter. Place on lightly greased baking trays at 2.5cm (1in) intervals. Bake in an oven preheated to 180C (350F) gas 4 for about 20 minutes or until golden. Cool on wire racks and store when cold.

Makes about 20

shoushmayov hatsig

sesame sticks

Simple bread sticks that are usually eaten at teatime with cheese or jam. I have to admit that I like to 'dunk' mine! Will keep for a long time in an airtight container.

15g (½ oz) fresh yeast or 8g (¼ oz) dried yeast
1 teaspoon sugar
75g (3 oz) lard
25g (1 oz) butter
120ml (4 fl oz) milk
450g (1 lb) plain flour, sifted
3 tablespoons sugar
1 teaspoon salt

Topping
1 egg, beaten
50g (2 oz) sesame seeds

Place the yeast in a small bowl with the sugar and 120ml (4 fl oz) warm water, stir to dissolve and set aside in a warm place until it begins to froth. Place the lard and butter in a small saucepan and set over a low heat to melt. Add the milk and heat until lukewarm. Pour the mixture into a large bowl. Add the yeast and gradually stir in the flour, sugar and salt. Gather into a ball and knead for 5-10 minutes or until the dough is smooth and elastic. Place in a clean bowl, cover with a tea towel and set aside in a warm place for 1-2 hours or until the dough has doubled in size.

Divide the dough in half and roll one part out on a floured work top to form a rectangle about 30 X 20cm (12 X 8in) and about 3mm (⅛in) thick. Brush the surface with egg, sprinkle evenly with half the sesame seeds and brush again with egg. Cut the dough into 1cm (½in) strips and each strip into 10cm (4in) pieces. Place on ungreased baking trays and set aside in a warm place while you prepare the remaining ball of dough in the same way.

Bake in an oven preheated at 180C (350F) gas 4 for 20-30 minutes or until golden. When all are cooked pile on to 1 baking tray, turn off the heat and return the tray to the oven. Leave until cold. The bread sticks will then be very crisp.

Makes about 70-80

tahinov hatz

sesame-cream cakes

Tahina/tahini is made from toasted sesame seeds. It is a must in the Armenian, Syrian-Lebanese and, in recent years, Israeli cuisines. It can be bought from most Indian, Middle Eastern and health food shops.

I have given two versions of this famed cake, one Armenian and the other Greek. This cake is traditionally prepared during the 40 days of Christian Orthodox Lent since it contains no animal products. Both versions will keep for a long time. They should be fairly sweet, but the sugar content can be varied according to taste. I, for example, like my Hatz very sweet.

15g (½ oz) fresh yeast or 8g (¼ oz) dried yeast
½ teaspoon sugar
225g (8 oz) plain flour
½ teaspoon salt

120ml (4 fl oz) vegetable oil

Filling
about 200ml (¹/₃ pint) tahina
sugar
ground cinnamon

Place the yeast and sugar in a small bowl with 180ml (6 fl oz) warm water, stir to dissolve and then set aside in a warm place until it begins to froth. Sift the flour and salt into a large bowl, make a well in the centre and pour in the yeast and the cooking oil. Mix together, gather up into a ball and knead for 5-10 minutes until the dough is smooth and elastic. Place in a clean bowl, cover with a tea towel and leave in a warm place until the dough has doubled in size. Pour some tahina into a bowl and stir until it is smooth.

Divide the dough into 6 balls. Lightly flour a work top and roll 1 ball out into a circle about 3mm (¹/₈in) thick. Spread 1 tablespoon of the tahina over the circle of dough and then sprinkle 1-2 tablespoons sugar over the top. Vary the sugar according to taste. Now sprinkle a pinch of cinnamon over the sugar.

Roll the circle up into a sausage, grasp it in your hands and squeeze gently. This closes the sausage and doubles its length. Cut the sausage in half. With each piece, fold the ends over the middle – one slightly overlapping the other. Press the cake down gently to secure the ends and flatten slightly. Repeat with the remaining balls of dough. Arrange on lightly greased baking trays. Bake in an oven preheated to 200C (400F) gas 6 for about 30 minutes or until golden. Cool on wire racks.

Makes 12

tahinopita

tahina cake

This cake includes tahina, orange juice, sultanas and nuts. Some Greek housewives substitute the tahina with peanut butter – a nasty habit!

200ml (¹/₃ pint) tahina
200g (7 oz) caster sugar
grated rind of 1 orange
150ml (¹/₄ pint) strained fresh orange juice
350g (12 oz) plain flour
¼ teaspoon salt
3 teaspoons baking powder
½ teaspoon bicarbonate soda
½ teaspoon mixed spice
75g (3 oz) finely chopped walnuts, almond or hazelnuts
75g (3 oz) sultanas

Place the tahina, sugar and orange rind in a large bowl and whisk until well blended. Add the orange juice and whisk thoroughly for 2-3 minutes. Sift the flour, salt, baking powder, soda and mixed spice into the bowl and fold thoroughly into the tahina mixture. Stir in the nuts and sultanas.

Grease a tin 20 X 25cm (8 X 10in), pour in the cake mixture and spread evenly, smoothing off the top with the back of a spoon. Bake in an oven preheated to 180C (350F) gas 4 for 40-45 minutes. Turn on to a cake rack and leave for 5 minutes before removing the tin. When cold cut into 2.5-3.5(1-1½in) pieces.

Makes about 40 pieces

tahina im egozim

tahina nut balls

An Israeli speciality which is related to Tahinov hatz (page 183).

Dough
350g (12 oz) plain flour
¼ teaspoon salt
110g (4 oz) margarine
50g (2 oz) sugar

Filling
110g (4 oz) walnuts, crushed
2 tablespoons finely chopped dates
½ teaspoon ground cinnamon
1½ tablespoons sugar
3 tablespoons tahina

Topping
1 egg, beaten
sesame seeds

Sift the flour and salt into a large bowl, add the margarine and rub it in with your fingertips until the mixture resembles fine breadcrumbs. Stir in the sugar. Add just enough cold water to mix to a soft dough. Gather up, transfer to a lightly floured work top and knead for a few minutes until soft and pliable. Prepare the filling by mixing all the ingredients together in a bowl. Roll out the dough until 3mm-½cm (⅛-¼in) thick. Cut into 7.5cm (3in) squares or circles.

Place a large teaspoon of the filling on each piece of dough and fold as follows: if cut into circles either draw the edges together and roll into balls, or fold the pastry over to form semi-circles and seal the edges with a fork; if the pastry is cut into squares then fold over to form rectangles and seal with a fork. Place on lightly greased baking trays, brush with the egg and sprinkle with sesame seeds. Bake in an oven preheated to 180C (350F) gas 4 for 30-40 minutes or until golden. Cool on racks before serving with tea or coffee.

Makes about 20

I cannot leave these recipes dealing with sesame seed-cream without
re-telling the amusingly tragic story of Kasim, 'the unworthy' brother of
Ali-Baba of the famed 'Ali-Baba and the forty thieves' from that magnificent
encyclopedia of medieval Middle Eastern customs, beliefs and dreams –
the *1001 Nights*. Kasim 'was stunned and dazzled by the sight of the bright
gold and the colours of the winking jewels; his desire to be the sole master
of these fabulous treasures increased and fastened to his heart; also he calculated
that he would need not one caravan of camels to empty the hoard but all the
camels which ply ceaselessly between the frontiers of India and Iraq. In the meantime
he contented himself with filling as many sacks as he thought his ten mules could carry
in the chests upon their backs. When the work was completed, he returned to
the gallery and cried "Open Barley!"

*'The wretched Kasim, unbalanced by the sight of so much gold, had forgotten the necessary
word. He shouted again and again: "Open Barley! Open Barley!" but the rock remained
impenetrable.*

'Then he cried "Open Oats!" But the rock remained impenetrable.

'Then he cried "Open Beans!" But the rock remained impenetrable.

*'Kasim lost patience and began to shout at the top of his voice
"Open Rye! Open Millet! Open Chickpea! Open Maize! Open Buckwheat! Open Corn! Open
Rice! Open Vetch!" But the rock remained impenetrable.*

*'Kasim stood shaking with terror before the cruel door and muttered over the names of every
cereal and seed which the hand of the Sower had cast upon the fields since the birth of time.
But the rock remained impenetrable.*

*'Ali-Baba's unworthy brother forgot one name, one magic name, Sesame,
that wonder-working word!'*
(from *The 854th Night*)

The coconut, on the other hand, makes only rare appearances in the Middle Eastern
cuisines and then usually in those of Iran and the Gulf States. There is nothing unusual
in this. Iran and the Gulf region have had longstanding cultural and trade intercourse
with the Indian subcontinent and, as the following recipes show, there are some
interesting coconut-based desserts worthy of note. A particularly good example is
the next one which is from the Caucasus. It is for finger-shaped biscuits of coconut
and pistachios coated with spiced icing sugar.

shakar madig

coconut and pistachio fingers

225g (8 oz) unsalted butter
110g (4 oz) caster sugar
2 egg yolks
1 teaspoon vanilla essence
½ teaspoon almond essence
1 teaspoon ground cinnamon
½ teaspoon ground cloves
½ teaspoon baking powder
½ teaspoon salt
225g (8 oz) plain flour
150g (5 oz) desiccated coconut
150g (5 oz) finely chopped pistachio nuts

Topping
50g (2 oz) sifted icing sugar mixed in a bowl with ½ teaspoon ground cinnamon,
½ teaspoon ground cloves and ¼ teaspoon ground cardamom

Place the butter in a large bowl and beat until pale and creamy. Beat in the sugar and egg yolks. Now add the vanilla and almond essences, cinnamon, cloves, baking powder and salt and mix thoroughly. Sift in the flour, add the coconut and nuts and mix thoroughly. Knead for several minutes until the mixture holds together and is easy to shape.

Flour a work top and divide the dough into 4 portions. Taking 1 portion at a time roll it into a sausage about 2.5cm (1in) in diameter. Cut the sausage into 5cm (2in) long pieces and arrange on greased baking trays. Repeat with the remaining portions of dough. Bake in an oven preheated to 180C (350F) gas 4 for 15-20 minutes. Do not allow the fingers to brown. Remove, toss one at a time in the spiced icing sugar and cool on wire racks. When cold sprinkle any remaining spiced sugar over the fingers and store in an airtight tin.

Makes about 40

loze-nargil

iranian coconut sweets

This sweet is sold all over Iran in small kiosks and is therefore seldom made at home. It is very similar to 'coconut ice'. Extremely quick and easy to prepare.

225g (8 oz) sugar
225g (8 oz) desiccated coconut
3 tablespoons chopped pistachio nuts

Generously grease a dish about 15 x 15cm (6 X 6in). Place the sugar and 180ml (6 fl oz) water in a saucepan and bring to the boil, stirring constantly until the sugar dissolves. Remove from the heat and stir in the coconut. Quickly pour the mixture into the greased tin, spreading it out evenly. Sprinkle the nuts evenly over the surface and press gently into the coconut mixture. Set aside to cool and when cold cut into small squares or lozenge shapes. Best eaten within a few days.

Makes about 20-24 pieces

hindistan cevizli biskuit

turkish coconut biscuits

A simple and tasty biscuit from Turkey.

2 egg whites
110g (4 oz) caster sugar
175g (6 oz) desiccated coconut
1 teaspoon baking powder
3 tablespoons white breadcrumbs
1 teaspoon lemon essence
2 tablespoons finely chopped pistachio nuts

Whisk the egg whites until stiff. Add the sugar and continue to whisk until the whites are glossy and stand in peaks. Add the remaining ingredients and mix in thoroughly with a metal spoon.

Drop dessertspoonfuls of the mixture on to greased baking trays about 2.5cm (1in) apart. Bake in an oven preheated to 120C (250F) gas ½ for 20-30 minutes or until a light golden colour. Remove and cool on the trays. Will keep in an airtight tin for several days.

Makes about 18-20

armavov katah

date and walnut cakes

There are many similar cakes made of dates, nuts and spices to be found all over the region. A typical example is this Armenian speciality which is a family recipe. Keeps well in an airtight tin.

Filling
50g (2 oz) butter
225g (8 oz) stoned dates, finely chopped
4 tablespoons milk

110g (4 oz) chopped walnuts
2 tablespoons rosewater
1½-2 teaspoons ground cinnamon

Dough
225g (8 oz) butter
50g (2 oz) sugar
1 egg, beaten
120ml (4 fl oz) milk
½ teaspoon vanilla essence
350g (12 oz) plain flour
2 teaspoons baking powder

Glaze
1 egg, beaten

First prepare the filling. Melt the butter in a saucepan, add the dates and cook gently. Add the milk and continue cooking until the dates form a soft pulp. Remove from the heat, stir in the remaining ingredients and set aside.

To make the dough beat the butter and sugar together in a large bowl until soft and creamy. Thoroughly stir in the egg, milk and vanilla essence. Sift the flour and baking powder together and then add, a little at a time, to the butter mixture, beating constantly until it is all well blended and a soft dough has formed. If the dough is a little sticky then knead in a little more flour. Now divide the filling into 6 and roll each out into a sausage.

Divide the dough into 2 balls. Lightly flour a work top and roll out 1 ball into a circle about 3mm (⅛in) thick. Place 1 date sausage over the dough near the edge of the circle closest to you.

Roll over twice and then cut from the remaining pastry so that you have a pastry sausage filled with the date mixture. Place another date roll along the cut edge and roll up to form another sausage. Cut from the remaining pastry and then place another date sausage along the cut edge and then roll up to form yet another sausage. Repeat with the remaining ball of dough and date sausages.

Slice each sausage into 2.5-3.5cm (1-1½in) pieces. Place 2.5cm (1in) apart on greased baking trays and brush with beaten egg. Bake in an oven preheated to 180C (350F) gas 4 for about 20-30 minutes or until golden. Cool on wire racks and store when cold.

Makes about 36

Klaicha is an Iraqi version of Armavov Katah. The filling is made up of
225g (8 oz) chopped dates fried in 50g (2 oz) butter until soft. The dough is
made by rubbing 225g (8 oz) butter into 350g (12 oz) flour and 50g (2 oz) sugar, stirring
in 2 tablespoons rosewater and kneading to a firm dough with just enough cold water.
Dough is broken into walnut-sized balls and flattened in the palm. A teaspoon of filling
is placed in the centre and the dough is moulded around it into a ball. Traditionally the
ball is pressed into especially carved moulds called *tabi*. Alternatively you can place
the ball on a greased baking tray, flatten it slightly with your palm and then pattern it
with the prongs of a fork. Cook as for Armavov Katah.

Kalampeh, an Iranian version, has a spicy date filling. The dough is prepared as for Klaicha. The filling is 175g (6 oz) coarsely chopped dates mixed with 75g (3 oz) chopped walnuts or pistachios, ¼ teaspoon each of ground cloves, nutmeg and cardamom. Break the dough into walnut-sized balls, press an index finger into the dough to make a hole and fill with some of the date mixture. Roll back into a ball and cook as above.

rahat lokum

turkish delight

The finest lokum comes from Istanbul, Turkey. The undisputed master of this sweet is a family-run business, established for over 200 years, called Hadji Bakir. Nothing beats the lokum of this establishment and the recipe below is in no way trying to equal or indeed do justice to this most famed (and perhaps most genuine) Turkish delicacy. For hundreds of years, ladies of the Orient indulged themselves with Rahat Lokum while passing their narrow, brief and languorous lives behind laced curtains in thickly carpeted cells.

1 teaspoon butter
450g (1 lb) sugar
1 teaspoon lemon juice
25g (1 oz) gelatine dissolved in 120ml (4 fl oz) hot water
½ teaspoon vanilla essence
1 tablespoon rosewater
3 drops food colouring, e.g. red, gold or yellow
1 tablespoon pistachio nuts, halved
50g (2 oz) icing sugar
25g (1 oz) cornflour

Grease a baking tin about 15 X 15cm (6 X 6in) with the butter and set aside. Put the sugar, lemon juice and 300ml (½ pint) water in a saucepan and bring to the boil. Continue to boil until the temperature reaches 121C (250F) on a sugar thermometer. If you do not have a thermometer, drop a little of the syrup into a bowl of cold water. If it has reached the required temperature it will form a hard ball. Remove the pan from the heat and leave for 10 minutes.

Stir in the dissolved gelatine and vanilla essence and beat with a wooden spoon until the mixture is well blended. Pour half the mixture into the baking tin. Stir the rosewater and colouring into the remaining mixture and stir well. Sprinkle the halved nuts over the mixture in the tin. Pour the remaining mixture into the tin and set aside in a cool place overnight.

Sift the icing sugar and cornflour on to a large plate. Turn the lokum out on to a clean board and cut into 2.5cm (1in) cubes. Toss the cubes in the sugar mixture and make sure they are thoroughly coated. Shake off excess sugar. Either wrap individually in waxed paper or store in an airtight container.

Makes about 30 pieces

Rahat Lokum comes in many colours, mixtures and flavours.

a) **Plain** – as the recipe above, but omit the food colouring and nuts.
b) **With nuts** – as recipe above or replace the pistachio nuts with almonds, walnuts, hazelnuts etc.
c) **Strawberry or mulberry** – cook the fruit in its own juice until soft, strain off the liquid, mash the pulp and incorporate into the lokum mixture. Omit colouring and nuts.
d) **With chocolate** – prepare as for plain lokum (a) and then dip each piece in melted chocolate and leave to dry on greaseproof paper.
e) **With coconut** – roll the cubes in desiccated coconut immediately after they have been cut.
f) **Orange lokum** – omit the vanilla and rosewater and add 2-3 tablespoons of orange blossom water and orange food colouring.
g) **Vanilla lokum** – omit the rosewater, colouring and pistachios and add 2 teaspoons vanilla essence and 3-4 tablespoons chopped toasted almonds.
h) A very popular lokum makes use of crème de menthe. Omit the rosewater and nuts and add 3 tablespoons crème de menthe and green food colouring.

As you can see the list is almost endless. You can create your own Turkish Delight by adding different nuts, essences and fruit mixtures.

nane shirini

shiraz biscuits

There are few sweets incorporating cocoa and chocolate, as both are recent arrivals to the area – as recent as 400 years! Obviously taste patterns change ultra-slowly in the Middle East. This recipe from Iran is popular in the region of Shiraz. Delicious biscuits flavoured with cocoa and lemon.

175g (6 oz) clarified butter (page 194)
175g (6 oz) caster sugar
1 egg yolk
1 teaspoon grated lemon rind
225g (8 oz) plain flour
2 tablespoons cocoa powder

Topping
1 egg white, beaten
2-3 tablespoons finely chopped pistachio nuts

Place the butter in a large bowl and beat until creamy. Add the sugar and continue to beat until well blended. Stir in the egg yolk and lemon rind. Sift in the flour and cocoa and knead until the mixture holds together in a ball. Refrigerate for 1 hour.

Lightly flour a work top and divide the dough into 2 portions. Roll 1 portion out until ½cm

(¹/₄in) thick. Cut out as many 5cm (2in) circles as possible using a decorative pastry cutter. Place on lightly greased baking trays. Repeat with the remaining dough. Brush the top of each with the beaten egg white and sprinkle with nuts. Bake in an oven preheated to 180C (350F) gas 4 for about 15 minutes. Cool on wire racks and store when cold.

Makes about 26-28

clarified butter

Middle Eastern housewives use clarified butter when making pastries, as well as sometimes when frying vegetables. Butter treated in this way does not burn at high temperatures. It is cleaner and, some say, healthier. You can buy a type of clarified butter in the shops – it is called 'ghee' and should be available at most Middle Eastern and Indian specialist stores.

900g (2 lb) butter

Melt the butter in a saucepan over a low heat. Skim off the foam with a spoon as it rises to the surface. Remove the pan from the heat and set aside for 5 minutes. Skim off any foam which still rises to the surface. Now spoon the clear butter into a bowl and discard the residue at the bottom of the pan. Refrigerate the butter until hard.

Makes about 675g (1½ lb)

ice creams and sorbets

Mid-summer, the air is still, stifling, streets and alleyways desolate; fugitive cats and dogs grovel in the dark of cellars, donkeys and mules quietly nod at street corners. Mid-summer, I, my brother and numerous cousins are out promenading down the cobbled street in search of a Dondur *maji* (ice cream shop). The famed Effendi emporium – restaurant, café, ice cream parlour and doner kebab take-out – was too expensive for us kids so we marched on to Ahmeds on the corner of Hart-Sisi. A small, dark shop with the shades down, some delapidated fridges and Ahmed – a tall, moustachioed man in his thirties, all smiles. '*Marhaba ya Shal Soujaqhan*' – Welcome brave lions. I stood, mouth agape, staring at the snow-white carcasses hanging from the ceiling.

'That's dondurma' someone whispered.

'But it's so hot yet it's not melting,' I protested.

'That's Ahmed's special ice cream.'

'Indeed' Ahmed joined in 'the greatest ice cream in the world.'

He was right. Dondurma Kaymakli is truely the great ice cream of the East. The secret (I found years later) is mastic – gum arabic – which acts as the glueing agent and hardens it. This is one ice cream I strongly recommend.

There is a great deal of nonsense written by people who should know better about the origin of ice cream. Anything whose source cannot be traced to Europe is immediately attributed to China. Thus, according to some, China is where one should turn for the origins of this dairy food. Others more subtly create a European connection – namely our dear friend the ubiquitous Marco Polo who, one way or the other, becomes the inventor or propagator of all things non-European. Nonsense! Before Marco Polo ever existed the Romans are known to have iced their wine and fruit juices and no doubt before them the Hitittes, ancient Egyptians and most certainly the Sumerians and Babylonians brought ice down from the hills to cool their thirst and they probably added fruit and fruit juices to it. Now, enough of Marco Polo!

Caliph Al-Mansur (10th century), while on a pilgrimage to Mecca ordered a huge caravan of camels to bring snow from the Zagros Mountains of Persia so he could drink cold sherbet flavoured with mulberry and orange juice. The Mughal Emperors (15th century) sent relays of horsemen to bring ice and snow back from the Hindu Kush to Delhi to make fruit-flavoured sherbets.

The word 'sorbet' comes from old Persian *sharbat* and ice cream as we understand it today made of cream or butterfat, milk, non-fat milk solids, sugar, flavouring and sometimes eggs was invented by a Paris café owner, a monsieur Tortoni, around 1786.

dondurma kaymakli

mastic ice cream

1 teaspoon powdered sahleb or 1½ tablespoons cornflour
900ml (1½ pints) milk
300ml (½ pint) single cream
225g (½ lb) sugar
1 teaspoon powdered mastic
1 tablespoon orange blossom water

Garnish
chopped nuts of your choice

Place the sahleb or cornflour in a small bowl, add a little of the cold milk and stir to dissolve. Pour the remaining milk, cream and sugar into a saucepan, place over a low heat and stir until the sugar dissolves. Bring to the boil. Pour a little of the hot milk into the sahleb or cornflour mixture, stir well and then pour back into the saucepan. Add the mastic and cook over a low heat, stirring constantly until the mixture thickens. Remove from the heat and stir in the orange blossom water.

Set aside to cool, beating frequently with a wooden spoon. Pour into a freezing tray and freeze for 2-3 hours. Remove, scoop the contents into a bowl and beat lightly. Return to the tray, smooth over the surface and re-freeze. Remove from the freezer 10-15 minutes before serving. Turn on to a dish and sprinkle with nuts of your choice.

Serves 6-8

funduk dondurmasi

hazelnut ice cream

A popular ice cream from Turkey and the Caucasus. Instead of hazelnuts you can use walnuts or almonds. Decorate with left-over nuts before serving.

4 egg yolks, lightly beaten
225g (½ lb) sugar
450g (1 lb) shelled hazelnuts
600ml (1 pint) milk
2 tablespoons orange blossom water

Place the egg yolks in a small saucepan, stir in half the sugar and cook over a low heat, stirring constantly until the sugar dissolves. Place in a refrigerator to cool. Grind three-quarters of the nuts. Bring the milk to the boil in a saucepan. Add the remaining sugar, the ground nuts and the

egg mixture. Reduce the heat to very low and cook until the mixture thickens a little, stirring constantly. Remove from the heat, stir in the orange blossom water and set aside to cool. Pour into a freezer tray and freeze for 2-3 hours.

Remove from the freezer, scoop into a bowl and beat lightly. Return to the tray, smooth over the surface and re-freeze. Transfer to a refrigerator about 30 minutes before serving. Turn on to a plate, decorate with the remaining whole nuts and serve.

Serves 4-6

gerasi baghbaghag
cherry ice cream

Fresh black cherries make a wonderful ice cream which leaves a tang on your lips.

600ml (1 pint) milk
300ml (½ pint) single cream
225g (½ lb) sugar
110g (4 oz) fresh black cherries, halved and stoned
thinly peeled rind of 1 lemon
1 teaspoon vanilla essence

Place the milk, cream and sugar in a saucepan and cook over a low heat until the sugar has dissolved, stirring constantly. Bring to the boil. Add the cherries, lemon rind and vanilla essence and cook over a low heat for about 10 minutes, stirring frequently. Remove from the heat and leave to cool, stirring frequently. Pour into a freezing tray and freeze for 2-3 hours. Remove, scoop into a bowl, beat lightly, return to the tray and return to the freezer. Repeat at least once. Place in a refrigerator 30 minutes before serving – this will soften it slightly.

Serves 4-6

şeftali dondurmasi
peach ice cream

Peach ice cream is delicious – as are ice creams flavoured with pears and quinces. Use the proportions below to make the ice cream of your choice. This particular ice cream is very popular in southern Turkey.

1 tablespoon powdered gelatine
175g (6 oz) sugar
5 fresh peaches
3 tablespoons lemon juice

1 tablespoon finely chopped pistachio nuts

Put the gelatine to soften in a small bowl with 4-5 tablespoons water taken from 350ml (12 fl oz). Place the remaining water in a small saucepan and bring to the boil. Add the sugar and continue to simmer for about 5 minutes. Remove from the heat, stir in the gelatine mixture until it dissolves and set aside to cool.

Blanch, peel and slice the peaches. Purée the flesh in a blender. Add the purée to the sugar mixture, together with the lemon juice and mix thoroughly. Transfer to a freezing tray and freeze for 2-3 hours. Remove, spoon into a bowl, beat lightly and then pour back into the tray. Return to the freezer for a further 2-3 hours and then remove and beat again. Repeat this process once more and then freeze until hard.

Place in the refrigerator 30 minutes before serving to soften a little. Turn on to a plate or spoon into dishes and serve sprinkled with the pistachio nuts.

Serves 4-6

dondurma mish-mish

apricot ice cream

A favourite of Damascus, this is a delicious ice cream.

1 teaspoon sahleb or 1½ tablespoons cornflour
600ml (1 pint) milk
225g (½ lb) fresh apricots, blanched, peeled, stoned and sliced or
225g (½ lb) dried apricots, soaked overnight in cold water
300ml (½ pint) single cream
150g (5 oz) sugar
2 teaspoons rosewater

Garnish
2 tablespoons finely chopped almonds

Dissolve the sahleb or cornflour in a little of the cold milk and set aside. Reduce the apricots to a purée in a blender, adding a little water if necessary. Pour the remaining milk into a saucepan with the cream and sugar and place over a low heat, stirring constantly until the sugar dissolves. Bring slowly to the boil. Add the puréed apricots and the sahleb or cornflour mixture. Cook over a low heat, stirring constantly until the mixture thickens. Remove from the heat, add the rosewater and beat thoroughly with a wooden spoon.

Leave to cool and then pour into a freezer tray and freeze. After 2-3 hours remove the tray, spoon the ice cream into a large bowl and beat lightly. Return to the tray and freeze until hard.

30 minutes before serving place the tray in the refrigerator. Serve the ice cream garnished with the chopped nuts and with fresh apricot slices if you have them.

Serves 4-6

'A glimpse of an everyday holiday at Ras-al-Bar on the Nile where children's thoughts turn to ice cream, the wife's to the continuity of a husband's affections and the husband's to 'pastures green' with white thigh!

'"Daddy – food – Mummy – ice cream!"

'Izzat turned round in search of the waiter. His gaze became riveted on the Casino entrance and he smiled, turning down his thick lower lip. His hand stretched out automatically and undid another of the buttons of his white shirt revealing a wider expanse of thick hair on his chest. The table behind Amal was taken over by a woman of about thirty who was wearing shorts that exposed her white, rounded thighs while her dyed blonde hair was tied around with a red georgette handkerchief decorated with white jasmine.

'Izzat clapped his hands energetically for the waiter who was actually close enough to have come at a mere sign. "Three – three ice creams."

'Amal was horrified at her husband's sudden extravagance. "Two's enough Izzat," she whispered, her face flushed. "I don't really want one."

'Izzat gave no sign of having heard her. He kept repeating "Three ices – ice creams – mixed – got it?" in an excited voice.

'Amal pursed her lips derisively. She and Izzat together, at last, really on holiday at a hotel in Ras-al-Bar! A fortnight without cooking or washing or polishing – she noticed Izzat's dark brown hand with its swollen veins and she was swept by an ungovernable longing to bend over and kiss it. The tears welled up in her eyes and she drew Midhat close to her with fumbling hands and covered him with kisses from cheek to cheek.

'"Three ice creams, two mixed and one vanilla."

'"I'll look after the vanilla old chap. Vanilla will do me fine," said Izzat, carefully enunciating his words and giving a significant smile in the direction of – which direction? A suggestive female laugh came back in reply. In reply to the smile? Amal cupped the iced glass in her hands and turned round as she watched him. White – vanilla – strawberry – pistachio – and the yellow ice? Would it be mango or apricot? Colouring, mere colouring? It can't be – it can't be. "Why don't you eat it?" asked Izzat.

'A second laugh rang out behind Amal. Her hands tightened around the iced glass from which cold, icy steam was rising like smoke. She raised her eyes and reluctantly turned her head without moving her shoulders, slowly lest someone see her, afraid of what she might see. She saw her, white as a wall, a candle, white as vanilla ice.'
The Picture by Latifa-el-Zayat. Modern Arabic short stories

dondurma-bil-moz

banana ice cream

An absolutely delightful Lebanese speciality.

1 teaspoon sahleb or 1½ tablespoons cornflour
600ml (1 pint) milk
300ml (½ pint) single cream
150g (5 oz) sugar
3 fairly ripe bananas
1 tablespoon orange blossom water
3 tablespoons coarsely chopped pistachio nuts
2 tablespoons sultanas

Place the sahleb or cornflour in a small bowl, stir in enough of the cold milk to dissolve and then set aside. Put the remaining milk in a saucepan with the cream and sugar and cook over a low heat, stirring constantly until the sugar dissolves. Bring to the boil and simmer over a low heat for 5 minutes.

Meanwhile peel the bananas and mash in a bowl until they form a purée. Stir a few tablespoons of the hot milk into the sahleb or cornflour mixture and stir back into the milk. Add the banana purée, orange blossom water, pistachio nuts and sultanas. Cook over a low heat, stirring constantly until the mixture thickens. Remove from the heat, beat thoroughly and leave to cool.

Pour into a freezing tray and freeze for 2-3 hours. Remove, scoop the ice cream into a bowl, beat lightly, return to the tray and freeze until hard. Place in the refrigerator 30 minutes before serving to soften slightly.

Serves 6-8

seghi baghbaghag

melon ice cream

An Armenian recipe. Melon ice cream is simply delicious and easy to prepare.

1 small ripe melon, e.g. ogen or honeydew
75g (3 oz) caster sugar
2 egg yolks, beaten until light and creamy
1 tablespoon orange blossom water
300ml (½ pint) double cream, lightly whipped

Garnish
2 tablespoons finely chopped pistachio nuts

Cut the melon in half and remove and discard the seeds. Remove the pulp and cut into 2.5cm (1 in) pieces. Place in a saucepan with the sugar and cook over a low heat, stirring very frequently until the sugar has dissolved and the flesh is reduced to a pulp. Stir in the beaten eggs and cook over a very low heat for a few minutes, stirring frequently. Pour the mixture into a bowl and leave to cool. Stir in the lemon juice, orange blossom water and whipped cream and chill for 1 hour. Transfer to a freezing tray and freeze for 2-3 hours. Remove, scoop the ice cream into a bowl and beat lightly. Return to the tray and re-freeze. Repeat this process once more and then freeze until hard.

Place in the refrigerator 30 minutes before serving to soften a little. Serve sprinkled with the pistachio nuts.

Serves 6

glidat egosim
pistachio ice cream

An Israeli recipe. Chef Roger Dabasque has created scores of new Israeli dishes and I think this is one of the finest.

3 eggs, separated
6 dessertspoons sugar
pinch of salt
300ml (½ pint) double or whipping cream
110g (4 oz) unsalted, shelled pistachio nuts, finely chopped
few drops of green food colouring

Place the egg yolks in a bowl with half the sugar and beat thoroughly. Add the salt, place the bowl over a pan of simmering water and cook, stirring constantly until the sugar dissolves and the mixture reaches a toffee consistency. Place in the refrigerator to cool.

Beat the egg whites in a bowl until stiff and then fold in the remaining sugar. Whip the cream in another bowl until stiff. Place the egg yolk mixture in a large bowl and then fold in the egg whites, cream, three-quarters of the nuts and just enough food colouring to give a pale green appearance. Sprinkle the remaining nuts over the bottom of a large freezing tray and pour in the mixture. Smooth over the surface and freeze. Place in a refrigerator 30 minutes before serving to soften a little.

Serves 6-8

paludeh

mulberry sorbet

The best sorbets that I know are made in Iran where they have deep historic traditions of sorbet making. This translucent sorbet has large crystals sparkling in it and is usually served with a fruit syrup poured over the top. Mulberries are a favourite choice in Iran, but you can use any fruit or syrup of your choice, such as strawberries or raspberries.

Sorbet
1 tablespoon powdered gelatine
275g (10 oz) sugar
2 tablespoons sultanas
1 tablespoon rosewater
2 tablespoons finely chopped pistachio nuts

Topping
90-120ml (3-4 fl oz) mulberry syrup or 225g (8 oz) mulberries mashed
with sugar to taste

Put the gelatine in a small bowl with 4-5 tablespoons water taken from 1 litre (1³/₄ pints), to soften for 5 minutes. Meanwhile bring the remaining water to the boil in a saucepan. Add the sugar and simmer for 5 minutes, stirring constantly until the sugar dissolves. Remove the pan from the heat, add the softened gelatine and continue to stir until it dissolves. Stir in the sultanas, rosewater and pistachio nuts. Pour the mixture into a freezing tray and set aside to cool. When cold place in the freezer for 2-3 hours. Remove and spoon the mixture into a bowl. Stir lightly to distribute the sultanas and nuts, return to the tray and freeze until solid. When ready to serve spoon the sorbet into individual dishes and pour a little syrup or mashed fruit over the top.

Serves 6-8

madznov sherbet

yoghurt sorbet

An Armenian favourite, yoghurt sorbet can be made with a variety of fruits the most popular ones being mulberries, strawberries and raspberries. This sorbet has a unique flavour and makes an ideal dessert.

225g (½ lb) strawberries, raspberries or mulberries
110g (4 oz) caster sugar
300ml (½ pint) yoghurt
1 tablespoon lemon juice
15g (½ oz) powdered gelatine
2 egg whites

Liquidise the fruit in a blender, pass through a sieve, discarding the seeds, and collect the pulp in a bowl. Add the sugar, yoghurt and lemon juice and mix well. Place the gelatine in a small bowl, add 5-6 tablespoons of water and set aside for a few minutes to soften. Place the bowl in a pan of hot water and stir until the gelatine has dissolved. Add to the yoghurt mixture and stir well.

Place the egg whites in a bowl and whisk until stiff. Fold into the yoghurt mixture and pour into a freezing tray. Place in a freezer for 2-3 hours. Remove, spoon into a bowl and beat lightly with a fork. Return to the tray and freeze until hard. Place in the refrigerator 30 minutes before serving to soften a little.

Serves 4-6

teyi baghbaghag

tea ice cream

A Caucasian favourite also very popular in Russia. A delicious, delicately flavoured ice cream. Use an aromatic tea such as jasmine.

3 teaspoons scented tea, e.g. jasmine
4 egg yolks
600ml (1 pint) milk
175g (6 oz) sugar

Place the tea in a small bowl, pour 120ml (4 fl oz) boiling water over it, cover and set aside to cool. Meanwhile place the egg yolks in a bowl and beat until light and creamy.

Bring the milk to the boil in a large saucepan, add the sugar and stir until it dissolves. Add a little of the warm milk at a time to the egg yolks, beating constantly. Return to the pan and cook over a very low heat, stirring constantly until the mixture thickens. Do not heat too quickly or the mixture will curdle. Remove from the heat, strain the tea into the mixture and stir until well blended. Pour into a freezer tray and set aside to cool. Place in a freezer for 2-3 hours.

Remove, spoon the ice cream into a bowl and beat lightly. Return to the tray and freeze until ready to serve.

30 minutes before serving place in the refrigerator to soften a little.

Serves 6-8

oghi sherbet
raki sorbet

An orange sorbet topped with raki-flavoured fruit. Raki is like the Greek ouzo, a spirit made from grape juice and flavoured with aniseed. A delicious sorbet which makes an ideal after-dinner dessert.

Sorbet
450ml (¾ pint) fresh orange juice
150ml (¼ pint) fresh lemon juice
350g (12 oz) sugar
2 tablespoons orange blossom water

Topping
12 strawberries or raspberries
1 small apple, peeled, cored and thinly sliced
1 small pear, peeled, cored and thinly sliced
1 apricot, peeled, stoned and thinly sliced
3 tablespoons raki

Strain the orange and lemon juice. Place the sugar and 600ml (1 pint) water in a saucepan and bring slowly to the boil, stirring constantly until the sugar dissolves. Simmer for 5 minutes. Remove from the heat and stir in the orange and lemon juice and the orange blossom water. Set aside to cool. When cold pour into a freezing tray and freeze for 2-3 hours. Remove, spoon into a bowl and beat lightly. Return to the tray and freeze until solid.

About 45 minutes before serving prepare the fruit mixture. Place all the prepared fruit in a bowl, add the raki, toss so that the fruit is coated and set aside to marinate. To serve place several scoops of sorbet into individual dishes and spoon some of the fruit mixture over each.

Serves 8

zaghqi sherbet

rosewater sorbet

A delightful and delicately flavoured Caucasian sorbet. It has a beautiful rose-scented aroma and a pale pink colour.

1 tablespoon powdered gelatine
350g (12 oz) sugar
1 large, ripe pomegranate
120ml (4 fl oz) rosewater

Put the gelatine into a small bowl with 4-5 tablespoons taken from 1 litre (1¾ pints) of water and set aside for 5 minutes to soften. Meanwhile bring the rest of the water to the boil in a large saucepan. Add the sugar, stir until dissolved and then simmer for 5 minutes. Add several tablespoons of this to the gelatine and stir until dissolved. Pour into the saucepan, stir well and remove the pan from the heat.

Halve the pomegranate and extract as much juice as possible. Stir the juice into the pan together with the rosewater. Set aside to cool. Pour into a freezer tray and freeze for 2-3 hours. Remove, spoon the sorbet into a bowl and beat lightly. Return to the tray and freeze for a further 2-3 hours. Remove, beat once more and re-freeze until ready to serve.

Place in the refrigerator 30 minutes before serving to soften a little.

Serves 8

'If the king eats one apple from the garden of a subject
His slaves will pull him up the tree from the roots.
For five eggs which the sultan allows to be taken by force
His soldiers will put a thousand fowls on the spit.
A tyrant does not remain in the world
But the curse on him abides for ever.'
(*The Gulistan of Sa'di*)

jams and preserves

The art of preserving food is very old and was of vital importance for maintaining supplies of winter food. This is not so today as commercially prepared preserves are available all year round. However, the recipes collected here are mainly ones that are unobtainable commercially or are still unknown to the western public in general.

A few general pointers:

1 Use undamaged and slightly under-ripe fruit – the pectin content will be at its highest and the jam will set well.
2 Granulated sugar is best, although in the past honey or grape-juice was used.
3 Jams and preserves should be boiled until they reach a temperature of 104C (220F). A sugar thermometer is most useful for this, but if unavailable use the tried and tested method for obtaining a perfect set – spoon a little jam onto a small plate and set aside in a cool place for a minute or two. When you push your finger through it the surface should crinkle. The jam is then ready so remove from the heat immediately.

incir reçeli
fig jam

I have given below two recipes for fig jam – one using fresh figs and the other using dried ones. Since fresh figs are virtually unobtainable in most parts of Britain and when they can be found are extremely expensive, I suggest you try the dried version as these can readily be bought at most grocers. Turkish dried figs are the best.

Fresh fig jam
900g (2 lb) fresh green figs, unpeeled, stems trimmed, washed
675g (1½ lb) sugar
juice of ½ lemon
thinly peeled rind of 1 lemon
1 teaspoon vanilla essence

Place the figs in a large saucepan and cover with boiling water. Bring to the boil and simmer for 15 minutes. Drain and rinse with hot water. Return the figs to the pan and cover again with boiling water. Repeat this boiling and draining process 4 times and on the 4th time cook the figs until tender. Drain, rinse under cold water and spread out to dry on kitchen paper.

Meanwhile prepare the syrup by placing the sugar and 450ml (³/₄ pint) water in a saucepan and bringing to the boil, stirring until the sugar dissolves. Add the lemon juice and rind and simmer for 10 minutes. Add the figs and simmer for a further 10 minutes. Remove from the heat, cover the pan and set aside for 18-24 hours.

Bring slowly back to the boil and simmer until the jam reaches 104C (220F). Remove from the heat, stir in the vanilla essence and set aside to cool. Pour into warm, sterilised jars and seal when completely cold.

Makes about 1.5kg (3 lb)

Dried fig jam: A Lebanese version
675g (1½ lb) sugar
1 tablespoon lemon juice
900g (2 lb) dried figs, coarsely chopped
4 tablespoons pine kernels
4 tablespoons walnuts or almonds, coarsely chopped
1 teaspoon ground aniseed
½ teaspoon powdered mastic

Place the sugar, 900ml (1½ pints) water and lemon juice in a large saucepan and bring to the boil, stirring constantly until the sugar dissolves. Lower the heat and simmer for 5 minutes. Add the chopped figs and simmer until they are tender. Stir frequently to prevent sticking. Stir in the nuts and aniseed and simmer, stirring frequently until the jam reaches 104C (220F). Remove from the heat immediately, stir in the mastic and set aside to cool. Pour into warm, sterilised jars and seal when completely cold.

Makes about 1.5 kg (3 lb)

ayva reçeli

quince jam

Quinces are abundant in Turkey and this jam is a great favourite with Turks, Kurds and the Caucasians. This is a fine jam with a delicious combination of fruit, cloves, cinnamon and rosewater.

6 large quinces, peeled, cored and quartered
450g (1 lb) sugar
2 tablespoons lemon juice
5cm (2in) stick cinnamon
3 whole cloves
3 tablespoons rosewater

Halve the quartered quinces. Place the sugar and 900ml (1½ pints) water in a large saucepan and bring to the boil, stirring constantly until the sugar dissolves. Add the quince pieces, lemon juice, cinnamon stick and cloves and boil for 3 minutes. Lower the heat and simmer until the jam reaches 104C (220F). Remove from the heat immediately and set aside to cool. Discard the cinnamon stick and cloves. Stir in the rosewater. Pour into warm, sterilised jars and seal when completely cold.

Makes about 900g (2 lb)

Quince jam –
to see . . . . *good and happy news on the marriage front*
to cook. . . . . . . *long life, satisfaction*
to eat . . . . *unbelievable happiness.*
The Book Of Dreams

In short – quinces are good for you!

ribat limon-em-egosim
lemon and walnut jam

An interesting Israeli recipe. It is of Central European origin, where Poles and Russians still eat it with a spoon accompanied by hot, sugarless lemon tea.

225g (½ lb) walnuts, halved
4-5 large lemons, peel and pith removed and reserved
900g (2 lb) sugar

Place the walnuts in a saucepan with some water, bring to the boil and simmer for 1 minute. Drain and set aside. Cut each lemon into 8 pieces and remove as many pips and as much coarse membrane as possible. Put the peel, pith, pips and membranes on to a piece of muslin and tie up into a bag. Place the sugar and 1.2 litres (2 pints) water in a saucepan and bring to the boil, stirring constantly until the sugar dissolves. Add the walnuts, pieces of lemon and the muslin bag. Lower the heat and simmer for about 20 minutes or until the jam reaches 104C (220F). Remove from the heat immediately and set aside. When cool, discard the muslin bag, stir the jam and pour into warm, sterilised jars. Seal when completely cold.

Makes about 1-1.25kg (2-2½ lb)

vişne reçeli
black cherry jam

This recipe is from Turkey, but cherry jam is popular throughout the region and particularly in Iran. The best jam is made with the black morello cherries.

1.5kg (3 lb) stoned black morello cherries, reserve the stones
juice of 1 large lemon
900g (2 lb) sugar

Place the cherry stones on a piece of muslin and tie into a bag. Put the cherries and lemon juice into a large saucepan and bring gently to the boil. Lower the heat and simmer for about 30 minutes. Remove and discard the bag of stones.

Add the sugar and cook over a low heat, stirring constantly until the sugar dissolves. Bring to the boil and simmer until the jam reaches 104C (220F). Remove from the heat immediately and set aside to cool. Stir, pour into warm, sterilised jars and seal when completely cold.

Makes about 1.5kg (3½ lb)

Particularly in Iran, dried cherry jam is very popular. These can sometimes be bought at Middle Eastern and health food stores. The cherries should be soaked in cold water for 24 hours first, then cooked in water (600ml/1 pint water to each 225g/½ lb fruit) until tender before adding sugar and proceeding as above.

murabba-bil-joz-el-hind

coconut jam

This is a Syrian speciality which is also popular in Turkey and Iraq. It has a snow-white colour, a delectable flavour. It is ideal for breakfast, but is often eaten as a dessert with a cup of strong black Arab coffee. It will not keep as well as a jam which has reached setting point. Do not keep for longer than about 4 weeks in the refrigerator.

225g (½ lb) desiccated coconut
2 tablespoons rosewater
225g (½ lb) sugar
1 tablespoon lemon juice
¼ teaspoon ground nutmeg
2-3 tablespoons chopped pistachio nuts

Put the coconut into a bowl. Sprinkle with the rosewater and 2-3 tablespoons cold water. Toss gently with your fingers until all the grains are just moist. Leave overnight to soften and swell.

Place the sugar, lemon juice and 150ml (¼ pint) water in a saucepan and bring to the boil, stirring constantly until the sugar dissolves. Simmer for a few minutes until the syrup thickens. Add the coconut and bring the mixture back to the boil, stirring constantly. Remove from the heat immediately and leave to cool. Stir in the nutmeg and nuts and spoon into sterilised jars when cold. Seal well.

Makes about ½kg (1 lb)

murabba-bil-amar
date jam

A classic Arab jam from Iraq, but popular throughout the Fertile Crescent. In Iraq it is prepared with a variety of date called *Berhi* – a light golden-yellow fruit with a tender skin. It is sweet with a touch of bitterness and has the texture of fresh sugar cane.

900g (2 lb) fresh dates
toasted blanched almonds
900g (2 lb) sugar
5-6 cloves
2 tablespoons grated orange rind
2 tablespoons lemon juice

Peel the dates, place in a large saucepan with 3.6 litres (6 pints) water and bring to the boil. Lower the heat and simmer for 1 hour. Using a slotted spoon transfer the dates to a large plate and reserve the cooking liquid. When cool enough to handle pull out the stone from the stem end of each date and discard them. Push a toasted almond into each date.

Sprinkle half the sugar over the base of a saucepan, lay the dates on top, scatter the cloves over them and spread the remaining sugar evenly over the top. Make the reserved liquid up to 1.1 litres (2 pints) with water if necessary, pour into the pan, cover and set aside overnight.

The next day bring the mixture to a quick boil, add the orange rind and lemon juice and boil until the jam reaches 104C (220F). Remove from the heat immediately, stir and set aside to cool. Spoon into warm sterilised jars and seal when completely cold.

Makes about 1.5kg (3 lb)

The Arabs' love for the palm and its fruit I have spoken of on several occasions, but I believe the anecdote below illustrates that deep affection and attachment much better than any words of mine ever could.

'When I looked on the desert arid plains which lie between Abusheher and the mountains and saw the ignorant, half-naked, swarthy men and women broiling under a burning sun, with hardly any food but dates, my bosom swelled with pity for their condition, and I felt the dignity of the human species degraded by their contented looks. "Surely" said I to Khojah Arratoon, "these people cannot be so foolish as to be happy in this miserable and uninstructed state. They appear a lively, intelligent race – can they be insensible to their comparatively wretched condition? Do they not hear of other countries? Have they no envy, no desire for improvement?"

'The good old Armenian smiled and said "No, they are a very happy race of people and so far from envying the condition of others, they pity them. But" he added, seeing my surprise "I will give you an anecdote which will explain the ground of this feeling. Sometime since, an Arab woman, an inhabitant of Abusheher, went to England with the children of a Mr Beauman. She remained in your country 4 years. When she returned, all gathered round her to gratify their curiosity about England. "What did you find there? Is it a fine country? Are the people rich – are they happy?"

'She answered "The country was like a garden; the people were rich, had fine clothes, fine houses, fine horses, fine carriages and were said to be very wise and happy." The audience was filled with envy of the English, and a gloom spread over them, which showed discontent at their own condition. They were departing with this sentiment when the woman happened to say "England certainly wants one thing."

'"What is that?" said the Arabs eagerly.

'"There is not a single date tree in the whole country!"

'"Are you sure?" was the general exclamation. "Positive" said the old nurse, "I looked for nothing else all the time I was there, but I looked in vain."

'This information produced an instantaneous change of feeling among the Arabs; it was pity, not envy that now filled their breasts; and they went away wondering how men could live in a country where there were no date trees!

'This anecdote was told me as I was jogging on the road alongside my friend Bluebeard, on our first march from Abusheher. I rode the remainder of the way (10 good miles) without speaking a word, but pondering on the seeming contradiction between the wisdom of Providence and the wisdom of man. I even went as far as to doubt the soundness of many admirable speeches and some able pamphlets I had read regarding the rapid diffusion of knowledge. I changed to a calculating mood and began to think it was not quite honest, even admitting it was wise, to take away what men possessed, of content and happiness, until you could give them an equal or greater amount of the same articles.'
Sketches Of Persia

vartanoush

rose petal jam

The greatest jam in the world! A most exquisite and tasty jam, one of the great delicacies of the East. I have tried preparing this jam using roses from my own garden, but the petals were too tough and there was little fragrance, but the addition of rosewater helps to counteract this.

450g (1 lb) fresh, dark red rose petals with as strong a fragrance as possible
juice of 2 lemons
450g (1 lb) sugar
3-4 tablespoons rosewater, depending on strength

Cut the white ends off the petals and then wash the petals thoroughly – especially if they have been sprayed. Place them in a bowl, squeeze over half the lemon juice and set aside for 10 minutes. The petals are often cooked whole, but because they may be tough I suggest you pass them through a mincer or chop finely. My mother used to knead them by hand, but this took her ages.

Put the petals in a large saucepan with any of the lemon juice left in the bowl - this will help set the jam. Add 600ml (1 pint) water, bring to the boil and then lower the heat and simmer until the petals are tender. This may take anything from 10 minutes to 1 hour. Add the sugar and remaining lemon juice and bring to the boil, stirring constantly until the sugar dissolves. Simmer, stirring frequently until the jam reaches 104C (220F). Remove from the heat, stir and set aside to cool. Pour into a sterilised jar and seal when completely cold.

Makes about 450g (1 lb)

Vegetables, as well as fruits and flowers, make excellent jams and preserves. The people of Kurdistan make a tasty jam of small courgettes, while in Mashad, on the borders of Afghanistan and Pakistan, Iranians prepare a spicy jam of rhubarb; while Armenians have a go with pumpkin jam and Israelis appear to have carried the beetroot in their wanderings all the way from 'Mother Russia' to produce 'Eingemachtes' – beetroot jam.

tutumi kaghtsr

pumpkin jam

An Armenian classic. The lime powder, or powdered hydrate of lime, is bought at the chemist's shop. It helps the fruit keep its shape.

1 small pumpkin, peeled and seeded; you need about 1.1kg (2¼ lb) flesh
2 tablespoons lime powder
1075g (2 lb 6 oz) sugar
2.5cm (1 in) piece cinnamon stick
3 cloves
2 tablespoons lemon juice
1 teaspoon vanilla essence
3 tablespoons slivered almonds or sliced pistachios (optional)

Cut the pumpkin flesh into ½cm (¼in) thick slices and then cut the slices into 3.5cm (1½in) squares, or grate the flesh. Mix the lime powder and 1.75 litres (4 pints) cold water together in a large bowl, add the pumpkin pieces and leave to soak overnight. Next day drain the pieces into a colander and then rinse very thoroughly under cold running water to remove all traces of the lime.

In a large saucepan bring 1.2 litres (2 pints) water and 900g (2 lb) of the sugar to the boil, stirring constantly until the sugar dissolves. Add the pieces of pumpkin, lower the heat and simmer for about 1 hour. Pour some of the syrup into a small saucepan and add to it the cinnamon, cloves, lemon juice and the remaining sugar. Bring to the boil, simmer for 2-3 minutes and pour the mixture back into the pumpkin pan. Lower the heat and simmer until the jam reaches 104C (220F) and then remove from the heat immediately. Stir in the vanilla essence and nuts, if using them, and set aside to cool. Pour into warm, sterilised jars and seal when completely cold.

Makes about 1.5kg (3 lb)

kayisi reçeli
apricot preserve

In the old days people used to keep their fruit preserves under the sun to thicken and there are still some who maintain that this is the best method of preserving apricots and peaches. Since one cannot guarantee the consistency of the sun's rays, alas! in this part of the world I suggest you follow this recipe. However, if you are fortunate enough to have much more sunshine where you live (than I do) then simply boil the apricots in the syrup for 5 minutes and then keep in the sun for several days until the syrup thickens – and then let me know if the old people were right!

1.75kg (4 lb) under-ripe apricots
900g (2 lb) sugar
2 tablespoons lemon juice

Wash the apricots very gently and then, with an apple-corer, remove the stones taking care not to bruise the fruit. Place the sugar and 900ml (1½ pints) water in a large saucepan and bring to the boil, stirring constantly until the sugar dissolves. Add the lemon juice and simmer for 5 minutes. Carefully drop the apricots into the syrup and boil for 2 minutes. Lower the heat and simmer gently. Do not stir, but just shake the pan occasionally. Remove from the heat and leave to cool. Spoon into warm, sterilised jars and completely cover with the syrup. Seal when cold and store in a cool dry place.

Makes about 3.5kg (8 lb)

touzi kaghtsr
green fig preserve

2 tablespoons lime powder dissolved in 900ml (1½ pints) water
900g (2 lb) fresh green or black figs
900g (2 lb) sugar
1 tablespoon lemon juice
3 tablespoons toasted sesame seeds
5cm (2in) piece of cinnamon stick
½ teaspoon powdered mastic (gum arabic)

Place the limed water in a large bowl, add the figs and leave to soak for 2 hours. Place the sugar, lemon juice and 450ml (¾ pint) water in a saucepan and bring to the boil, stirring constantly until the sugar dissolves. Simmer for 5 minutes.

Drain the figs into a colander and rinse thoroughly under cold, running water. Carefully add the figs to the syrup, together with the sesame seeds, cinnamon stick and mastic, lower the heat and simmer until the syrup is thick. Remove from the heat and leave to cool. Discard the cinnamon stick and spoon the figs into warm, sterilised jars; cover completely with the syrup and seal tightly when cold. Store in a cool, dry place.

Makes about 1.5kg (3 lb)

engouyzi anoush
green walnut preserve

A great Caucasian classic which is absolutely magnificent – dark, soft, sweet walnuts floating in syrup. Serve with strong, black, Arab coffee at the end of a meal.

about 50 fresh green walnuts
8 tablespoons lime powder
900g (2 lb) sugar
1½ tablespoons lemon juice
5 cloves
10cm (4in) piece of cinnamon stick

Pierce the walnut shells with a strong needle in 3-4 places to check that the inner shells are still soft – there should be no resistance.

As walnuts will stain your hands black wear rubber gloves when handling them. Remove the outer green walnut shells and discard. Place the walnuts in a large bowl and soak in cold water for 2 days. Change the water 3 times a day. On the third day drain the nuts, add fresh water, stir in the lime powder and soak the nuts for 24 hours. Next day drain the walnuts and rinse very thoroughly under cold, running water. Pierce each nut in several places with a thin skewer and then soak in fresh water for a further 2 days. Drain into a colander.

Place the sugar, lemon juice and 600ml (1 pint) water in a saucepan and bring to the boil, stirring constantly until the sugar dissolves. Lower the heat and simmer until the syrup is thick enough to coat the back of a spoon. Add the walnuts, cloves and cinnamon and cook for 3 minutes. Remove the pan from the heat and leave to cool. Return the pan to the heat, bring to the boil, simmer for 1 minute and remove. Repeat this process twice more. Finally remove the pan from the heat and discard the cloves and cinnamon stick.

When cool spoon the walnuts into warm, sterilised jars and cover with the syrup. Seal tightly when completely cold.

Makes about 1.75kg (4 lb)

murabba-al-bousfeir

orange preserve

A popular Middle Eastern preserve where the orange peel is rolled up and cooked in syrup until tender. You can prepare grapefruit and lemon peel in the same way, as well as the finest preserve of this type called *Muraba-al-Kabbad* which is the peel of the bitter Seville orange.

6 large oranges
560g (1¼ lb) sugar
1 tablespoon lemon juice

Lightly grate the surface of the oranges to remove the shine. Cut the rind into 6 vertical sections and peel them away from the flesh. With a sharp knife carefully remove as much of the white pith as possible from the pieces of rind without cutting them. Tightly roll up each piece of rind and then, with a needle and heavy thread, string up the rolls. I suggest 18 rolls (from 3 oranges) on each string. Tie the ends of the threads together to form 2 garlands. Put the threaded rolls into a large saucepan, cover with water, bring to the boil and then drain. Repeat this process at least 2 more times – this will remove the bitter taste.

Place the rolls in the saucepan, cover with cold water again, bring to the boil and cook for about 30-40 minutes or until the rolls are tender. Drain and pat dry. Place the sugar, lemon juice and 750ml (1¼ pints) water in a large saucepan and bring to the boil. Add the strings of rolls and simmer for about 45 minutes or until the syrup is thick and the rolls are beautifully glazed. Remove from the heat and leave to cool. Carefully remove the strings and store the rolls, in their syrup, in sterilised jars. Seal tightly when cold and store in a cool place. Serve 2-3 rolls at a time, with a little of their syrup, as a dessert or with coffee.

Serves 6

murabba-al-griffon

preserved grapefruit rolls

Follow the recipe above *but*
    a) use 4 grapefruit
    b) cut the rind of each into 8 vertical sections
    c) boil in water 4 times instead of 3 to remove bitterness.

loligi mourapa

green tomato preserve

A classic Armenian preserve. Use small, green tomatoes no more than 2.5cm (1in) in diameter.

900g (2 lb) small, green, unblemished tomatoes, washed and drained
1.2kg (2½ lb) sugar
1 tablespoon lemon juice
5 cloves
5cm (2in) piece cinnamon stick
seeds of 3 cardamom pods

Bring some water to the boil in a large saucepan, drop in the tomatoes and simmer for 10 minutes. Drain and leave to cool.

Meanwhile prepare the syrup by placing the sugar, 450ml (¾ pint) water and the lemon juice in a large saucepan and bringing to the boil, stirring constantly until the sugar dissolves. Drop the cooled tomatoes into the syrup, remove from the heat and set aside for 2 hours. Place the cloves, cinnamon stick and cardamom seeds in a small muslin bag, tie tightly and hang by a piece of string into the syrup.

Return the saucepan to the heat and simmer very gently for 30 minutes. Remove from the heat and set aside for a further 2 hours. Repeat this process once more. Return the pan to the heat and cook over a low heat until the syrup is thick. Remove from the heat and set aside until cool. Discard the spice bag. With a slotted spoon carefully drop the tomatoes into sterilised jars and cover with the syrup. Seal tightly when cold and store in a cool place.

Makes about 1.5kg (3 lb)

sekhi mourapa

melon preserve

This is a great Caucasian speciality. Seeds of the cantaloupe melon were transported from their natural habitat (the region of Lake Van in modern Turkey) some 400 years ago by Catholic monks – no! for a change not by Marco Polo. They were cultivated, variegated and exported to the rest of the world. The old monks did not stay long enough to note down this recipe so here, a little late, I offer you this fragrant preserve which is served on the breakfast table of any self-respecting Kurd, Georgian or Armenian.

900g (2 lb) semi-ripe melon flesh, cantaloupe or ogen
2 tablespoons orange blossom water
450g (1 lb) sugar

675g (1½ lb) sugar
1 tablespoon lemon juice

Cut the melon flesh into 2.5cm (1in) cubes and place in a large bowl. Sprinkle with the orange blossom water and 450g (1 lb) sugar, toss gently and set aside for about 3 hours.

Meanwhile prepare the syrup by placing 450ml (¾ pint) water, the sugar and lemon juice in a saucepan and bringing to the boil, stirring constantly until the sugar dissolves. Boil gently for 5 minutes and then pour the syrup over the melon pieces. Mix carefully and set aside for 24 hours.

Next day carefully drain the syrup back into the saucepan. Bring to the boil and simmer for 2 minutes. Poor over the melon pieces, mix gently and set aside for a further 24 hours.

On the third day pour the contents of the bowl into a large saucepan and cook gently until the melon is translucent and the syrup is thick enough to coat the back of a spoon. Remove from the heat and set aside to cool. Spoon the preserve into warm, sterilised jars and seal when completely cold.

Makes about 1.5kg (3 lb)

tsmerougi mourapa

watermelon preserve

A unique speciality from the Ashtarag region of Soviet Armenia. This preserve is golden-red in colour with the most delectable flavour imaginable.

900g (2 lb) watermelon flesh
3 tablespoons lime powder dissolved in 900ml (1½ pints) water
1.5kg (3 lb) sugar
1 tablespoon lemon juice
2 tablespoons vanilla essence

Remove and discard any whitish flesh from the watermelon and then cut the flesh into 2.5cm (1in) cubes. Place in a large bowl with the limed water and soak for 1½ hours. Drain the melon into a colander, rinse thoroughly under cold, running water and leave to drain.

Place the sugar, 450ml (¾ pint) water and the lemon juice in a large saucepan and bring to the boil, stirring constantly until the sugar dissolves. Add the pieces of watermelon and simmer over a low heat for 20 minutes. Remove from the heat and set aside for 2 hours.

Return to the heat and cook for a further 20 minutes, by which time the syrup should be thick. Remove from the heat, stir in the vanilla essence and set aside to cool. Spoon the cubes into warm, sterilised jars, top up with the syrup and seal when completely cold.

Makes about 1.5kg (3 lb)

Aubergine, 'Queen of Vegetables' as a Persian poet proclaimed a long time ago, is truely the 'Vegetable of the East'. Used in soups, salads, stews, kebabs etc it also makes a marvellous sweet. There are several jams and preserves made with this vegetable. I have included two, both from the Caucasus, though I hasten to add that this preserve is equally popular as far away as Crete and Southern Iran.

badrijani murabba

aubergine jam

From Georgia, but also popular with the Laz people who live on the NE Black Sea coast of Turkey.

1.75kg (4 lb) small aubergines
2 tablespoons salt
4 lemons
4 cloves
2.5cm (1in) piece of fresh root ginger, peeled and bruised
1.5kg (3 lb) sugar
4 tablespoons raisins
110g (4 oz) crystallised ginger, chopped

Peel the aubergines and cut into ½cm (¼in) cubes. Place them in a large colander, sprinkle with the salt and set aside for 30 minutes. Pare the rind from the lemons and cut into thin strips. Squeeze and reserve the juice.

Rinse the aubergine cubes under cold water and pat dry. Place in the top of a steamer and half fill the bottom part with water. Or put in a colander over a saucepan of water and cover with a lid. Bring to the boil and then steam the aubergines until tender – about 10-15 minutes. Remove from the heat and transfer the cubes to a large pan and add the lemon juice. Put the lemon rind, cloves and root ginger into a muslin bag, tie tightly and add to the pan. Add the sugar, mix thoroughly, cover the pan and leave to stand undisturbed for at least 24 hours.

Next day bring slowly to the boil, stirring constantly until the sugar dissolves, and then simmer for 10 minutes, stirring frequently. Add the raisins and crystallised ginger, raise the heat and boil vigorously until the jam reaches 104C (220F). Remove from the heat, discard the muslin bag and set the jam aside to cool. Spoon into warm, sterilised jars and seal when cold.

Makes about 3kg (6 lb)

This is how the poet Iraj (1874-1924) describes his beloved
when he compares her to an auhergine!

'Pet onion!
In your layers of veil and gown;
All beauty is one mirror, or
a turnip in a sack?

No matter where I look;
up or down,
You are not my pet or sweet
or even a human bean –
Wrapped in that black and purple skin
You are an aubergine.'
A Veiled Girl

The final preserve recipe, from the land of Iraj, Hafiz, Saidi and the other Persian poets – fragments of whose poems I have used – comes from the city of Qum. Here the Ayatollahs, seated in dark corners, quote or misquote and generally pontificate on matters of universal importance. My humble quote is a preserve for cucumbers which tastes sweeter than all the honey of Shiraz and is more fragrant than the gardens of Isphahan.

mourapa-ye-khiar

cucumber preserve

900g (2 lb) cucumbers
2 tablespoons lime powder dissolved in 1.1 litres (2 pints) water
900g (2 lb) sugar
2 tablespoons lemon juice
1 teaspoon ground cardamom
3 tablespoons rosewater

Peel cucumbers and cut into 1cm (½in) pieces. Place the limed water in a large bowl, add the cucumber pieces and set aside for 24 hours. The next day, drain the cucumber pieces into a colander and rinse thoroughly under cold, running water. Place the pieces in a pan with a little water and simmer for 10-12 minutes or until tender. Drain and set aside.

Place the sugar, 300ml (½ pint) water and the lemon juice in a large pan and bring to the boil, stirring constantly until the sugar dissolves. Add the cucumber pieces and cardamom, stir well and boil until the jam reaches 104C (220F). Remove from the heat immediately, stir in the rosewater and set aside to cool. Pour into warm, sterilised jars and seal when completely cold.

Makes about 1.5kg (3 lb)

drinks and sherbets

'the usual Drink is Sherbet, made of water, juice of lemmons and Ambergeece, which they drink out of long thin wooden spoons, wherewith they lade it out of their bowls.

'Sherbets are made of almost all Tart pleasing fruits as the juice of pomegranats, lemmons, citrons, oranges, prunellas, which are to be bought in the Markets. Thus by Diet, as well as Air, they procure not only a firmness of Constitution, but properness and tallness of body, for none excel them either for beauty and stature.'
John Fryer *A New Account of East India and Persia 1672-1681*

On a hot day in a Middle Eastern home guests are served a sweet fruit-flavoured drink called *Sharbat* – from old Persian meaning 'King's water', i.e. wine. Today viniculture is non-existent in most Muslim countries due to the Prophet's prohibition of all intoxicants: 'O ye who believe, liquor, gambling, idols and divining arrows are but abominations and Satanic devices so turn away from each one of them.' *Koran 'Al-Maidah'*. But Middle Easterners do produce and consume alcohol – this particularly applies to non-Muslims such as Jews and Christians. Cypriot wines and sherries are already well known in Britain. In recent years Israeli wines and liqueurs have made a tentative appearance while the excellent brandies, wines and vodkas of Armenia and Georgia are almost unknown. But it is to the fruit and herb-flavoured drinks we must return to better appreciate that peculiar 'oriental' characteristic that has so struck numerous travellers in the East. James Baillie Fraser was so impressed by the street vendors and their wares while on his travels through that land: 'The dishes are brought in on large metal trays – and contain pilaus, stews, sweetmeats, and other delicacies; while bowls of sweet and sour sherbets, with long-handled spoons of pear-tree wood swimming in them, are placed within their reach.' (James Baillie Fraser Esq *Persia*. Harper & Bros 1834)

Poets may have sung numerous songs in praise of wine, but the people drank water or fruit-flavoured water. For the man in the desert the most precious commodity on earth is water. Springs, rivers and lakes were, and still are, worshipped and the Prophet suggested that when a believer finds no water he 'have recourse to pure dust and having placed your hands on it pass them over your face and forearms.' I recall as a child drinking ice cool water placed outside most shops for the convenience of passers-by and sampling the numerous 'miraculous' springs visited for the purification of body and soul. But the most vivid memories of my childhood are of the sherbet-sellers who passed up and down the sun-drenched streets of Aleppo, Idlib and Beirut, chanting the coolness and flavour of their wares. 'What are those itinerant vendors crying?' asked Wilfred Blunt* of the tinkling water-seller rattling his brazen cups. 'Ya'atshan, es-sebil – Oh thirsty one, the distribution; of the fruit juice-seller, 'Balak snunak' – take care of your teeth; by the hawker of nose-gays; 'Salih hamatak – appease your mother-in-law'; of the cress-seller,

'Tender cresses from the spring of Ed-Du'iyeh; if an old woman eats of them she will be young again next morning.' These street sellers were an integral part of my childhood. The drinks they served were made of herbs, fruits and vegetables and I have included many of them below.

A Persian Spring by Wilfred Blunt. Barrie 1957.

sahlab

resin drink

Sahlab (salep) – *orchis hircina Satyricum hircinum* – is a resin. It is usually sold in a hard resin form and unfortunately it is not easily available in the West. It can be bought from some Middle Eastern shops and chemists and should be crushed before use. This makes an excellent winter drink and is popular throughout the Middle East.

600ml (1 pint) milk
1 teaspoon ground sahlab
2 teaspoons finely chopped pistachios or a mixture of almonds and walnuts
pinch of ground cinnamon

Heat the milk in a saucepan. Add the sahlab, stirring constantly until the mixture comes to the boil. Lower the heat and simmer for 10-15 minutes, stirring frequently. Pour into small dessert cups, sprinkle with the nuts and cinnamon and serve.

Serves 4

sous

liquorice drink

This is a very popular Middle Eastern drink sold by street vendors in beautifully decorated brass containers. A must in the heat of the Arabian summer, *sous* is made of liquorice mixed with water and is drunk ice cold. Use either root of liquorice or, for convenience sake, its powdered version both of which can be purchased from most health food shops. A beautiful drink.

4-6 liquorice roots 7.5-10cm (3-4in) long or
10 teaspoons liquorice root powder

Bring about 1.5 litres (2½ pints) water to the boil in a large saucepan. If using roots crush them with a hammer and add to the boiling water. If using powder stir it into the water. Simmer for 2-3 minutes then remove from the heat and set aside to cool. Strain the liquid through muslin into a jug, refrigerate and then serve with ice cubes.

Serves 4

asal ou kouzbara

coriander honey

This is a sweet, delicious and aromatic drink from Arabia. It can be drunk hot or cold, and the old women highly recommend it for colds and flu.

2 teaspoons honey
½ teaspoon ground coriander

Warm 1 cup (usually 250ml/8 fl oz) water in a small saucepan, add the honey and stir until dissolved. Stir in the coriander and serve warm as a refreshing drink.

Serves 1

zaghgi osharag

rosewater syrup

A fragrant drink especially popular in Greece, Turkey and Armenia. If you like the smell of rosewater you will love this drink. Ideal with cakes and gateaux.

900g (2 lb) sugar
juice of 1 lemon
150ml (¼ pint) rosewater
2 tablespoons red food colouring

Place the sugar, 600ml (1 pint) water and the lemon juice in a saucepan and bring to the boil, stirring constantly until the sugar dissolves. Lower the heat and simmer until the syrup thickens and coats a spoon with a thin film. Stir in the rosewater and food colouring and simmer for a further 2 minutes. Remove from the heat and leave to cool. When cold store in sterilised bottles and seal. Serve diluted with water and ice cubes.

In Iran 'Land of Poetry', Hafiz, Nizami, Jami, Saidi and the host of great poets –
not forgetting the ubiquitous Omar – sang the praises of wine, but I suspect
went home to quench their thirsts with a glass of sherbet. Hafiz, perhaps
the most romantically lyrical of them all sang:

'Rang through the dim tavern a voice yesterday;
"Pardon for sins! Drinkers of wine, drink! Ye may!"

'Such was the word; hear the good news, Angel-borne;
Mercy divine still to the end holds its way . . .

'Bear her away, Reason the Dull, tavern wards,
Here shall the red wine set her pale veins a-play.

'Still is my ear ringed of His locks ringletted,
Still on the wine-threshold my face prone I lay.

'Hafiz, awake! Toping on more counts for sin,
Now that our Lord Royal hath put sins away.'
Versions From Hafiz by W. Leaf Grant Richards 1898

His favourite drink, it is rumoured in the chiaroscuro bazaars of Iran,
was no! not wine (red or white) or *arak* from Iraq and made of grape juice
or dates, but the juice of a humble vegetable – rhubarb. Yes! Sharbat Rivas.
No doubt he also liked *Sekanjabin* – a drink that is often mentioned by
European travellers and is still very popular throughout Iraq and Iran.

sharbat rivas

rhubarb syrup

450g (1 lb) fresh rhubarb
560g (1¼ lb) sugar

Wash and trim the rhubarb and cut into 2.5cm (1in) pieces. Place 600ml (1 pint) water in a
saucepan and bring to the boil. Add the rhubarb, lower the heat and simmer for about 20
minutes or until soft. Remove from the heat and leave to cool for 10 minutes. Strain the mixture
through muslin into a bowl. Squeeze to extract all the liquid. Measure the juice and make up to
600ml (1 pint) with water if necessary.

Return the juice to the pan, add the sugar and bring to the boil, stirring constantly until the
sugar dissolves. Boil for 5-6 minutes and then set aside until cold. Pour into sterilised jars and
seal. To serve pour 5-6 tablespoons of the syrup into a glass, stir in 6-7 tablespoons of water
and crushed ice.

sekanjabin

sweet and sour mint syrup

350g (¾ lb) sugar, or more to taste
120-180ml (4-6 fl oz) wine vinegar
4 large sprigs fresh mint, washed and drained

Bring about 500ml (17 fl oz) water to the boil in a saucepan. Add the sugar and stir constantly until it has dissolved. Add the vinegar and simmer for 20 minutes or until the syrup has thickened and coats the back of a spoon. Add the mint, stir well and set aside to cool. The syrup should now have the consistency of thin honey. Strain the syrup when cold into a sterilised bottle and seal.

To serve
a) For breakfast or as a dessert – separate the leaves of a Cos lettuce, wash and pat dry. Pour some syrup into a bowl. Fold the leaves, dip into the syrup and eat – very refreshing.
b) As a drink – about one-third fill a glass with syrup. Top it up with water or, as in fashionable circles, with mineral water or soda water. Stir, drop in some ice cubes and serve.
c) As a punch – grate a small, sweet cucumber into a punch bowl. Add syrup, ice cubes and soda water. Stir well and garnish with mint springs and cucumber slices.

seghi osharag

melon drink

When melons are over-ripe in the shops buy them – they ought to be cheap and they make a lovely drink which is very refreshing in the summer. Watermelons, pineapple, and other soft, ripe fruit can be used in the same way. Never waste!

1 medium-sized, ripe melon, peel and seeds discarded
2 tablespoons sugar
2 teaspoons rosewater
seeds of 2 cardamom pods, powdered

Chop the melon flesh into small pieces, place in a blender and blend to a pulp. Transfer to a large jug and stir in the remaining ingredients and 450ml (¾ pint) water or soda water. If you wish strain the mixture into another jug and then chill. Serve with ice cubes.

Serves 4

tamar hindi
tamarind syrup

This is a thick, dark syrup which has a sweet and sour flavour and is made of tamarind – an Arabic word meaning 'date of India'. This syrup is sometimes sold in Middle Eastern shops, but tamarind is easily found in Indian groceries where it is sold in 450g (1 lb) blocks named *tamarindo*. When using tamarindo soak it overnight in cold water so that the pods become soft.

450g (1 lb) tamarind pods
900g (2 lb) sugar

Leave the pods to soak in water overnight. Drain. Now rub the pods through a fine sieve, pushing hard with a wooden spoon until all the juice is removed. Discard the seeds and thick fibres. Strain the juice through muslin into a saucepan. Add the sugar and bring to the boil, stirring constantly until the sugar has dissolved. Lower the heat and simmer until the syrup is thick. Remove and leave until cold. Pour into sterilised bottles and seal. To serve dilute with water and ice cubes.

vişne şerbeti
cherry syrup

By far the most famed and loved drink of Turks and Persians. Poets have called it 'The Queen of Queens'. Has a sweet yet tart flavour.

900g (2 lb) sugar
450g (1 lb) large, dark, sour cherries, washed
¼ teaspoon vanilla essence

Place the sugar and 600ml (1 pint) water in a large saucepan and bring to the boil, stirring constantly until the sugar dissolves. Lower the heat and simmer for 15 minutes. Add the cherries and simmer for a further 20 minutes, stirring frequently until the syrup thickens. Remove from the heat and cool for 10 minutes.

Strain the mixture through a muslin bag into a bowl. If possible suspend the bag over the bowl and let the liquid drip through. When cold squeeze the bag tightly to extract all the juice. Pour the cold syrup into sterilised bottles and seal. To serve dilute to taste with water and ice.

sharbat-e-tout-ferangi

strawberry syrup

Iran is famed for her strawberries. They are large, dark red and very sweet. You can use the same recipe for raspberries or, as with another popular Iranian syrup, a 50-50 mixture of strawberries and raspberries. All these make excellent drinks.

900g (2 lb) sugar
450g (1 lb) strawberries, rinsed
½ teaspoon vanilla essence

Place the sugar and 450ml (³/₄ pint) water in a large saucepan and bring to the boil, stirring constantly until the sugar dissolves. Lower the heat and simmer for about 10 minutes. Add the strawberries and simmer until the syrup thickens and coats the back of a spoon. Stir in the vanilla essence. Remove and cool for 10 minutes. Strain through muslin into a bowl and leave until cold. Pour into a sterilised bottle and seal. Serve diluted to taste with water and ice.

portakal şerbeti

orange syrup

A sweet orange syrup that makes an excellent summer drink. Lemons and tangerines can be prepared in the same way.

About 10-12 large, juicy oranges
grated rind of ½ orange
1 teaspoon lemon juice
sugar

Halve the oranges and extract the juice. This should yield about 600ml (1 pint) juice – measure the exact volume. Place the juice in a saucepan with the rind, lemon juice and 1½ times the volume of sugar. Bring slowly to the boil, stirring constantly until the sugar has dissolved. Lower the heat and simmer for 5-7 minutes. Remove from the heat and leave for 10 minutes. Strain the syrup through muslin into a jug and when it is cold pour into sterilised bottles and seal. Serve diluted to taste with water and ice.

tan

yoghurt drink

Yoghurt, one of the major ingredients in the Middle Eastern cuisine, makes a fine, refreshing drink called *Tan* or *Ayran* or *Dough*. Probably the most popular cold drink of all it is served at home, in restaurants, by street vendors and, in recent years, ready-made in supermarkets.

2 tablespoons yoghurt
¼ teaspoon salt
¼ teaspoon dried mint
some ice cubes

Spoon the yoghurt into a glass and very slowly stir in 300ml (½ pint) water to make a smooth mixture. Stir in the salt and mint. Drop in a few ice cubes and serve. If preparing for more than 1 person mix all the ingredients together in a jug first.

Serves 1

VARIATION

In Iran soda water is often substituted for the water. Sometimes a few drops of lime juice or lemon juice are added to each glass of Tan. An interesting variation from Eastern Iran is *Dough-e-Miveh* – fruit and yoghurt drink. For 1 person mix together –

150ml (¼ pint) yoghurt
150ml (¼ pint) water
2 teaspoons honey
½ tablespoon lemon juice
50g (2 oz) finely chopped soft fruit, e.g. apricots, strawberries, peaches, melon etc.

Yet another variation, this time from Caucasian Armenia is *Salori Tan* – prune and yoghurt drink. For 1 person mix together –

150ml (¼ pint) yoghurt
150ml (¼ pint) prune juice
½ teaspoon lemon juice
pinch of ground cinnamon

Serve with ice cubes.

chay

tea

Tea arrived in the Middle East via Persia where it still retains its pre-eminence as the national drink. From Iran it spread into modern Iraq, the Gulf States, Asia Minor (modern Turkey) and up through the Caucasian mountain range into Russia. Centuries later it was confronted by coffee which arrived via Arabia, and in the ensuing struggle between these 2 thirst quenchers certain territorial readjustments were made. Tea is still supreme in Iran, Iraq, the Gulf States and most of Turkey. Coffee reigns in Syria, Lebanon, Jordan and the rest of Turkey.

In the Middle East tea is never drunk with milk, nor is it sugared. It is consumed neat in small cups straight from a samovar. An Iranian will put a sugar lump between his teeth and drink his tea through it. My father recalled his childhood when a lump of sugar crystal was passed from person to person as they supped their brew. Amongst Arabs and Armenians tea is drunk strictly for medicinal reasons and then only in the cold, winter months.

One final point – the tea is very often flavoured with herbs and spices as the recipe below indicates.

chay-bi-yanasoun

aniseed tea

1 teaspoon tea
½ teaspoon powdered aniseed
sugar to taste

Make the tea in the ordinary way. Add the aniseed powder and sugar, if required, stir and allow to settle. Serve.

Serves 1

The Armenians, not to be outdone, have a delightful tea made with cinnamon and cloves which they claim has great medicinal qualities.

haygagan tey

cinnamon and clove tea

2.5-4cm (1-1½in) piece of cinnamon stick
2 whole cloves
1 tablespoon tea leaves
sugar to taste

Place 900ml (1½ pints) water, the cinnamon and cloves in a small saucepan and bring to the boil. Lower the heat and simmer for 5-7 minutes. Turn off the heat, add the tea leaves and stir well. Strain into a teapot and serve with sugar.

Serves 4

chay-bi-nana

mint tea

The finest mint is reputed to come from the region of Meknes in Morocco and mint tea is the drink of Morocco. It is a very refreshing infusion of tea (green variety) and fresh mint. Mint tea is considered to be good for upset stomachs, colds and flu. There is a great deal of ceremony connected with the serving of this tea in Morocco, but here is a simple method eliminating all pomp and circumstance.

3 teaspoons green tea
handful of fresh, whole mint leaves or 1 tablespoon
dried mint
sugar to taste

Warm the pot with a little hot water and discard it. Add the tea leaves, pour a little more hot water into the pot, swirl around again and pour out the water, but not the leaves! Add the mint and the amount of sugar required. Add about 900ml (1½ pints) boiling water and steep for 5 minutes. If any mint surfaces remove it. Taste and serve. Do not add any sugar once it has been poured into the cup.

Serves 4

ainar

tea with nuts

A Lebanese speciality which is traditionally served when a child is born. A very fragrant brew drunk as most Middle Easterners, except Iranians, still drink their tea – by taking it, a sip at a time, from a teaspoon.

1 tablespoon ground caraway
1 tablespoon ground cinnamon
1 tablespoon aniseed
$^1/_8$ teaspoon ground nutmeg
5-7 tablespoons nuts – pine nuts, walnuts, almonds or a mixture
sugar to taste

Place all the spices in a small pan with 5 cups of water and bring to the boil. Simmer for 5 minutes and then strain through muslin into a teapot. Place 1 tablespoon, or a little more, nuts into the bottom of each of 5 cups. Add the required amount of sugar. Fill the cups with the hot, spiced water and serve. Drink from a teaspoon, a sip at a time.

Serves 5

qahwa (kahwa)

arab coffee

There is a standard way of preparing Arab coffee, although there are local variations. You can have it a) with sugar b) without sugar or c) very sweet – it is all a matter of tradition and taste. The coffee beans should be 100% pulverised and they will prepare it for you in this way in most coffee shops.

The recipe below is for 1 person. If you wish to make it for a number of people simply increase the proportions accordingly and use a larger *jaswah* – a coffee pot usually made of brass. It has a long wooden handle and the pot is narrower at the top than at the bottom - essential for getting the all important froth. The jaswah is also known as *kanika, cezve, ibrik, briki* or *surlap*. They can be bought in most Middle Eastern, Indian and large departmental stores.

1 teaspoon sugar
1 teaspoon coffee

Mix the sugar and 1 coffee cup of water together in the jaswah and bring to the boil, stirring until the sugar has dissolved. Add the coffee, stir well and bring to the boil. As the coffee froths up remove the jaswah from the heat and allow the froth to subside. Return the jaswah to the heat until the froth reaches the brim. Remove once again. Repeat this process 2 more times. Remove from the heat and pour into the cup. Do not add more sugar and do not stir or you will disturb the sediments at the bottom of the cup.

Serves 1

VARIATIONS

Armenian – As above, but add 1 crushed cardamom pod and 2 drops orange blossom water.

Anatolian – As above, but add 2 drops rosewater.

Cypriot – As above, but add a few drops of cold water to the coffee in the cup.

Ottoman – This is the version first popularised in the West – it is thick and very sweet. Allow at least 2 teaspoons of sugar per person.

Bedouin – Known as *Kahwah-al-Hilo* this coffee is very thick and flavoured with cardamom and saffron:

1 teaspoon coffee
1 coffee cup water
½ crushed cardamom pod
½ teaspoon powdered saffron

Combine the ingredients in a jaswah, stir to dissolve and bring to the boil. Reduce the heat to very low and leave for 20 minutes until reduced and thick. Add sugar to taste – normally very little if any at all. The coffee will have a slightly bitter flavour. Drink a few sips at a time.

After the coffee is drunk, cups are turned upside down and left to rest for 5-10 minutes. In that time the cups must not be touched – such is the law of 'fortune telling'. This unwritten law from time immemorial is part and parcel of Eastern culture. There are 3 methods of coffee cup 'fortune telling' – Arab, Persian and Indian. In the Arab method one's fortune is read after the coffee has been drunk and the cup turned upside down and left awhile. The Persians read the cup immediately after the coffee has been drunk, while with the Indian method the coffee is allowed to cool and then ceremoniously thrown away. One can never read one's own cup.

A well known Indian fakir Sounkam Brahmin, who was famed for his fortune-telling prowess, wrote a book *How to read a coffee cup** where he scientifically-cum-astrologically expounded his beliefs. Briefly – a cup of coffee is the universe, the sediments the stars. 'Turn your face to the east whence light and all knowledge comes. Thence the coffee "line" and our physical "line" come.' The best time for 'telling' is from dawn to noon. The sun is the supreme controller of our destinies, the moon does not play any part in that process. A warning! Never let your cup be read on Thursdays for according to Mr Sounkam 'I have read over fifty thousand cups of coffee and of my Thursday predictions 85% have been thoughts and deeds of misfortune (sickness, death, accident) while 5% only have been of happier events. I studied the people whose cups I was reading. They were both physically and emotionally normal. So I warn all not to permit their coffee cups to be read on Thursdays. The remaining 10% were cases of permanent neurosis.' Nice fellow this Sounkam!

My late aunt Makroohi had a method of her own. Everyone had a letter (or telegram) coming bearing news, which could be good, not so good and sometimes bad. There was always a visitor on the move, i.e. someone was coming who could be a relation, a friend, an acquaintance, etc, etc. My aunt had diagnosed the 4 main criteria of a good life as food, shelter, health and money and she brilliantly played variations on them. Mr Sounkam Brahmin made science out of art and that, in fortune telling, is not on.

The great fortune tellers of the East were and still are all women who have experienced life's sweet-sorrow ups and downs and have acquired a thorough knowledge of the human psyche. They do not need all that Indian mumbo-jumbo, besides Indians know nothing about coffee! Let them stick to their aromatic teas and leave the work of coffee to my aunt and her kind. And may Allah be praised that the sediments are arranged such that we all receive abundant health, wealth, happiness and dreams.

'Inshallah Sahten' – the will of God and good health to us all!

*published about 1925. Bombay, India.

basics

home-made baklava filo

This recipe explains how you can make your own filo. It is not difficult, but needs patience and practice to get as thin a filo as possible. Good commercially prepared filo is very thin and it is unlikely you will be able to achieve a similar thinness. I suggest therefore that when using home-made filo to prepare Baklava or similar sweets you use half the number of sheets recommended in the recipe.

675g (1½ lb) plain flour
1 teaspoon salt
3 tablespoons olive oil
cornflour

Sift the flour and salt into a large bowl. Make a well in the centre and add 450ml (³/₄ pint) tepid water, little by little, kneading until you have a soft dough. Gather into a ball, transfer to a work top and knead for 5 minutes. Now knead in the oil, 1 tablespoon at a time, and knead for a further 20 minutes by which time the dough should have a smooth, satiny texture. Place the ball of dough in a clean bowl, cover with a tea towel and set aside for 4 hours.

Divide the dough into 18 equal portions and roll each between your palms to form a ball – about 3.5-5cm (1½-2in) in diameter. Lightly dust a work top with cornflour and, taking 1 ball at a time, roll out into circles about 15-17.5cm (6-7in) in diameter. Place the first circle on greaseproof paper and stack the others on top of it. Cover with a damp cloth and leave for about 45 minutes.

To shape the dough take a round and stretch it over the backs of your hands. Pull your hands carefully apart stretching the dough out until it is uniformly paper thin. Work carefully but with speed because the pastry dries quickly. When you have stretched a sheet to about 30 X 45-50cm (12 X 18-20in) place it on a work top dusted with cornflour and trim off the thick edges to a rectangle about 27.5-40cm (11 X 16in). Cover immediately with a damp cloth and prepare the other sheets of filo in the same way. When all the sheets have been prepared proceed with the recipe of your choice.

Makes 18 sheets

home-made kunafeh filo

I have included this recipe more for its curiosity value since to make this filo is impossible without a special kunafeh container. This is a deep brass dish with numerous holes in it, like a large sieve, and it is virtually unobtainable in the West. However, if you happen to have a friend or relative 'passing through' the Middle East ask them to bring back one for you. Until then use commercially prepared filo.

675g (1½ lb) plain flour
300ml (½ pint) milk
110g (4 oz) clarified butter, melted (page 194)

Sift the flour into a large bowl. Make a well in the centre and gradually add 300ml (½ pint) tepid water and the milk, kneading until you have a soft dough. Now start thinning it out by adding a little more water. Stir constantly until the mixture has the consistency of a batter.

   Place a large metal griddle over a low heat. With a large ladle pour some of the batter into the kunafeh container. The batter will drop on to the hot metal griddle in rope-like form and the ropes will solidify in a matter of seconds. Carefully lift them off and deposit in a large bowl. Repeat until you have used up all the batter. Pour the melted butter into the bowl containing the filo and gently rub between your fingers until all the strands are coated with butter. Proceed with the recipe of your choice.

kaymak (ser)

This is the Middle Eastern cream. Known as *kaymak* in Turkey and Iran, *eishta* in the Arab lands and 'ser' in Armenia. The rich, thick cream can be literally cut with a knife. It is usually made with the milk of buffalo or sheep, but you can make your own by using double cream and milk.

900ml (1½ pints) milk
300ml (½ pint) double cream

Pour the milk and cream into a large shallow pan and bring slowly to the boil. Lower the heat and simmer very gently for 2 hours. Turn off the heat and leave to rest for 6-8 hours. Refrigerate for several hours. By now there should be a layer of cream about 1-2cm (½-¾in) thick. Slide a knife around the edge to loosen it and lift on to a plate. Serve on pastries or eat with honey.

otov ser
whipped kaymak

This is a more decorative version of the above cream. The cream is bubbled while cooking and then set.

1.1 litres (2 pints) double or whipping cream

Pour the cream into a large shallow tray and bring slowly to the boil. Lower the heat and, with a ladle, lift out some cream and pour it back in until bubbles start rising. Continue doing this for 30 minutes to 1 hour – the longer you do it the larger and softer the bubbles will be. Turn off the heat and leave for 3-4 hours. Refrigerate for at least 6-8 hours. Run a sharp knife around the edge to loosen and carefully lift out on to a large plate. Roll up and slice.

There is no substitute for kaymak. The nearest you can get is clotted cream. I suggest you try making kaymak if you have the time.

bekmez
tahina and carob syrup

Bekmez is the Turkish name given to one of the most interesting sweet spreads in the world. It is a mixture of syrup and *tahina* (sesame cream) and throughout the Middle East, particularly in Turkey, Armenia, Syria and Lebanon, people very often in the morning or at teatime (children almost all the time) spread this sweet over bread and munch their way through happiness.

There are 2 basic syrups:
a)   grape syrup – this is the true *bekmez* which is made from pure grape juice;
b)   carob syrup – also known as locust bean or St John's bread.

Carob is the fruit of a Mediterranean shrub and it is very popular in Chinese and Middle Eastern cooking. You will be able to buy bottled carob syrup in most Middle Eastern, Greek or Chinese shops. The grape juice is rather difficult to find. If you want a sweet yet earthy flavour as a change from marmalade and jams then try this recipe.

120ml (4 fl oz) carob syrup or grape syrup
120ml (4 fl oz) tahina paste

Mix the 2 ingredients together in a bowl until well blended. Now spread a little – or a lot depending on taste – on to a slice of bread.

index